Yohogania County

Ohio

Fairfax
Stone

County

Hampshire County

Monongalia County

Augusta County

Greenbrier County

Montgomery and Fincastle
Counties

N

	miles	
0		50
0	kilometers	60

Western Virginia
c. 1780

Absentee Landowning and Exploitation in West Virginia 1760–1920

Barbara Rasmussen

Absentee Landowning and Exploitation in West Virginia 1760 – 1920

THE UNIVERSITY PRESS OF KENTUCKY

Library of Congress Cataloging-in-Publication Data

Rasmussen, Barbara.
    Absentee landowning and exploitation in West Virginia, 1760–1920 /
Barbara Rasmussen.
        p. cm.
    Includes bibliographical references and index.
    ISBN 0-8131-1880-8 (acid-free paper)
    1. Land use—Virginia—History. 2. Land use—West Virginia—
History. 3. Land tenure—Virginia—History. 4. Land tenure—West
Virginia—History. 5. Absenteeism—History. I. Title.
HD211.V8R37 1994   94-5096
333.73'09755—dc20

For Norval, Sara,
and
Christopher

Special histories therefore contribute very little to the knowledge of the whole and conviction of its truth. It is only indeed by study of the interconnexion of all the particulars, their resemblances and differences, that we are enabled at least to make a general survey, and thus derive both benefit and pleasure from history.

—*The Histories of Polybius*, bk. 1, 264–146 B.C.

Contents

Acknowledgments

Completion of this project is the result of much assistance from many people, all wise and kind. I wish to acknowledge, with much gratitude, the help I have received during the preparation of this work. Ronald L. Lewis, Kenneth Fones-Wolf, John R. McKivigan, and Robert Blobaum have all given time and goodwill. Portions of the research included here were supported by a research assistantship at the West Virginia University Regional Research Institute. Others to whom I am deeply indebted include Larry Sypholt, Annette Cotter, Christelle Venham, and David Bartlett of the West Virginia and Regional History Collection, a magnificent repository of documents pertaining to Appalachian history.

Richard Fauss of the West Virginia Department of Archives and History assisted with county records. I wish to acknowledge also John Maxwell, William T. Doherty, Rosemarie Zagarri, and the late Dennis O'Brien for many hours of help. Gordon McKinney's suggestions for revision proved overwhelmingly helpful. Lastly, I wish to thank Mary Lou Lustig for her wisdom and support through the final stages of this work. Her mastery of colonial history strengthened the entire manuscript. Boundless support from Norval, Sara, and Christopher Rasmussen has kept this project alive. All of these individuals have contributed a great deal to the strengths that may lie in this book; any error of fact or judgment is mine alone.

Introduction

Insecure claims to their lands and a state government system that was prejudiced against their interests in eighteenth-century settlement days created a symphony of hardship for the original settlers in much of what is now West Virginia. Long-standing speculation in land and absentee ownership greatly influenced the fortunes of some mountain counties, while active local control of land guided affairs differently in others. The pattern of landownership has been crucial to the history of many West Virginia counties. I will study Randolph, Tucker, Pocahontas, Monroe, and Clay counties in the ensuing chapters.

Four of these counties were dominated by absentee ownership early in their histories; one, Monroe, was not. If the experience of these counties is representative of the region as a whole, then this episode in American history reveals that Appalachia is economically distressed because residents and resources were consciously exploited by identifiable others. Such evidence would undermine contentions that Appalachia is victimized by its own regional and cultural characteristics.

Once an area of breathtaking scenery and lavish virgin forests, these five counties were settled by commercially minded frontiersmen who were bringing to the West the successful agricultural patterns and social organization that characterized the early days of settlement in the Shenandoah Valley, just a few miles to the east. The mountain farming culture was defeated, however, by the ever-widening grasp of speculators and absentees, who by 1880 were sufficiently powerful to engineer a rapid and devastating industrial transformation within the region. Mining and timbering competed with agriculture for control of the land, which could not sustain all three economic pursuits.

From the earliest colonial days, Virginia's political system was carefully structured to protect the interests of those who owned vast lands, not the independent mountain farmers who generally claimed fewer than five hundred acres apiece. In these early years, absentees, speculators, and low country slaveholding planters shared common cause: they fought high taxes on their land that would adversely affect the profitability of their enterprises. Despite an increasing population in the West, this alliance between investors and large planters remained unassailable. Elites successfully retained control of Virginia's politics. When combined with Virginia's land-granting history, this political system made early Virginia farmers extremely vulnerable to the desires of speculators and industrialists.

As the mid–nineteenth century blossomed, the interests of speculators turned more and more toward development of their landholdings, particularly the exploitation of coal and timber resources within the mountains. The Civil War strained the alliance between planters and investors, but the change brought no benefit to politically weak mountain farmers, who remained underrepresented in state government, despite their growing numbers. At the close of the war, industrialization was firmly entrenched. Increasing appetites for natural resources changed the way of life within the mountains, and the indigenous farmers' power and political influence declined even further.

During the Gilded Age, population increased rapidly. Farmers and their descendants were outnumbered, as manufacturers brought tens of thousands of desperate immigrant workers to the Appalachian Mountains for numerous industrial jobs. Both immigrant and native workers supplied the manpower for timbering in Tucker, Randolph, and Pocahontas counties. Within fifty years these forests were laid waste. The underground resources in these counties, as in Clay County, were assaulted. This transition to extractive industries, accomplished with the unthinking assistance of native workers, proved generally devastating for all residents of the region. The attitude that permitted—even encouraged—such devastation was rooted in the perspectives of those first settlers who claimed Virginia for the Crown of England. This attitude spread westward as an earlier generation of immigrants populated the western reaches of Virginia long before the American Revolution. Settlers, trappers, traders, schemers, and investors all rushed to the West for land, which appeared to be endlessly available. During the revolutionary era, land remained the dominant aspect of social and political status.[1] Hunger for land was the prime motivation for all who crossed the Appalachian Mountains in the years 1763–83. It followed, then, that loss of land was cataclysmic in an agricultural society where land determined status.

The changing ways in which mountain lands have been used must be considered over the long term. The familiar segments of colonial, middle, and recent American history muffle the continuing significance of land in the region's past. Considering a broad span of time allows the theme of land to assert itself with clarity. This previously obscure past looms large. The complexity of events and interrelationships over so many years provides a daunting challenge. To investigate the *longue durée*, one must be willing to take up a "whole new way of conceiving of social affairs." Historical actors "who make the most noise" may not be the most authentic—"there are other, quieter ones too."[2]

So it is for Appalachia. Speculation in land and absentee ownership have influenced the region's affairs since the earliest English footfalls upon Virginia's soil. The evolving ownership of the land is an unprobed mystery of Appalachia's past. Understanding the quest for land illumines the history of the Appalachian people. Geography influences the region's history in dramatic ways. Appalachian history must be studied from this perspective because its problems are posed and revealed by place.

Regional historians have embraced this concept of place. New interpretations are bringing keener appreciation of the enduring significance of broad historical themes.[3] When this approach is applied to Appalachia, an intriguing vision emerges. Although the region is widely perceived as "different," careful study reveals another theme that is common in America's frontier history. In Appalachia, this common thread of culture, economy, opportunity, and politics produced a region still lagging in economic development. The history of land partially explains this perplexing Appalachian reality.

The period from 1760 to 1915 demonstrated the overarching importance of land to the settlers who farmed western Virginia. It also revealed the relentless efforts of speculators and absentees who captured control of the land. Within these 155 years occurred exploration, settlement, political defeat, and, ultimately, economic exploitation of the region and its residents.

I studied the counties of Randolph, Tucker, Pocahontas, Monroe, and Clay in the context of landownership, national politics, state politics, and civil war. In four of the counties, land use moved steadily and inexorably away from agriculture toward industrial development in the form of resource extraction. At the heart of this transition lies the question of why the farmers of the region gave up their way of life. Many farmers did not welcome the change. Industrialists successfully exploited the region because they controlled the land and the political system. Their power allowed them to exploit callously the local culture, the natural resources, and thousands of immigrant workers. Clay, Tucker, Randolph, and Pocahontas counties yielded to the transformation. Monroe County did not. Farmers there did not have to deal with an industrial presence, nor did local farmers give up control of their land. Monroe County did not grow rapidly, nor did its agricultural emphasis change.

Settlement patterns, geography, and economic activity in these five counties are similar in most respects. Located just west of the Northern Neck of Virginia proprietary lands of Lord Fairfax are the contiguous counties of Tucker (established 1856), Randolph (1787), and Pocahontas (1821). These counties were originally part of Virginia's district of West Augusta. Some areas were settled as early as 1755. Large portions of Tucker, Randolph, and Pocahontas are now included

in the Monongahela National Forest. Tucker County's Fairfax
Stone, at the source of the Potomac River, was set in 1746, although explorers found the site ten years earlier. According to
early land records, settlers came west into the mountain region after the American Revolution to cash in their veterans'
pensions for virgin farmland. Their settlement imitated the
commercial farming of the neighboring Shenandoah Valley,
which was already settled and successful. The Valley of Virginia offered inspiration to settlers going further west, who
took with them a model and a method of agriculture that had
flourished since the 1720s.

In Monroe County, farther south, settlement proceeded
from about 1760. Political division from Greenbrier and Botetourt counties in 1799 gave these mountain farmers a closer
courthouse than the old one at Lewisburg. Clay County lies
farther west than the other four, and its history demonstrates
that by 1810, Virginia's frontier had advanced beyond the
mountains and into the Allegheny Plateau. At that time settlers began farming in the region along the banks of the Elk
River, which bisects the county and exposes rich outcrop-
pings of coal.

Monroe, Clay, and Tucker counties are, by West Virginia
standards, small. Pocahontas and Randolph are two of the
state's largest. Size, however, is not the critical difference
among them. The critical difference is the presence of mineral wealth. All but Monroe are endowed with recoverable
coal. All five counties were similarly covered with a nearly
impenetrable stand of eastern hardwood, fir, and spruce trees
for many years after they were settled. All five counties were
settled by farmers, generally of Ulster, German, or English
stock. Chosen for this study because they are so similar, Pocahontas, Randolph, Tucker, and Clay counties were also selected because they underwent a tremendous upheaval
through industrialization. Monroe County is included because it was settled in the same fashion and at the same time
as the others but did not undergo industrial transformation.

Monroe County's history suggests what might have happened to the other counties if the industrialists had never
come. The absence of coal muted outside interest in this

county. Dispersed landholdings among the residents strengthened the gentry's political power. Farming remained in place.

Regional records of land agents, deeds, court documents,
local histories, and pertinent personal papers make possible
four observations on the history of these counties. First, speculators and absentee landowners were present at the outset of
settlement and exploration. Their needs and desires generally
directed the course of political events within the region. After
the Civil War, absentees and speculators began to develop
their lands. Their power and influence left local inhabitants
helpless to defend themselves against the rapid increase of
absentee-led extractive industries in the 1880s.

Second, the ascent of absentee control was facilitated by
specious land claims, chicanery, ejectment, and deceit. Long
before the Civil War, the usurpation of land occurred hand in
hand with political defeat for western mountain dwellers.
Continued domination of the state political system by eastern
Virginia planters and later by industrialists was essential to
the rise of absentee-guided industry. Before the war, western
Virginians constituted a popular majority in the state but did
not have sufficient political power to legislate a tax system to
finance improved transportation and communications. Such
a success for western Virginians would have greatly harmed
the economic interests of the eastern planter class. It also
would have eroded the control elites wielded over the land.
Constitutional revisions in Virginia and West Virginia secured the industrial and absentee control of the region. By
1880 corrupt control of political institutions by industrial
leaders ensured their continued tenure in office and silenced
their critics.

Third, local courthouse records make it clear that the agricultural residents of the region worked diligently to reduce
isolation and to secure and advance their society. They were
defeated politically and crippled culturally by powerful business interests.

Lastly, few clear lines delineated the actors in the region's
transformation. For the sake of argument, I will refer to farmers, settlers, industrialists, speculators, and absentees as distinct groups. In fact, many individuals crossed some or all of

the lines between these groups. Between the clear extremes of self-sufficient farmers and absentee speculators, there existed a gray area of economic activity, where, for a while, roles and interests overlapped. The region's history has revolved around the quest for its land. To understand the people, we must first understand their relationship to the land.

The significant events studied in the following pages were not the only important influences at work within the region during the transition years. Other developments were unfolding as well. The roles of powerful, profit-driven outsiders, however, rest at the heart of the transition that changed the Monongahela region of the Appalachian Mountains. Indigenous western Virginians first chartered corporations for improving transportation and navigation; absentees created the mining, timbering, and railroad companies. The presence of small operators and local participation in industrial activities were short-lived.[4]

Farmers of the Monongahela, like their predecessors in the Shenandoah Valley, were commercial men with capitalist aspirations and traditional social networks. Court records confirm that an active political organization within the region effectively enforced civil tranquillity and administered justice. Mountain families paid their taxes, answered the census, created schools, and built churches of established denominations.

Records of an early slander suit in Tucker County indicate that the residents of the region maintained economic links to other towns, cities, and states.[5] The suit further demonstrates that the members of a community respected credit ratings and acknowledged the important role of banks in their lives. Transmontane farmers sought to emulate and join the larger commercial world, not flee from it. It does not appear that mountain farmers were shunning commerce and capitalism.[6] Subsistence farming was not the lifestyle of choice; subsistence status for them was transitory. Tucker, Randolph, and Pocahontas counties are geographically remote, but this does not mean the early settlers were escaping from unwanted social systems. They left evidence demonstrating that from the first they were devoted to the same standards championed by

Virginia society at large. Their records challenge the core of traditionally held opinions about the region and its citizens. These mountain farmers worked hard to develop a commercial economy. Monongahela farmers took advantage of water routes to the port of New Orleans to market their agricultural products: flour, potatoes, apples, and pork. Free navigation of the Mississippi was a firm demand of Virginians in the revolutionary Congress. Flour was Virginia's "second" crop. Wheat grew where tobacco could not—in the West.[7]

The steady stream of migrants westward and the ever-increasing population in the mountains make it doubtful that settlers were eschewing commercial development. The region now comprising all of West Virginia contained only thirteen counties in 1800. In response to demands from the rapidly growing West for more governmental services, twenty-seven additional counties were formed over the next fifty years. Only fifteen of West Virginia's fifty-five counties were formed after 1850. The West's increasingly sharp demands for more state services and appropriate political representation reflected increasing populations and developing commerce. Struggles to enhance the economy of the West form a major theme in Virginia's history.

Despite this history, many interpretations examine the motives of early settlers. Some analyses suggest that rugged, solitary mountain dwellers were inherently different from other early farmers in America because they sought to avoid economic growth. Strong bonds of religion, kinship, and family economic unity theoretically enabled transmontane farmers to cling to noncapitalist social relations. Such interpretations overlook the nascent capitalism that was present before industrialization began.[8]

The complacence of modern residents of Appalachia is misunderstood as a long-standing cultural characteristic. Residents of Clear Fork Valley in central Appalachia have resigned themselves to a life of relative powerlessness as a direct result of industrial and absentee control of the region. Their passivity is not a valid indicator of the preindustrial cultural background of the residents.[9] Southern mountain farmers were as commercially motivated as other American farmers were, but they were hampered by isolation. New England's farmers were descended from migrants who came to the New World to preserve Puritan ideas of social reform. Virginians came for fortune and freedom, expressed as land. This key difference must be considered in any assessment that views mountaineers as rejecting capitalist economic systems.

The economic transformation of Appalachia was stressful for the region's farmers because they were less well equipped to navigate the economic and political waters. When New England farmers competed with industrial interests, they were buttressed by clearer titles to their farms. They were less isolated. They faced no quest for coal. Their political system of townships gave them a more active voice in local affairs. Thus protected, these farmers were able to negotiate more advantageously in the face of economic changes. This leeway was not available to trans-Appalachian farmers.

New England's merchant capital formed a major aspect of the Monongahela's early history, however. Transmontane farmers were exploited when their agriculture was crushed in favor of industrial development. Early mountain Virginians struggled to maintain their land claims against challenges from powerful outsiders. Overlapping conveyances, deception, and remoteness of locale weakened the certainty of many early land claims. As demand for mountain lands increased, this uncertainty deepened and significantly influenced the history of the region.

New England's farmers and Virginia's farmers thus differed in the security of their claim to land. In most other ways they were similar. Mountain farmers' embrace of religion, kinship, and family economic unity sustained Appalachian society in eclipse. It did not define their economic preferences. These values were a strong influence, but probably no more so than the New England farmers' Puritan heritage of righteous living in an unrighteous world. Family ties and spiritual reassurance comforted farmers caught up in an economic maelstrom they could not harness.[10] This is not the same as retreating to religion to avoid change. Moreover, the universally human emotional anchors of family, religion, and kinship noted in such an interpretation point to the similarities between northern and southern farmers, not to their differences.

Acceptance of capitalism is another similarity between these groups of farmers. In the form of commercial agriculture, capitalism was already in place in the mountains of Virginia long before industrialization. This nascent capitalism, though, was destroyed by the intrusion of merchant capital. Distant investors financed the West Virginia Pulp and Paper Company, the Baltimore and Ohio Railroad, the West Virginia Central Railroad, the Davis Coal and Coke Company, and multitudes of other extractive enterprises, whose charters can be found in abundance among the acts of the Virginia and West Virginia legislatures. Industrial control of western land by the end of the Civil War was so prevalent that it rendered farmers helpless to influence the course of the transformation of the region. Deed books in many of the mountain counties reveal brisk legal activity surrounding land that was unsettling to mountain society. Incidents of obvious collusion between industry and government are evident in Clay County records. Deed fights forced farmer after farmer to court to defend their claims of landownership.

Many mountain farmers wished to help direct the changes in their region, not resist them. They were sorrowfully perplexed when the changes passed them by. Current analysis of the Hatfield-McCoy feud assigns a great deal of significance to outside industrial designs on the Tug Fork timberland that Hatfield owned. In the industrial era, a petty local dispute was manipulated by absentees and their local helpers to discredit indigenous residents and exploit the resources of the area.[11] Hatfield was forced to court so often that he had to sell the lands that outsiders coveted to pay his legal fees. Despite the colorful description of "Devil Anse" Hatfield as a lawless, bloodthirsty, and backward mountain man, he left a long record of patient legal attempts to solve his problems. His calm rationality is a jarring contrast to the reputation that survives him.

Such evidence of rational response to rapid change forces a reexamination of the region's history. How likely can it be that a small farming community could be so abjectly different from other American communities of similar background? Mountain farmers were typical American farmers at the beginning of the national experience. Time worked a peculiar hardship into the mountain lifestyle. These farmers entered modern society as victims of a process that transferred their agricultural wealth to industrial coffers.

The important differences in the security of land are accompanied by equally important aspects of locale. The Monongahela region is more southern than northern in cultural identity, but with its proximity to Maryland and Pennsylvania, Deep South analogies must be evaluated as skeptically as New England ones. During settlement, Virginia's transmontane residents experienced many of the political problems of Kentucky and early Carolina, but Virginia is nevertheless different in significant ways from the rest of the South.

Originally Virginia was an investment for British merchants, while Carolina was a political experiment born of the Age of Enlightenment. Virginia produced little cotton, the economic mainstay of the Deep South. In the transmontane, Virginians grew only small quantities of tobacco. Without the "bonus crop" that agriculturalists in other areas enjoyed, the farmers of western Virginia were economically compelled to develop diversified agriculture, internal improvements, and self-sufficiency. Implicit in their economic behavior is an acceptance of the market's role and a flexible attitude that could accommodate the market's changing demands. The switch from tobacco to wheat in early Virginia may have been prompted by soil exhaustion, but it was encouraged by an expanding European demand for food.[12] In other words, the farmers of Virginia responded rationally to market changes.

In governance, Virginians steadfastly upheld county government and the gentry that dominated that system.[13] Local gentry and itinerant Methodist or Baptist preachers were the dominant influences in social, political, and religious life in the mountains of Virginia. In the low counties, established churches were usually Episcopal.

There were other differences too. Southern mountain farmers elsewhere enjoyed legal protections that mountain Virginians lacked. Upcountry Georgia contained an independent mountain farmer class much like the western Virginians, even though they were deep in the slaveholding South. Established as a refuge for debtors, Georgia protected its farmers with a homestead exemption that partially spared them from loss of property if they defaulted on taxes or loans.[14]

The great size of Virginia was another reason its transformation differed from New England's. Slavery was the issue of greatest contention between eastern and western Virginians. Mountain farmers had little need for slaves on their diverse commercial and self-sufficient farms, and they frequently rejected the institution.[15] Tidewater planters required slavery to succeed.

Abolitionist agitation west of the Blue Ridge, mounting attacks on slaveholders' political power and tax privilege, and the ultimate dissolution of the commonwealth "belie Virginia as a closed society committed to the . . . philosophy of the Deep South."[16] If the planters had not silenced this mounting cry for greater democracy in Virginia, they would have faced serious financial problems stemming from increased taxes. Never solidly proslavery or prosecession, Virginia might never have seceded or divided had it been more democratic.

Hence Virginia, whether eastern or western, was neither purely northern nor purely southern. It was a hybrid of both cultures, with a healthy nod to the commercial tendencies of the middle states in its northern sections. The disdain for slavery reflected a northern commercial outlook, but not ethical similitude: a great many Virginians eschewed emancipation in favor of black colonization.[17]

In the lapse of time between the founding of Virginia, the first successful colony, and the founding of other colonies, English politics, commercial interests, and technology had changed drastically. Nearly fifty years separated the birth of Virginia from that of Carolina, its younger southern neighbor.

The issues of settler motive, time, climate, agriculture, and terrain influenced the outlook of all new arrivals to America.

Each of these issues carried the seeds of diversity. They all must be considered when evaluating events of nineteenth-century Virginia.[18] Regional peculiarities are sufficient to invoke a skepticism about the usefulness of North-South comparisons. A more characteristically Virginian explanation for the industrial development of the region is necessary.

Nowhere else in the United States did one state contain two economic ideas that were so mutually antagonistic. One view called for high property taxes to fund growth and development; the other found such levies to be a direct threat to survival. Political struggle was unavoidable. In other ways, eastern and western Virginians were alike. Virginia's gentry-led social structure prevailed in the mountainous regions, despite a widespread aversion to slaveholding. Honest and powerful, Virginia's gentry governed well.[19]

In the mountains, social status was defined by land alone; in the coastal regions of the state, both land and slaves defined high social standing. The first settlers in the mountains, in the 1750s and 1760s, brought no slaves with them, but they were imbued with the Virginian ethic (by then more than one hundred years old) that no record was more important, nor more carefully kept, than title to land.[20] Economic activity became more commercial as farmers sought improved markets for their agricultural products. They also worked politically to improve their fledgling economic system.

In coastal Virginia, economic activity was also agricultural. Plantations grew staple crops and commodities. Growth did not come from expanding market exchanges. Tidewater success was derived largely from political power. The planter elite kept taxes low and enforced a system that extracted surplus labor from unfree workers. Mountain Virginians as well as lowland Virginians pursued commerce, but in different ways.

Traditionally, western farmers exchanged goods and services. This activity allowed them to preserve cash for other needs, such as taxes. Cash was always scarce in frontier and agricultural regions, but this was a function of shortsighted federal monetary policy, not mountain economic preferences. Absence of cash did not necessarily equal poverty, nor did it signal a rejection of commerce. For a farmer, land meant wealth. It was more valuable than cash. Landlessness constituted a distinctly lower social class of whites that did not include farmers. Land is the key to making an otherwise difficult distinction between yeoman farmers and poor whites. Aspirations for land or possession of land defined the early patterns of settlement and development in the mountains. Nearly all efforts were directed toward a commercial agriculture that was optimistic about future long-term successes. Western Virginians shared the perspectives of farmer-frontiersmen in other early American locales.[21] Scholars have amply discussed and debated, without resolution, the cultural influences upon the choices and behaviors of mountain farmers.[22]

Sectional politics drastically shaped the history of transmontane Virginia. Taxation and apportionment bedeviled Virginians. Elections were won or lost on issues of tax reform, representation, and internal development. Eastern Virginia's political hegemony precluded democracy, before and after the Civil War; in this respect Virginia was like most southern regions.[23] Thus capitalism was at a disadvantage and could not flourish.

Merchant capital was diligently applied to the purchase, sale, and development of gigantic land grants that were secured in the Virginia land office before the American Revolution was won. Because many of these transactions took place in faraway cities, their impact was not immediately felt in the mountains. This land business required political resources to keep property taxes low. Internal improvements for growth within the mountains required political resources to increase state revenues. Thus, conflicting economic interests grievously strained harmony among Virginians. By 1851 the proponents of land businesses and the planter class had presided over two revisions of the Virginia state constitution. They secured the political power necessary to protect their interests. The farmers and entrepreneurs of the mountains were defeated in their attempts to obtain public funding for internal improvements.

After the Civil War, the Monongahela region was thoroughly dominated by absentee owners—corporations and individuals—whose economic interests did not include commercial agriculture. Even though they were far outnumbered by the farmers, they had garnered sufficient power to thwart the will of the majority. These absentee owners had acquired enough land and political power to unleash a relentless economic transformation. With astonishing rapidity, industrialization was thrust upon these mountain regions. People had no time to resist or to object; they were caught up in a terrible turmoil. When the industries left the region fifty years later, their sudden departure was as numbing as their sudden arrival had been. The population was about the same as before, but everything else was gone.

1

Imperial Politics
Early Speculators and the Leather Stocking Assault upon Virginia's Transmontane

Petroglyphs, pictographs, and carvings on trees provide evidence that for centuries humans have lived and hunted within the Appalachian mountain ranges that now constitute modern West Virginia. Long before the arrival of settlers in leather stockings or investors in silk stockings, ancient Indian tribes populated the mountains. Mysteriously abandoned by those resident tribes, the region became the coveted hunting grounds of later, rival Indians. By the seventeenth century, the powerful Iroquois dominated the area and its lucrative fur trade. From that time on, Iroquois, Europeans, and Americans—individuals, corporations, and sovereigns—focused their desires for empire on the Appalachian Mountains and whatever lay beyond.

The land, game, and timber first lured explorers west. Although vast beyond measure, these attractions were but a portion of the bounty that nature bestowed on the region. Beneath the surface of the earth, coal, gas, limestone, and sandstone lay awaiting discovery. Each of these resources represented one more dimension of the idea of property as it evolved into more and more complex dimensions in the minds of the ambitious men who would seek to capture the wealth of the mountains. The concept of property would be asked "to embrace a broad range of resources" as people and ideas moved westward across the continent.[1]

Eons in the making, these gifts from the geologic past were created while all of western Virginia was the floor of a huge sea into which poured many ancient rivers. The silt, sand,

and pebbles from these rivers accounted for the rich sandstone deposits found in the eastern edges of the state. Farther west, at the deepest part of the ancient sea, marine shells and skeletons formed the thick limestone layers now found in Greenbrier and Monroe counties. In the plentiful shallower portions of this sea, swamplike conditions prevailed, hosting vegetation that became the vast seams of coal that undergird most of West Virginia's counties. Nearer to the edge of the Ohio River, plentiful oil and natural gas deposits were formed.

As mountains hove out of this sea and the waters disappeared, the Appalachian range stood as a barrier to westward movement, save for the relatively recent Indian hunting trails.[2] Beyond the Allegheny Front, seemingly endless waves of mountain peaks deterred almost all advances except for those of the Iroquois, who controlled the region. Susquehannas from what is now Pennsylvania and Senecas from the Illinois region traversed the mountains, although they were subjugated by the Iroquois. Indians protected their commercial interests in the area: French traders sought game and pelts.[3]

Until the era of exploration and war in the eighteenth century, the Virginian transmontane was nearly devoid of settlement, Indian or white. When the source of the Potomac River was marked for Lord Fairfax in 1736 and the first Fairfax Stone was laid there in 1746, white settlement of what is now West Virginia began. Lord Fairfax was a single proprietary owner who leased his lands in the English fashion, planning to sell none. His land, in the Shenandoah Valley of Virginia, had been given to his ancestors by a grateful King Charles II.

The Shenandoah Valley was well populated during early colonial days, with settlement being facilitated by the reasonably traversable landscape. Both settlers and the leadership of Virginia looked westward during the eighteenth century. Lieutenant Governor Alexander Spotswood in 1710 planned to interrupt French trade with the western Indians. By 1716 he claimed the entire Valley of Virginia for the king of England. Spotswood's expansionist ideas were later carried on by Governor Robert Dinwiddie, who pressed western exploration and settlement. To enhance settlers' safety, he negotiated treaties of protection with the Indians. To ensure settlers' economic success, he exempted them from taxes and quitrents. In the first third of the eighteenth century, Mecklenberg (later Shepherdstown) was established, and further settlements punctuated Jefferson and Berkeley counties.[4]

In this era Indians resisted white settlement in their hunting grounds, and most of the transmontane remained under the control of native Americans or their French allies. Dominated by the Iroquois nation, Indian fur trade was lucrative. Hunting territories were jealously protected by various tribes.[5] Difficult and life-threatening, English settlement continued, despite French and Indian resistance. Settlers and land agents pushed west with an indomitable fervor.

To encourage western settlement and finance his estate, Lord Fairfax began in 1720 to issue some land leases for portions of his Northern Neck of Virginia property. His tenants paid composition money, or down payments, and annual quitrents. This feudalistic approach to land management was not wholly successful in the New World, and Fairfax was not to enjoy a trouble-free flow of income from the rent. Plagued by the mismanagement and duplicity of his agent Robert Carter, a prominent Virginia planter, Fairfax reluctantly came to America in 1747 to tend his lands for himself.[6]

In the same period, other settlement led by frontiersmen proceeded without respect for proprietary owners' rights to leases or quitrents. These settlers wanted full title, in fee. Creeping westward, they settled along the Shenandoah and South Branch rivers, reaching present Pendleton County and the spine of the Appalachian Mountains by the 1740s.[7] This region marked the western edge of the Valley of Virginia and was attractive to early settlers and speculators because it was reasonably accessible from eastern Virginia.

From these first days of settlement in the eighteenth century through the establishment of the Monongahela National Forest in the early twentieth, absentees and speculators dominated enough of the Monongahela's land to secure their control of the affairs of the region. Although frontiersmen were numerous, they never controlled nearly the amount of land that remained in the hands of absentees and speculators.

Fairfax's proprietorship, the Levi Hollingsworth survey, Albert Gallatin's lands, George Washington's claims, and the Deakins family claim, all in place within the transmontane of Virginia before the writing of the U.S. Constitution, accounted for vast portions of the Monongahela region. They are all examples of the early influence of absentees and speculators within the region.

Aside from these great landholdings, settlers also held land in parcels of various sizes. Pushing into the region and bringing traditional Virginia mountain farming culture with them, these farmers claimed land. Their claims were in many cases insecure, but they had no way to apprehend that their descendants would suffer ejectment in the next century.

Governor Patrick Henry, who opposed the earlier land policies of Governor Dunmore, in 1776 attempted to protect the rights of settlers in the West. He signed the first land law to grant actual settlers preemption rights to four hundred acres of land. These claims could be validated by taxes paid, even in the absence of a deed. Henry also chaired a committee that questioned the right of the king to sell vacant lands and that urged future settlers not to accept lands under such conditions. This feeble attempt to protect western settlers came in the throes of Revolutionary War fervor and was short-lived.[8] During the years of the Revolutionary War (1776–83), Virginia honored early settlement claims, but subsequent challenges by speculators and absentees clouded many of them. Virginia's 1779 land law failed to resolve land contests and became instead a source of strife on the frontier. Early farmers and graziers were frustrated from the start by provisions of that law that allowed the holders of preemption rights and military and treasury warrants to transfer them to other purchasers.[9] This device allowed wealthy purchasers to gather a great deal of land very cheaply. Persons who sold their claims remained in the East with their cash, leaving westward settlement to others.

The Virginia Land Law of 1779 attempted to impose order on the chaotic rush for western lands. The law for a few years recognized and legitimated the unrecorded claims of settlers and Revolutionary War pensioners, but this security began to erode shortly after 1783. In the years after the Revolutionary War, owners of large tracts of land and developers were able to defeat settlers' claims with increasing success. A few fortunate pioneers held on to their land in spite of challenges from powerful land agents and absentees. Generally, however, the challenges to land claims of transmontane settlers were successful, especially in regions where deeds were not recorded meticulously, or in cases where Virginia treasury warrants were held by those who sought the lands claimed by settlers. Those settlers who were confronted with challenges in early years frequently gave up and moved farther west. By the eve of the Civil War, this solution was no longer possible. Many farm families were forced to accept disheartening compromises or to fight ejectment proceedings.[10]

Within the boundaries of modern Tucker County, the western limit of Lord Fairfax's Northern Neck adjoins the Deakins family's grants. Settlers who wanted to claim their own land were attracted to the region also. The Potomac River rises in Tucker, and its feeder streams and those of the northerly flowing Cheat River form an attractive site for logging and milling, as well as for farming. Similar geographic elements exist in Randolph and Pocahontas counties. All these counties were settled by farmers early in the nation's history.

These counties lie along the eastern edge of the Allegheny Plateau. The sharply defined geography of the Valley and Ridge province significantly affected the settlement, as well as the isolation, of the region. Nearly impenetrable from the east, the mountains forced settlers moving west to drift south through valleys, in search of mountain passes. Pocahontas and Pendleton counties form the highest part of the plateau region that covers a third of the state, sweeping in a curve to the southwest.[11] Numerous rivers began within these hills, luring settlers ever westward.

Indian trails through the mountains were plentiful. These rough paths were the only passages through the region for almost one hundred years after white explorers found the area. The McCullough trader's trail led from Moorefield via Patterson's Creek and Greenland Gap, across a spur of the Alleghenies to the North Branch River, west of Oakland, Maryland, to the region of Bruceton Mills, on the Pennsylvania–West Virginia border. A branch of the trail traversed Tucker County through Lead Mine Run and Horseshoe Run to the Cheat River, where it connected with a branch of the trail through Parsons and ultimately intersected the Seneca Trail at Elkins. From Elkins, the trail headed south to the Greenbrier River, passing through Pocahontas County at Mingo Flats, west of the Marlinton Pike, crossing the mountain and splitting into two branches on top of Middle Mountain. One branch continued to Old Field Fork, and the other to Clover Lick.[12]

The predominant route through the Monongahela region was the legendary Seneca, or Shawnee, Trail, which connected the South Branch with the Tygart River Valley. This trail was heavily traveled by settlers in the early 1800s, and it ultimately delineated some modern transportation routes. Cattle were driven eastward to market on this trail, and packhorses carried out iron and salt. The trail ascended the South Branch and followed the North Fork and Seneca Creek, crossed the Alleghenies twenty miles south of the North Branch Trail and the branches of the Cheat River above the mouth of Horse Camp Creek, and passed near Elkins and Beverly to the vicinity of Huttonsville in Randolph County.[13] These trails were difficult, but all were well traveled.

This region contains rugged mountains and narrow valleys, watered by often fickle rivers. The Cheat, Greenbrier, Tygart, and Blackwater rivers run full, flooding in the early spring months, and dwindle to a trickle by the advent of summer. This geographic characteristic aided nineteenth-century efforts to harvest timber in the region. In settlement days, pioneers were blessed and cursed equally by these temperamental mountain streams. Spring floods were as dangerous as summer droughts. Encouraged by the plentiful water supply, however, settlers followed quickly after the rivers were found by European trappers, traders, and explorers. The Greenbrier River was discovered in 1749 by General Andrew Lewis, of the Greenbrier Land Company, while he was surveying the firm's one hundred thousand–acre grant of land in the region.[14] Near modern Marlinton, Lewis encountered

Jacob Marlin and Stephen Sewell, who had been living in the area for several years.

Settlement and exploration in the Monongahela region were further hastened by the 1748 formation of the Ohio Company, which received at least half a million acres of land along the Ohio River, between the Great Kanawha and the Monongahela rivers.[15] Settlers were drawn to the area because of bottomland along the river. Both settlers and speculators seized upon the potentials for the region. Land along the Horseshoe Bottom of the Cheat River, claimed by settlers as well as land agents, became the locus of the scramble for timber and wealth for nearly two hundred years after its settlement.

Tentative settlements within present Randolph and Preston counties came in the 1750s, but permanent settlement required a negotiated peace with the Indians. The Treaty of Logstown in 1752 provided some accommodation with the Iroquois but upset the Delawares, who were threatened by the prospect of dispossession for a second time.[16] In 1763, at the end of the Great War for the Empire between England and France, Ottawa chief Pontiac sought a confederacy of Huron, Shawnee, Delaware, and Ottawa tribes to push back white intruders and recapture the transmontane. Pontiac led his warriors in 1763 in plundering white trading businesses along the Ohio and Monongahela rivers.[17] In 1765 General Henry Boquet finally negotiated a treaty with Pontiac that brought peace to the region for another ten years.[18] Boquet had a personal stake in western peace. He owned stock in the Ohio Company equivalent to twenty-five thousand acres of land.[19]

In this era, Americans as well as Britons were taken by land fever. Everyone with "any ambition and capacity, it seems, on both sides of the Atlantic, sought some profit from what promised to be the greatest land boom in history." Officials of colonial America, British politicians, and planters and merchants from everywhere were as eager to capture an interest in land as were the poorer but braver settlers who undertook to farm the land.[20]

During the peaceful interlude negotiated by Boquet, settlers poured over the mountains, heedless of King George III's
1763 royal proclamation that banned settlement west of the
spine of the Allegheny Mountains. The Crown, and many influential Britons, feared that the lure of free land in America
would result in a depopulated England. Alarm increased
when the Board of Trade realized that not only the poor were
leaving England; many persons of talent and potential were
also looking to America for improved opportunity and prospects. By closing the frontier, many Britons believed, the lure
of American land would be dulled.[21] Complaints about emigration came from the landed and commercial classes in England, but these same classes were simultaneously investing
in great land companies, seeking to profit from the western
regions themselves.

Pioneers who settled the region were variously squatters,
war pensioners, fugitives, adventure seekers, Indian traders,
and trappers. Others came after discovering they were too
late to claim land in the Valley of Virginia. Despite the initial
differences in their backgrounds, once in the West most settlers turned their energies to farming.

Settler claims to western lands almost immediately overlapped each other and the great conveyances of the Virginia
land office. In some cases, pioneers simply packed up and
moved farther west. Others were forced to repurchase their
lands when their claims were contested. Sometimes surveyors could not locate granted land. Some Virginia conveyances
were only for acreage, not a particular parcel, and it was up
to the grantee to locate, survey, and register the claim.[22] Virginia's government attempted to legislate a resolution to the
chaos. Virginia passed laws extending the time for patenting
claims and registering surveys, but the rules did little to resolve the imbroglio.

Various types of owners—land companies, speculators,
and individual absentees—battled among themselves and
against settlers to tighten their grips on their Virginia claims,
which usually overlapped like shingles on a roof. The land
companies were generally organized in England as stock

companies, or they held proprietary bequests from the Crown. The venturers either speculated on their grants of land or leased land for annual quitrents.

The Ohio, Loyal, Greenbrier, and Indiana companies claimed some of the same territory within the Monongahela region that was also claimed by various individual owners. The Indiana Company was formed by wealthy traders who were caught in the hostilities in the Ohio country during Pontiac's War and demanded land as damages for their "suffering." These traders included George Croghan, William Trent, Samuel Wharton, David Franks, John Coxe, Thomas McGee, Robert Callender, and Alexander Lowry.[23]

In the 1768 Treaty of Fort Stanwix, the Shawnee Indians agreed to a gift of land to the "suffering traders" and the New England merchants who backed them.[24] Their gift included about 2,862 square miles of what is now the state of West Virginia, north of the Little Kanawha River. The treaty stipulated that the land was for the exclusive use of the traders, but in fact Virginia also claimed the territory. Thomas Walker, a member of the Loyal Company, signed the treaty on behalf of Virginia.[25]

To resolve the dispute between Virginia and the traders, in 1770 Samuel Wharton traveled to England, where Benjamin Franklin introduced him to influential Britons. Wharton pleaded for a royal confirmation of the traders' "Indiana grant." British legal experts assured Wharton such a step was not necessary. No longer impressed by the Indiana plan, Wharton worked instead for a new colony that would incorporate the entire Fort Stanwix cession. Wharton's plan for the Grand Ohio Company included purchasing land directly from the Crown and forming a fourteenth colony of Vandalia. Indiana Company stockholders who proposed Vandalia were Britons Thomas and Richard Walpole, George Grenville, and Thomas Pownall and Americans Benjamin Franklin, Joseph Galloway, Joseph Wharton, Samuel Wharton, Sir William Johnson, George Croghan, and William Trent.[26]

The project failed because of a morass of political considerations in England, including the fear that the motherland would suffer depopulation. But one good thing came of the proposal: the despised Lord Hillsborough, secretary of state for America, resigned his post rather than recant his earlier policies that forbade settlement and claims in the West. Benjamin Franklin particularly hated the secretary; Hillsborough had rejected his diplomatic credentials as an emissary from America. Furthermore, Hillsborough had derailed the Vandalia plan. This animosity made Britain's diplomacy on western issues all the more difficult.[27]

Holders of the old Indiana Company stock were distraught by what they perceived to be ingratitude and treachery by Wharton, and they in turn acted to protect their individual interests. As relations between England and the colonies deteriorated further, the Vandalia plan was abandoned. Indiana holders acted quickly to retrieve their lands. The Indiana Company announced plans to sell lands before 1777, but this triggered an immediate hostile response from Virginia.[28]

In the throes of the American Revolution, Virginians wrote into their state constitution a ban on claims to land based on Indian treaties until the legislature could determine ownership or grant state sanction. Nearly all out-of-state claimants relied on such Indian treaties. Virginia further declined to recognize the sovereignty of the United States over western lands conveyed to Virginia in its charter from England. The "utmost limits of Virginia" included all of present-day West Virginia, Kentucky, Ohio, Indiana, and Illinois.[29] The dispute quickly heightened. The American wing of the supporters of the old Vandalia plan joined the fray, taking the problem to the Continental Congress, where the battle became a material issue in the debates over western lands. The fate of the land companies dominated these debates. Many congressmen had personal investments in western lands and were vitally concerned with the outcome. James Wilson of Pennsylvania was a backer of the Wabash land plan, and Samuel Wharton of Delaware was intimately involved in the Vandalia plan and the Indiana Company.[30]

While the congress debated the fate of western lands and speculators, other difficulties were unfolding in the West. Within the Monongahela region, boundary disputes caused complications for settlers. Virginia and Pennsylvania were embroiled in controversy over the political boundaries of the Monongahela region. Virginia claimed the transmontane as part of West Augusta, but the northern limits were poorly delineated, and Pennsylvania claimed portions of the region as well. The district of West Augusta was formed when settlers in the region, manipulated by powerful speculators and absentees, petitioned the governments of Virginia and Pennsylvania for relief from oppression and threats to land titles. Because no definite boundary existed between the two colonies, controversies ensued. Virginia governor Lord Dunmore dangled promises of Virginia land grants to Pennsylvanians in hopes of turning their loyalties to Virginia.[31]

The controversy between Virginia and Pennsylvania clouded many intrigues and proposals that were in the making on the eve of the Revolution. Ever hopeful that something might yet come of their investment in the Vandalia scheme, Benjamin Franklin and the Whartons secretly formulated a plan for a new state in the transmontane to be called Westsylvania.[32] With the same area as the proposed Vandalia colony plus some additional Pennsylvania territory, the new state was enthusiastically championed by frontier speculators Thomas Cresap and George Croghan, who had also been associated with Vandalia. There was much opposition to the plan, however, because many persons believed Virginia was already disproportionately large and as such threatened the Union. The only lasting result of the proposal was to strengthen Virginia's political presence on the frontier and to further confuse and demoralize the settlers there. The intrigues and duplicity of these powerful Vandalia investors— some of whom were simultaneously lobbying the Continental Congress for recognition of their claims—brought the added hardship of political uncertainty to the Monongahela region and set the tone for Virginia's approach to western settlement.[33] The unrest lasted until 1779, when the Mason-Dixon Line was extended west to separate Virginia from Pennsylvania. That settlement placed most of Yohogania County in Pennsylvania, while Monongalia and Ohio counties remained largely in Virginia.

Pennsylvania had opened a land office in 1769 to sell lands acquired from the Indians in the 1768 Treaty of Fort Stanwix—lands as far west as the Ohio and Allegheny rivers—with the proviso that actual settler claims would be respected. Virginia followed suit in 1774, selling land in the same region much more cheaply than the Pennsylvanians. Governor Dunmore, alert to the potential of expansion, contended that under a Virginia claim, the land was the king's and therefore was at the governor's disposal.[34] He used this interpretation to enhance Virginia's presence along the frontier. By undercutting Pennsylvania's price and at the same time waging unprovoked war upon the Indians, Dunmore contributed even more instability to the region.

After the signing of the Declaration of Independence, Virginia appointed backwoodsmen and self-promoting speculators as commissioners to oppose the appointees of Pennsylvania. One such appointee was George Croghan.[35] The jurisdictional confusion prompted many settlers to embrace the new-state scheme, but in 1776 Virginia blocked the idea because of the state's plan to monopolize the western lands for Virginia alone. Soon after the 1779 extension of the Mason-Dixon Line, Pennsylvania law declared the new-state proposition treasonous because it would violate the terms of the compromise between Virginia and Pennsylvania that had allowed the line to be struck further west. The frontier was "divided into two armed camps" until Indian problems on the Ohio River diverted Virginia's military resources. Pennsylvania's spies, the "threat that settlers' lands would be sold, and Congress' cool reaction finally quieted the westerners." Even with this temporary abatement, "the dispute on the Monongahela carried over into the Revolution, seriously hampered the war effort, and set the stage for civil strife between Tory and Patriot partisans."[36]

While the claims of the Vandalia organization and the Indiana Company came to nothing, their individual stockholders as well as other absentees managed, with varying degrees of success, to retain ownership of tremendous amounts of land. The Wharton brothers alone controlled more than 2 million acres. Virginia speculators were by no means inactive. Thomas Walker and the Loyal Company claimed 200,000 acres in the transmontane. George Croghan and Thomas and Michael Cresap claimed holdings along the Cheat River Valley, and Francis and William Deakins controlled the Horseshoe Bottom of the Cheat River Valley. George Washington owned thousands of acres in the transmontane. His holdings lay as far west as the Ohio, Kanawha, and Little Kanawha rivers, as well as throughout other portions of Virginia. Washington "not only obtained western lands by bounty warrants and by purchase, but he became interested in various land companies—the Walpole Grant, Mississippi Company, Military Company of Adventures, and the Dismal Swamp Company." He estimated his estate at 60,200 acres in his will, but in fact, "Washington was land poor. He possessed a princely estate in acreage, but little of it was productive."[37]

There were other owners of vast lands in the West. Many of them never ventured into the region, but their influence would be felt in later decades. Merchants who backed the Ohio Company, planters who lived in Virginia's Tidewater region, and New England investors were influential in the affairs of transmontane Virginia, even though they did not reside within the region. Robert Morris, Henry Banks, Robert and Samuel Purviance, Levi Hollingsworth, and Henry Lee were a few such individuals.[38] Their vast claims were upheld by deeds recorded in the Virginia land office. These deeds formed the core of evidence that was used in the nineteenth century as the legal basis to force many mountain farmers to give up some or all rights to their land.

2

Settler Politics

Jostling for Place and Power
in the Brand-New West

Some of the wealthy landowners lived within the Monongahela region. Michael Cresap, George Croghan, Saveray de
Valcoulon, Albert Gallatin, and Thomas, sixth Lord Fairfax
were prominent western speculators.[1] Along the Cheat River,
Francis and William Deakins conducted a land business that
brought them into frequent contact with settlers. The fortunes of these and other speculators were mixed. Two centuries of encroachment and counterclaims ultimately reduced
Lord Fairfax's proprietary from five million acres to two
million acres. The land was ultimately dispersed after the
American Revolution to a syndicate led by James Markham
Marshall, son-in-law of Revolutionary War financier Robert
Morris.[2] The Deakinses faced frequent challenge from settlers. Nevertheless, speculator interests, if not these individuals, remained powerful influences within the transmontane
for decades after the Revolution.

Some speculators, including Cresap, acquired their lands
by negotiating land treaties with various Indian leaders. Iroquois and Wyandottes negotiated with white explorers for
land rights and hunting areas. Also, numerous squatter-
speculators settled, legally or not, and later sold their home-
steads to others before moving on westward.[3] This chaotic
activity in land claims was worsened by the absence of uni-
form record-keeping systems. Despite the hardship and risk,
some land agents received grants of land and ultimately
moved to the area to manage their land-based business affairs. In the region that became Pocahontas, Randolph, and

Tucker counties, the Deakinses, from Georgetown, Virginia, began their land business in the Monongahela before 1781. This family received a 1783 conveyance of 6,130 acres from the state. A relative, perhaps Francis and William Deakins's father, surveyed in 1788 the "Deakins Line" that runs from the Fairfax Stone north to the Mason-Dixon Line, forming the boundary between western Maryland and West Virginia. The Deakins family quickly claimed some 36,000 acres as the basis of their land business.[4]

Exploring and claiming the land was arduous, but even greater dangers accompanied settlers. Shawnee Indian raids were terrifying realities for the earliest settlers, who faced the constant threat of attack. One assault took place near St. George in 1781. Returning from registering their claims for land along Horseshoe Bottom, a group of settlers led by John Minear was attacked by Indians. Three, including Minear, were killed, but two settlers survived.[5] After the Revolution, raids in 1787 and 1789 prompted Virginia to send militia to protect western settlers. Raids continued until General Anthony Wayne's victory over several Indian tribes at Fallen Timbers in 1794 and the removal of the Shawnee and eight other tribes to the West. Only then were whites free of Shawnee, Miami, Ottawa, Chippewa, Potawotomi, Sauk, Fox, and Iroquois raids within the mountains.[6]

Spurred by fears of Indian raids and British treachery, the leaders of Virginia moved quickly to charter towns in the West and to create local governmental units. Virginia's government had already begun to address the westward population growth by creating new counties from the old West Augusta district. The 1776 division of West Augusta into Monongalia, Ohio, and Yohogania counties was revised, and additional counties were formed. As settlement increased and population rose, Virginia created Harrison County in 1784 from Monongalia; in 1787 Randolph was partitioned from Harrison. Pocahontas County was formed in 1821 from parts of Bath, Pendleton, and Randolph counties. Tucker was formed from Randolph in 1856.

Pocahontas County contains 942.61 square miles, and Tucker, 421.67 square miles. Randolph, despite the loss of territory to other counties, is the largest county in West Virginia, at 1,046.34 square miles. All of these 2,410.62 square miles of territory were explored, claimed, and settled in the eighteenth century by a wide array of claimants that included kings and commoners, merchants, Indians, and soldiers. Despite the variety of themes and guises, the quest for empire clearly guided the westward push.

Those who came west brought familiar institutions with them. The earliest settlers installed the traditional Virginia county government system. This system of deferential leadership placed much trust in the idea of an educated elite. From among themselves, farmers elected a strong and honest local leadership. Wealthy farmers in the mountains, as in the Tidewater, were chosen by their constituents to govern their counties. The mountain county courts fulfilled the same social and governmental role as the county courts of the eastern counties. Society in the transmontane became increasingly stratified with the rapid increase of population. As in the eastern part of Virginia, wealthier families in the West who controlled the courts acted in the interests of local hierarchies. During the revolutionary period, mountain farmer gentry retained a firm grip on local government. Traditional Virginia society established itself west of the mountains, where the population extended Virginia's successful planter and general farming culture beyond the Blue Ridge, into the Shenandoah Valley, and beyond.[7]

In Virginia's political system, local elections gave small farmers political control of their leaders. Accountability was important to political success. There was extensive small farmer participation in the early Virginia political system. The gentry, though undefined by any firm set of characteristics, was thoroughly understood by all Virginians to be an upper class. Somewhat below them fell the "solid and independent yeomanry looking askance at those above, yet not venturing to jostle them." Farmers sat on juries, held petit offices, and, most important, voted. By the time of the American Revolution, the southern mountain region, including transmontane Virginia, was being rapidly settled by a multitude of small farmers who grew grain and raised livestock.

This "virtual agricultural revolution" expanded the ranks of small farmers in the region of the South open to them. Settlers came from Pennsylvania, New York, England, Ulster, and the Palatine.[8]

Among early settlers, those from Ulster were important migrants to Virginia's West. They were among those whose land claims predated the Virginia 1779 land law as well as the American Revolution. These Scotch-Irish formed the largest group of Europeans to migrate to America before the Revolution, and many of them drifted in a southwesterly pattern into the Appalachian Mountains. In the mid-1700s, natives of Ulster came first to Virginia, Maryland, and Pennsylvania.[9] Some of these settlers were prosperous men who paid their own way to the New World. Men of modest success, these immigrants sent representatives ahead to find good soils for agricultural pursuits in America, often availing themselves of the opportunities in western lands. Ulstermen Samuel Glass and Andrew Vance and German-speaking Jost Hite were important settlers in the Appalachian transmontane. Self-made men who were interested in speculative and commercial lands, they were not of the same class as the desperate immigrants who traded freedom for passage out of England in the seventeenth century. With the assurance of land awaiting, these later, more affluent immigrants moved quickly to positions of influence in Virginia's West. Other immigrants came as tenant farmers, confident of quickly acquiring their own land. But regardless of financial standing, most of these eighteenth-century settlers were farmers, coming from the British Isles to continue farming.[10]

Mountain settlers were taking their first steps toward an agricultural society, basing their farm production on the demands of an increasing population in the Ohio Valley and New Orleans, as well as European markets. The markets of New Orleans and the inability of Europe to feed itself offered attractive opportunities for American farmers who could produce foodstuffs for export.[11] They followed the agricultural practices of the Shenandoah Valley, whence some of them came. These practices suited their values, goals, and resources. Settlers in the early Shenandoah were determined to build an agricultural society in the West. They were not "reduced to a raw state of economic evolution," nor were they distinguished by "geographical isolation, complete self-sufficiency and marginal living standards. Such conditions lasted one to two years at most."[12]

Settlement of the Shenandoah lands had begun in 1720, and within twenty-five years farmers were pressing into the Monongahela region, aiming to expand agriculture and carry on traditional Virginia farmer cultural patterns. Like the early Shenandoah Valley farmers, trans-Appalachian farmers were engaged in a determined pursuit of a commercial economy based on agriculture. By 1790, 19 percent of Virginia's population lived west of the Blue Ridge. Westerners lacked a "miracle crop" such as easterners had with tobacco, but they managed to create "a complex, diversified, expanding and well-integrated foundation for their economy." Of necessity they were self-sufficient in food, but these mountain farmers were at heart commercial men. They sought to expand their networks and to enhance their profitable agriculture. Their economic community was successful and growing.[13]

Virginia farmers were particularly willing to raise wheat; their low country soils were exhausted by the demands of tobacco, and mountain farms lay outside the climatic zones that favored the weed. For Virginia's farmers, "European population growth had enhanced the value of the little man's harvests, not the rich man's staples." These dynamics also blurred "the old textbook distinction between the commercial agriculture of the South and the subsistence farming of the North."[14] Commercial agriculture, then, spurred westward settlement. Early settlers brought to the mountainous West the ways of those they left behind. They quickly became self-sufficient and used their agricultural surpluses to generate a commercial enterprise. Although scholars continue to debate the significance of the cultural background of these mountain farmers, cultural identity did not seem to be associated with farmers' economic fortunes until well into the nineteenth century. At that time concessions and compromises in lifestyles became necessary for survival in the region.[15]

More pertinent to the fortunes of early mountain farmers is the notion that individual entrepreneurs could not withstand the pressures of more wealthy and powerful business competitors under the provisions of the new federal Constitution. The "double edges of the Constitutional sword" cut both ways.[16] Although the 1789 document protected individual rights, it also allowed for the centralizing of wealth and power. The powerful edge of wealth was amply illustrated within the mountains of Virginia, where the political power of speculators and absentees increased, ultimately to dismantle the farmer-led local political system.

The pace of westward migration quickly moved the politically weaker small farmers and settlers farther from seats of Virginia government, where the more powerful landowners controlled affairs. Registering deeds was nearly impossible because of distance, so claims to lands were made by planting, building homes, and marking trees. Land offices were not located on the frontier, and sometimes settlers claimed, innocently or not, lands that were not available for settlement.[17]

The geographic reality of Virginia's transmontane further destined the West's history to unfold differently from that of the eastern areas of the state.[18] Water routes were available from these high mountain regions via the Cheat and Monongahela rivers all the way to New Orleans. The 1795 Treaty of San Lorenzo obtained Spanish recognition of U.S. boundaries and free navigation of the Mississippi River, which increased the markets open to western farming. A further provision of the treaty opened the Spanish-held port of New Orleans to American trade, enabling commerce along the Ohio River to increase. Mountain farmers were thus stimulated to plant crops for commercial purposes. Flour, potatoes, apples, and pork were among the crops raised in the transmontane for the New Orleans markets.[19]

Rugged mountains and west- and north-flowing rivers compelled western dwellers to look north and west for markets. The canal-building projects along the Potomac, James, and Kanawha rivers, which would have linked the East and West by water, were abandoned because of their high cost.

Western farmers remained limited by the imposing mountain crossing that lay between them and eastern markets. Hence, western farmers availed themselves of existing water transportation routes. The Monongahela River flowed north and converged with the Allegheny at Pittsburgh to form the Ohio River, which flowed to the Mississippi and thence south to New Orleans. This route, in the era before railroads, was the only commercial route, except for horseback, for those mountain residents who were too far west to use the Potomac River route to the Atlantic seacoast markets profitably. Cattle, which could transport themselves to market on the hoof, continued to be herded to the eastern markets of Baltimore and Philadelphia.[20]

This fledgling economy, however, would suffer from a scarcity of land, ultimately falling victim to Virginia's policies that made it easy for wealthy purchasers to amass vast lands. The Land Office Act of 1779 was an assault upon democracy in Virginia because it discouraged small landholdings. Such small holdings are recognized as "one of the most satisfactory means that has ever been devised" to secure democracy.[21] Under the provisions of transfer in that law, speculators could acquire millions of acres of western land cheaply by purchasing grantees' rights for cash.

As a result of the act, within a few years Robert Morris and Alexander Wolcott garnered two and a half million acres of Virginia's western lands, and "most of that remaining fell into the hands of other absentee speculators who paid, in depreciated currency . . . about fifty cents the hundred acres." Henry Banks, Wilson Carey Nicholas, Robert Morris, James Welch, and James K. Taylor each obtained half a million acres under this system. German immigrants Bernard and Michael Gratz, who settled in Philadelphia and became successful merchants, were active in land speculation ventures, participating early in trade with Indians and later in the Indiana, Illinois, and Wabash land schemes.[22]

Ironically, Thomas Jefferson, as governor of Virginia, participated in the drafting of this law, which so drastically undercut his own belief in the value of commercial farming. Virginia's dire need for revenues from land sales helped

nudge the governor to a more pragmatic stance. Nevertheless, Jefferson was acutely aware of political discrimination
against smallholders in the transmontane. He observed that
19,000 men "living below the falls of the rivers . . . give law
to upwards of 30,000 living in another part of the country."
He also foresaw that the planter class of Virginia would have
very different interests from the mountain farmers of the
West.[23]

Virginia's land law recognized four basic types of land
claims. Settlers relied on the provision that the state would
recognize and honor their prior claims, as evidenced by actual settlement and improvements. Treasury warrants conveyed acreage at the price of forty pounds per hundred acres.
Bounty warrants for land were issued as payment of state
debt or as a reward for service. Exchange warrants allowed
grantees to claim allowed acreage anywhere unpatented land
could be found. Possession of warrants did not by itself convey land; the grantee was compelled to find, survey, claim,
and patent the lands before the claim was secure.[24] Claims
were sometimes registered in frontier courthouses, but patents were only recorded in the Richmond land office. In cases
of dispute, the Richmond records generally prevailed as the
final authority.

Settlers often experienced much anxiety when they were
unable to defend their farms against challenges from other
claimants, even though the law stipulated that their preemption claims and military warrants took precedence over
speculator-held treasury warrants conveyed by the state land
office. For example, a survey for Noah Haden was recorded
on December 6, 1783, registering his claim to 594 acres of
land in Monongalia County on the Dry Fork of Cheat River,
part of a 1,000-acre warrant issued on October 16, 1782.
Haden also registered a 1,000-acre claim to land along Red
Creek at the Monongalia County Courthouse. This claim was
never patented in Richmond. The presence of documentation
of this nature in the Deakins family papers demonstrates
that, at least part of the time, settlers and land agents were
claiming the same land and that holders of treasury warrants
sometimes considered challenging settlers. The continued

pressure of speculation on the frontier added to the confusion. Investors were actively involved in influencing developments along the frontiers. Since 1760 they had been the largest and most powerful owners of Virginia's transmontane.[25]

Settlers within the Monongahela region were long established in Romney and along the South Branch River, Pattersons Creek, and the Maryland side of the Potomac. In fact, Thomas Cresap, Abram Johnson, Solomon Hedges, and Henry Van Metre entertained George Washington in their homes on his westward journey of 1748.[26] Later settlers moved westward along the Cheat. John Crouch arrived in 1766, and James Parsons settled in 1769. Adam Hyder followed in 1772, claiming four hundred acres along the Cheat River. John Minear brought a group of settlers in 1774. Also in 1774, John McNeil and others from the Valley of Virginia settled in the Little Levels district of Pocahontas County. Between 1772 and 1774 the Horseshoe settlers constructed a fort in modern Tucker County, and two other forts were built at the sites of present Beverly and Huttonsville.

David Minear in 1776 claimed one thousand acres along the Cheat River. The site may approximate the present location of the town of St. George, where David's brother John located a group of settlers before moving along the Cheat and establishing what surely must have been the first of many sawmills that would soon dominate the region.[27] James Parsons's sons in 1774 settled along Horseshoe Bend, claiming about four thousand acres. John Brannon, Noah Haden, Samuel Bonnifield, Isaac Booth, Salathiel Goff, and John Rush arrived between the end of the American Revolution and 1800.[28] Goff alone registered a county court claim for nearly five thousand acres.[29]

The settlers were attracted to the Cheat Valley's bottomland. The Deakinses' initial 1783 grant of 6,130 acres lay along the river, a lucrative site for timber and farming. Over the ensuing years, the supply of land would be inadequate to the demands for it, and controversy would frequently accompany land transactions.

After the Revolution, despite increasing numbers of challenges to land claims on the frontier, Virginia continued to sell land at a reckless pace, largely because no one knew the limits of western lands. People believed the supply was inexhaustible. Under the governorship of Edmund Randolph, the land office granted the Deakinses another two thousand acres west of the Cheat River. Two additional conveyances, dated October 31, 1788, contributed to the Deakinses' ultimate holding of at least thirty-six thousand acres.[30]

Since settlers also claimed land that was covered by these conveyances, controversy was common. This misfortune befell many of the original settlers in the transmontane. Contesting some of the Deakinses' claims, Thomas James Goff in September 1781 successfully petitioned the Monongalia County Court for verification of a claim of eight hundred acres on the Yohogania River as a preemption right, to include improvements made there in 1775. Ruling in Goff's favor were commissioners for claims to unpatented lands for Monongalia, Yohogania, and Ohio counties, formerly the old district of West Augusta. Commissioners John P. Duval, James Neal, and William Haymond, the surveyor, issued the directive.[31]

Land agents, surveyors, and speculators were careful to keep good records. In a report to the Deakinses dated April 3, 1793, surveyor John Compton reported converting an earlier Horseshoe Bottom survey, dated 1792, for Friend and Downard. But this did nothing to ameliorate the contradictory claims that were made for the bottomland. In the same period, land was surveyed for William Hilton, who was settling on the east side of the Cheat River adjacent to Thomas Parsons. Hilton's Coburn's Run parcel of 151 acres was a part of a larger land office treasury warrant. Still another very early claim was made in the Monongahela region by William Parsons. On December 1, 1783, he received fifty acres from a four-thousand-acre tract described in the Deakinses' records. Courthouse records show he claimed one thousand acres.[32]

A survey the Deakinses commissioned from W. Pettyjohn on July 12, 1784, may have been contested by other claimants in the region. Salathiel Goff that year received a grant of 240 acres from Virginia governor Benjamin Harrison, conveyed from a survey made in 1781 by Samuel Hanway.[33] Goff was a member of the Monongahela region's gentry. In 1787 he was appointed by the governor to be a justice of the peace for Randolph County, and that court subsequently elected him its first president.[34]

The Deakinses' May 1784 claim to 1,696 acres on the eastern shore of the Cheat probably overlapped with several settler claims in the same region, particularly those of the Parsons brothers. In 1791 David Minear claimed 500 acres along the bottom, and in 1793 Thomas and Elie Parsons claimed 303 acres.[35] In 1776 Minear had registered his claim to 1,000 acres along the Cheat in the Monongalia County Courthouse. It is not clear whether in 1791 he was settling an overlap with the Deakinses or claiming additional land.

Despite their wealth and power, the Deakinses were regularly confronted with challenges and other difficulties. A certificate issued on November 19, 1792, by Joseph Nevill, a Randolph County surveyor, brought the bad news that the lands the Deakinses had been assigned by Mary Walker could not be located. Only 200 acres of the 7,000 granted could be found by survey. Another survey report indicated that a plat of 23,500 acres claimed by the Deakinses was, by June 1794, "lost in prior rights." The family's prospects brightened when Governor Robert Brooke in November 1796 granted an additional 7,209 acres in Monongalia County to them.[36]

In 1798 a trial was held in Morgantown to resolve a dispute between "Deakins and Goff" over title to lands. An amicable settlement was reached in 1799. The Deakinses also were involved in disputes with John Threlkeld over a six-hundred-acre tract adjacent to their lands.[37]

All of these controversies arising from conflicting claims led farmers to repair faulty local land records. The impossibility of the task is illustrated by the experience of the Randolph County Court, which investigated land claims and the surveyor's records in 1803. Citizens William Wilson and William B. Wilson and Sheriff Asahel Heath were directed by the court to examine the records and discuss them with surveyor Henry Jackson. They were to determine whether there were two books of entries and to review "all other papers and records relative to said Office and make return on Oath to next Court."[38] Edward Jackson had been the first county surveyor and an early sheriff; Henry Jackson was appointed surveyor in 1793.[39]

Upon completion of their assignment, the three reported a parade of error, omission, and malfeasance. Indeed there were two survey books, and the entries did not match. Eight surveys were not recorded in the old land book but were in the new one. At issue were about ten thousand acres of land. Pages were torn out of the old land book, and comparison of entries in the two books revealed serious discrepancies in acreage and owners of record. The investigators found so many mistakes that they observed that noting all the errors would bring great expense to the county and inconvenience to themselves. The more egregious activities included surveyor Henry Jackson's scratching out old records and reentering them in his own name. Other entries, the group asserted, "materially alter the meaning of the entries when first made." In 1804 the county removed surveyor Hezekiah Rosecrance (a founding trustee of the town of Beverly) from his post, but the fate of Henry Jackson remains obscure.[40]

Aside from challenges, sloppy record keeping, and outright fraud, the history of these early land conveyances has been further obscured because political divisions have changed county boundaries greatly since colonial days. Rarely did records of old land transactions move to new county courthouses. More important, political differences within the Virginia statehouse led to confusion on the frontier. Claims made after independence but before the Virginia land office was established frequently were in conflict and often were found to be invalid. Despite the lack of securely recorded titles and claims, settlement continued, even though many of the settlers' claims were ever at risk of a challenge from land companies.[41]

Western settlers enjoyed the support of liberal (Democratic-Republican) Virginians who favored populating the interior. These leaders were led by some landowners who hoped to get rich by selling lands to settlers and at the same time stabilizing the republic with the presence of many small landowners. Their ranks included Richard Henry Lee, Thomas

Jefferson, George Mason, George Wythe, John Taylor, John Tyler, Sr., and James Madison. These liberals found themselves arrayed against conservative (Federalist) Virginians including Benjamin Harrison, Carter Braxton, Archibald Cary, and Edmund Pendleton.[42] The conservatives preferred to withhold sale of their property, speculating on price increases and higher profits from future sale of their lands. Western settlement and development would bring pressures for expensive governmental services, and that prospect threatened to bring higher taxes for wealthy land speculators. Because of a dispute with Thomas Jefferson, Patrick Henry, also a speculator, sided with the conservatives, even though he favored states' rights. The conservatives owned lands, but they also maintained social and economic ties with the mercantile trade, a characteristic not found in the liberal faction.[43]

Conservative Tidewater and Piedmont planters were "practical men" with ties to the merchants of New England. They espoused government of "the rich, the well-born, and the able," echoing the preferences of Alexander Hamilton. They worked to "steer the ship of state into channels that would prove profitable to themselves."[44] Many of them apparently hoped to continue the preindependence pattern of proprietary ownership, collecting rents and dues on their vast estates. Others wished to hold land for future use. Ultimately, all of them opposed land taxes.

Dividing Virginia's leaders was the dilemma of public finance, an issue that had long troubled leaders in other colonies as well. New York governor Robert Hunter in 1711–12 struggled with the question of who should bear the greatest burdens of taxation, merchant or landowner. Benjamin Franklin, in his brief stint as a Pennsylvania assemblyman, encountered difficulties in 1753–54 in getting Pennsylvania's proprietary owners to agree to very modest taxes on their lands to provide for collective security in dealings with the Iroquois League.[45]

Proprietary aspirations of some Virginia leaders continued into the era of the new republic. Elite landowners Americanized the concept, and with their amassed power and wealth they often managed to shift the tax burdens to merchants and their customers. Great landowners in Virginia and other colonies manipulated public policy to enhance their private interests.[46] The political divisions over public finance had significant influence upon the land policies of Virginia in the years after independence, reverberating into the twentieth century.

Liberal voices urged policies to facilitate settlement and the profitable sale of lands to individual frontiersmen. Conservatives favored speculation because many of them owned western lands and would risk losing their wealth in an onslaught of settlers' preemption claims and rising demands for public services.[47] Discouraging settlement also removed a need for new tax-supported institutions. Hence, the conservative position was cheaper for the taxpayers, and it won public support. In subsequent years, Virginia continued to tax livestock and personal property to ease the burden on conservative landowners and planters.

None of this tax controversy slowed the movement west. Frontier farmers moved on, establishing their own society along traditional Virginia patterns. The West became more attractive to settlers as population increased. Nearly all of the transmontane was settled before Jefferson's presidency began in 1801. Ohio achieved statehood in 1803, revealing how far west the frontier had pushed in the years since American independence. Settlers continued to move westward, but the land regulations and administration of them by Virginia never kept pace. Confusion over rules combined with hope for land to assure that chaotic record keeping stayed in lockstep with settlement.

Virginia continued to flourish and grow, but by 1830 the interests of the East and the West were sufficiently different to constitute threats to the welfare of each region. A white aristocracy was essential to maintaining eastern planters' investment in slaves. A minority in Virginia, the planters nevertheless retained political control by refusing to reapportion the state equitably as the populations in the western counties increased. Politically weak though numerically strong, westerners were cast into permanent political inferiority.[48]

Between the War of 1812 and the issuance of Andrew Jackson's Specie Circular of 1836, the owners of vast western lands gathered political power and cemented their control over Virginia's land policies, but these years also provided time for commoners to find their voices and demand a more generous share of political and economic opportunity. They echoed Thomas Jefferson's belief that natural commercial tendencies would serve to strengthen individuals and help them grow and flourish in a free market. Their outlook was democratic, capitalist, agrarian, and commercial.[49]

Jackson's Specie Circular was designed to help settlers acquire land by crippling the speculators' ability to purchase land with paper money. His direct attack blocked speculators' designs on the middle frontier lands, so they could not hoard it or buy it cheap to sell it dear. Whatever else Jackson's paradoxical administration may have brought the nation, this measure of beneficence afforded settlers of the middle frontiers a degree of security in land that had been denied the settlers of Virginia's transmontane.

Virginia's leaders, in the first half century of the republic, aligned themselves politically along national issues, and this allegiance directed their behavior toward local issues. If they had been able, or willing, to devote their energies to the problems of land in the West, perhaps a resolution to the confusing policies could have been achieved. Instead, Americans were overwhelmed with more immediate problems presented by Indians and British and French imperial designs. Western land policies were ignored. The new Whig party in the West was echoing the Federalist political traditions of centralized political power and industrial development. Farmers turned to the local courts to resolve a multitude of land controversies in western Virginia, but the state took no action to clear up the confusion within its boundaries.

In this regulatory vacuum, settlers continued to scramble for lands in the West. Until the land ran out on the frontier, conflicts among claimants were apparently settled by compromise or local court directives. Such homegrown resolutions as these, however, would not satisfy absentees in faraway cities, who defined their ownership with ancient grants, Virginia treasury warrants, Indian deeds, and private transactions, all duly recorded. Conversely, frontiersmen and farmers defined their claims by the crops they grew, the fences they built, and the taxes they paid. The line between settlers and speculators blurred. Ambitious entrepreneurs in the West often shared, at least temporarily, the perspectives of absentee landowners. Over time, however, transmontane dwellers and investors divided themselves into two large, loosely aligned groups. Some sought a proactive government devoted to transmontane development. Others wished for government to remain uninvolved in the West, keeping taxes low and development to an inexpensive minimum. Conflict between the groups was unavoidable. Ultimately, the descendants of both frontiersmen and speculators would discover that all too often they were claiming the same lands. In the inevitable struggle that ensued, the weak would lose their inheritance.

3

Backcountry Politics
Planter Economics and Frustrations in the West

Despite the obvious difficulties and disadvantages that accompanied settlers when they crossed the Appalachian Mountains, multitudes of them continued to stake their hopes for their futures on lands in Virginia's transmontane. They could not yet know of the many tribulations that lay in wait for them as they began to construct their new world in the West. Between 1800 and 1851 the white population of western Virginia grew to exceed that of the eastern part of the state, but carefully planned political maneuvers prevented westerners from realizing their potential as the political majority in Virginia's statehouse.

As the population grew, political activity and industrial interest in the region began to reflect the attitudes of the most powerful forces within western Virginia. Original settlers and their descendants faced difficulties after the War of 1812. National and state disputes over the tariff and slavery triggered political action by Virginia that was harmful to western development. Ignoring pleas for state assistance with internal improvements, the eastern-dominated state government legislated a permanent political inferiority for the West in the form of taxation policies that crushed all hopes of state-funded construction of roads and bridges. The East and West had mutually exclusive economic goals, but the East maintained political dominance sufficient to direct affairs as it chose, at the expense of the West. Eastern elites also nurtured an economic liaison with absentee landowners.

In spite of these political struggles, Virginia chartered

more and more corporations, both domestic and absentee. The state never objected to privately financed development, and consequently western-based organizations undertook internal improvements. At the same time, absentee firms and eastern interests tended with increasing frequency to focus on coal mining or timbering in the West. After 1805 these companies were located in coal-rich areas, and their charters proclaimed their intent to mine coal. Such new endeavors increased pressures for land and brought an unanticipated influence on local communities. These developments foreshadowed economic hardships in future years.

By the early nineteenth century, the idea of a national republic secured by freeholding commercial farmers was yielding to the pressure of an increasing population. The demand for land far exceeded its availability.[1] This shift occurred even before Thomas Jefferson, who espoused the aims of freeholders, left the presidency.

To satisfy their demands for land, Americans continued to look to the frontier. Despite rising population and conflicting land claims between 1810 and 1830, Virginia continued to grant land in portions of the Appalachian Mountains and the Ohio River Valley. The "real" frontier, however, was reaching past the Ohio River and extending into the Indiana country. Settlers and immigrants who could not meet the asking price of lands in the eastern regions of Virginia were willing to undertake the uncertainties and risks necessary to push westward into the mountains, or they could strike out for a settlement claim in the unbroken frontier West, far beyond the Alleghenies. Merchants and investors likewise looked to the West for gain.[2]

In Virginia, East-West struggles were compounded throughout the nineteenth century by increasingly prevalent absentee influences. From the outset of settlement, there was an unrelenting struggle over deeds and surveys along the Virginia frontier. The surviving records of the era show that vigilance was required of all claimants. William and Francis Deakins fought a continuing battle with settlers to preserve their land office warrants. Their claims to Randolph County lands dated from 1781, yet preemption, overlaps, and challenges from other settlers played havoc with their land business. Other claims and surveys were recorded in courthouses along the frontier but were never patented in the state land office in Richmond. Courthouse records were considered inferior to land office records until 1831, when a constitutional revision equalized all future records. For settlers and farmers in the West, this reform came too late. In the former district of West Augusta, some settlers registered their claims at the Monongalia County Courthouse between 1766 and 1794, but those claims, apparently, were never forwarded to Richmond for entry in the state books. They languished there until their rediscovery in 1920.[3] Local resolutions of land controversies, likewise, were rarely forwarded to Richmond. Although local resolutions seem to have been satisfactory at the time, subsequent decades brought more substantial challenges to descendants of original settlers.

Public attitudes concerning such land transactions often reflected the prevailing public policy concerning sale of public lands. The federal government has regulated the disposition of federal lands since 1785, but various congressional regulations have manifested "the divergent interests of squatters, farmers, speculators, and of government itself."[4] Generally, after 1828 pioneers settling west of the Ohio River found a more sympathetic federal attitude toward their rights and claims than did their predecessors in the Appalachian transmontane. The changed governmental attitude was expressed by definite policies that were designed to protect settler interests rather than the interests of speculators.

When the trans-Allegheny region was first settled in the 1760s, those who would later frame the new American government personally controlled great amounts of western land. In the nation's formative years, they used their positions of leadership to enhance their personal fortunes while they created the new republic. Robert Morris, Albert Gallatin, Wilson Carey Nicholas, Patrick Henry, Thomas Jefferson, George Washington, Benjamin Franklin, and George Mason were among these prominent national leaders.[5]

By the time of Andrew Jackson's presidency, most of the framers of the Constitution were dead, and the settlers' interests, not speculators', received the federal government's attention. Jackson was particularly opposed to the advantages that merchant capital and speculation could achieve, and he directed his policies at limiting their influence in society. He curtailed sale of federal lands to speculators, and he crushed the Second Bank of the United States. The deflation that followed was ruinous to the classes he defined and targeted, but settlers and farmers in the middle frontier were relatively unharmed. In fact, they flourished.[6]

Differences in perspectives and economic interests among westerners predated sectional identities. Class struggle, rather than sectional strife, explained much of the political behavior of the era: "More can be understood about Jacksonian democracy if it is regarded as a problem not of sections, but of classes." This interpretation, advanced in the 1940s by Arthur M. Schlesinger, Jr., has been challenged by those who see Jacksonian politics as a "vehicle for cultural conflict between hostile ethnic and religious groups." Yet the experience in Virginia during this era supports the notion that economic interests, and therefore class, directed political behavior.[7]

By 1830 a more democratic outlook characterized the young nation. Abandoning their deferential attitudes, more and more citizens attained greater participation in determining the affairs of the nation. Jackson introduced the notion of class into American thought, and frequently the concept was used to fuel attacks on wealth and elitism, or at least attacks on the power that wealth and elitism could command. Jacksonian thinking aroused a sentiment for a return to old republican values. Jackson touted the worth of the "people," as opposed to the "money power," and this thinking captured the attention of smallholders and ambitious common folk throughout the nation.[8]

Jackson's devotion to the "fundamental rules of simplicity and economy" and the "separation of the political power from the conduct of economic affairs" was attractive, but the actual result of this Jacksonian thrust to American affairs had a different influence on Americans who lived in the Appalachian Mountains. His Specie Circular, which curtailed sale of public lands to speculators, helped the pioneers of the middle frontier, because it enabled settlers to buy land directly from the government at deflated prices they could afford. Yet Jackson's support of the separation of government and business hurt the descendants of transmontane Virginian settlers, who belonged to the producer class Jackson supported. They suffered when Jackson's laissez-faire approach to business allowed the silk-stocking speculators, whom he detested, to profit from their investment in land within the Appalachian Mountains, unimpeded by federal interference.[9]

While federal acquiescence and the Specie Circular helped settlers on the newer frontiers, government's distancing attitude from business allowed it to ignore the economic assault upon the fortunes of those who had settled the older frontiers. Their descendants were beginning to lose ground to holders of Virginia treasury warrants, who used the political mood of litigiousness and broader participation in the democracy to defeat the land claims of residents in the Virginia mountains. Circumstances in Virginia earlier in the century serve to amplify this paradoxical development. After the War of 1812, national politics were more influential in determining Virginians' political allegiances than were local issues. Despite persistent accounts of western Virginians as isolated, apolitical mountain dwellers, they were in fact organized politically and involved in national, state, and local affairs. By 1815 farmers within the trans-Allegheny region were largely Democratic-Republican, but the Valley of Virginia and the Tidewater remained Federalist. Virginia was hotly divided on the issue of internal improvements that was then being debated in the U.S. Congress as well as in the Virginia statehouse. The implied powers of the federal Constitution were cited by congressional backers of improvements (western Whigs and Democratic-Republicans) as the source of federal authority to undertake development projects in the interior. In most of Virginia, states' rights proponents and the planter elite (former Federalists and eastern Whigs) feared loss of political control and higher taxes if the government funded internal improvements. But in the western portions of Virginia, citizens united to speak for the concept. Because westerners believed the region's economic growth depended on inter-

nal improvements, the western desire for roads and canals transcended political ideology. Congressional and state
representatives who had constitutional reservations about
federal participation were unprepared to vote against an issue of such importance to their constituents west of the
Alleghenies.[10]

Western Virginians were also closely watching, and con-
demning, the convolutions of the Northern Neck land case,
Fairfax's Devisee v. *Hunter's Lessee*.[11] In 1816, in a precedent-
setting decision, the Supreme Court resolved the ownership
of the remains of the Fairfax proprietary lands in favor of the
heirs of Thomas, sixth Lord Fairfax. The ruling came even
though Fairfax was a British subject whose lands should have
been confiscated after the Revolution. Chief Justice John
Marshall, who wrote the decision, profited from it. His
brother James Markham Marshall had earlier taken the justice's advice to form a syndicate to disperse the lands at a
profit.[12] The status of landowners who had received grants or
made purchases since confiscation was lowered by the ruling,
which respected title and property rights before American
citizenship.[13] The ruling gave the practical advantage to
speculators and absentees, who in later years used royal conveyances and Virginia land grants as evidence of clear title.[14]
Transmontane Virginia settlers were extremely careful to
record their claims, but standards of secure title changed
over the years.

Another national issue that caused East-West friction in
Virginia was the 1816 tariff of 30 percent. The domestic industry that had developed nationally during the War of 1812
welcomed the protection afforded by the 30-percent tax on
competing imports in peacetime. Most American industry
was located in New England, where support for the tariff was
nearly unanimous, but infant extractive industries in transmontane Virginia found themselves arrayed against the eastern planter class on this issue. With international trade
restored after the War of 1812, the industries wanted the support of the tariff. The members of the planter class opposed
the tariff because they heavily depended on imports, which
were far more costly with a high tariff in place.[15]

The role of these economic influences in the Appalachian transmontane has not been fully explored for the antebellum period, yet it is clear that tariff issues delineated key economic differences between the transmontane and the East. The "Tariff of Abominations" in 1828–30 only made things worse by logrolling special congressional interests into an equally high tariff package. South Carolina's response of nullification drew more public attention, but the tariff caused problems in Virginia as well. Westerners voted for the measure; easterners did not.[16]

Transmontane Virginians were farmers or small business owners. Traditionally they have been incorrectly perceived as independent of the vagaries of the commercial, industrial world. It is important to remember that the major holders of land in the transmontane were not simple frontiersmen. They were speculators, corporations, and land companies, intimately involved in the fluctuations of the financial community and equipped thoroughly to deal with its changing character. Settlers in the transmontane wanted internal improvements to enhance rising local commercial agriculture, and they wanted tariffs to protect local industry. The more powerful absentees and eastern elites saw only heavier land tax bills that would hamper speculation and erode plantation profits.

Speculators fought taxes and public spending. They objected to tax-funded improvements such as roads and public construction. Sometimes they refused to pay their assessments. As a result, mountain farmers, the actual beneficiaries of public spending, had to tax themselves and their smaller resources even more heavily to finance local schools, bridges, and highways. In the Federal era, transmontane Virginia simply had too few settlers to carry this burden alone. By the time settlement had increased, the West was so thoroughly controlled by absentees and speculators that taxes were shifted permanently away from land.[17]

Absentee speculators and Tidewater planters both opposed increased taxes on land, to the detriment of western Virginian entrepreneurs. In the West, Virginians found welcome economic shelter in the tariff on imported iron and hoped that higher taxes on land would bring long-sought internal improvements. In effect, because their economic interests were similar, the New England–based absentees and the eastern Virginia planters were allied against the occupants of Virginia's western regions. Northern and western similitude on tariffs could not withstand differences concerning land taxes. Within the Monongahela, agriculture required the boost that tax-funded road construction could bring. More and more farmers were moving to the region. Increasing political organization accompanied population growth.

Modest but organized local communities were in place within the mountains early in the nineteenth century, and by midcentury they were electing local governmental leaders. In 1855 Jesse Parsons was elected constable of the region of the Horseshoe Bottom where he lived, and William R. Parsons was justice of the peace. Before the formation of Tucker County in 1856, this section was still in Randolph County. For the year 1857, Jesse Parsons's list of tithables gave 258 white males. Three free Negroes and 21 slaves were also reported. Taxable property of these individuals included 425 horses and mules, 5,114 head of cattle, sheep, and hogs, 1 pleasure carriage, 28 watches, and 117 clocks. Fees of office paid during the year numbered 368.[18]

The following year, Parsons's records list 241 white males, 3 free Negroes, and 20 slaves. Property comprised 450 horses and mules, 5,147 head of cattle, sheep, and hogs, 2 pleasure carriages, 23 watches, and 105 clocks. Fees of office paid numbered 538.[19] "Fees paid" suggests an articulate and conscientious populace, committed to a stable and respected social order, not random settlers cast away from organized communities. These numbers also indicate that farmers went to court twice a year to transact business and take care of their taxes and other legal affairs. Knowledgeable, conscientious, litigious, and political, these Horseshoe Bottom farmers did not in any way resemble the ignorant mountaineers of folklore and popular fin de siècle travelogues. Their passage through these years resembles that of the residents of the younger settlement of Cades Cove, Tennessee, for whom the Monongahela settlers might have provided an example.[20]

Cheat River settlers were an organized and cohesive society of Virginia mountain farmers who were actively involved in commerce and agriculture.

The early records of Tucker County's government contain a lengthy portion of the records of a slander suit that transcended county and state boundaries. In *William J. Harper* v. *William W. Parsons, William J. Harper* v. *William R. Parsons,* and *William J. Harper* v. *Solomon Parsons,* the plaintiff complained that the defendants had ruined his credit by circulating rumors that he planned to default on a debt to the Weston branch of the Merchant Exchange Bank of Virginia. Harper asked for six thousand dollars in damages. The records of the court contain evidence, transcripts, and depositions from as far away as Baltimore. The suit, filed in 1856 in Randolph County, continued for years but in 1858 was moved to Tucker County, where it continued at least through 1860. Earlier still, but less far-reaching, was administrator George Lean's 1853 suit against Arnold Bonnifield, seeking repayment of debt to the estate of George Long plus twenty dollars in damages. Lean also sued David Moore and Robert Johnson in 1855 on behalf of the Long estate. Bonnifield was clerk of the county, but his position did not spare him the anguish of another suit in 1855, for debts owed the Long estate. His co-defendants were two Bonnifield relatives, Samuel and Arnold T.[21]

In 1855 Almira Butcher sued William Vick for breach of promise and trespass. She sought attachment of Vick's land in Randolph County and an award of two thousand dollars because he broke his promise of marriage. In 1857 the circuit court heard eleven suits for debt recovery and proceedings concerning foreclosures on three properties. In 1858 Caleb Boggess and John Hoffman sued Job Parsons for unpaid debts, and August F. Hartman sued William J. Harper for trespass and damages. Harper was fined fifteen dollars for impregnating Hartman's stepdaughter.[22]

These court records and Jesse Parsons's lists of tithables indicate that residents were active members of a community that clearly articulated its rules, responsibilities, and expectations. Remoteness, and the self-sufficient nature of the farming community, apparently led to imprecise outside observations about these transmontane farmers and their social system by the 1890s.

Seventy of Parsons's 1858 tithables reappeared on the 1870 federal manuscript census of agriculture. In addition, many more of the same surnames appeared, suggesting that many grown children remained in the region and successfully carried on traditional agricultural pursuits.

Transmontane Virginians' desires for economic development and internal improvements were reflected in legislation that offered lucrative inducements to privately financed industrial development. Local leaders sought supportive legislation to encourage development. For example, coal and timber were exempt from property taxes.[23] Banking services to western entrepreneurs were improved with the establishment of the Hampshire County Bank in 1860. Sometimes investors' interests overlapped: John Pancake, for example, an incorporator of the Preston Coal and Iron Company, was also affiliated with the banking venture. William A. Kuykendall, Isaac Parsons, Jacob Myers, John Heiskell, and Hanson Dawson also signed the March 9 charter.[24]

Westerners believed that appropriate industrial development, by and for westerners, would enable the West to develop economically for their own benefit. They were wrong. Absentee landowners and speculators successfully defeated the western campaign for regional growth and development by manipulating the political environment to suit their own purposes. The vast number of corporations and the potential legal contests over ownership of desirable land combined to create great pressures upon the resident landowners of the Monongahela region. As the timber and mineral wealth of the region appreciated, local residents were compelled to cope with overwhelming demands for the development of the resources. Their options were to sell out to developers or be forced out by legal maneuvers that challenged land titles.

A few corporate charters indicate that at first, local investors were included in the industrial development. Other native residents may have wished to remain in farming or local commercial pursuits, but they faced tremendous pressures to sell their land. Farmers who wished to expand could not successfully bid for good land because prices exceeded farming resources, but industrialists were always ready to buy. As the supply of farmland dwindled, it became more and more difficult for farmers to maintain their influence in the region. At the same time, the pressure mounted for them to sell their own holdings to industrialists.

State government, meanwhile, continued to grant lands that were probably already occupied, and corporate influence in the region continued to grow. For instance, in 1857 the Virginia legislature was still granting land in Tucker County to absentees and speculators. George and W.B. Dobbin of Baltimore received title to 27,188.5 acres on Black Run and Dry Run and the Black Fork of the Cheat River. William F. Deakins was awarded 5,357 acres on Coburn's Run, Horseshoe Run, Clover Run, Black Run, and Dry Run. Even after statehood, West Virginia in 1868 granted Jonathan Arnold 2,146 acres on Leadmine Run.[25]

As the demand for land continued to grow, some local owners undoubtedly sold out quickly, and with relief. For those owners of highly desirable tracts of land who did not wish to sell, there were other pressures, including legal challenges, partnerships with absentees, or compromise settlements. Hence, accommodation between industrialists and residents was essential, although locals quickly lost control and became redundant.

In the face of this insatiable appetite for land, settlement claims made by frontiersmen in the transmontane between 1779 and 1795 were by the 1880s found to be insecure. For many mountain farmers who had inherited their land from these settlers, this development spelled disaster.

4

Robber Baron Politics
Tax Breaks for Industry and Legislated Defeat for Western Residents

In the decades after 1830, interest in the economic potentials of the West gathered momentum. Absentee holders of Virginia treasury warrants took advantage of the federal government's laissez-faire policy toward business to eject descendants of early transmontane settlers, who were by then called squatters.[1] These absentees, for so long unseen and unheard, began to consolidate their holdings in the interest of coal, oil, railroading, and timber. These developments proved stressful for the mountain economy.

Other changes also adversely affected growth in the economy of the transmontane. As the nineteenth century advanced, partitioning of the large western Virginia counties into smaller and smaller political units sometimes had the effect of removing indigenous dwellers even farther from their land records, despite the general idea of the times that a courthouse ought not to be more than a day's ride away from any settler. Even though county courthouses were erected in these smaller, newer counties, transfer of land records was erratic and unreliable. Before 1800 Monongalia County had given up territory to form Harrison and Randolph counties. Thus, a landowner in a new county might still need to travel to the original county seat or to the land office in Richmond to prove his deed.

Separated from Kanawha, Greenbrier, Nicholas, and Braxton counties in successive partitions over many years, Clay County, Virginia, offers an instructive example of hidden and confusing land records. Residents suffered when their new county's court in 1858 was deluged with land disputes, deed challenges, and ejectment actions. Absentee industrialist William H. Edwards challenged local landowners who were residing, as descendants of settlers, on 105,000 acres of land that Edwards also claimed. He based his claim on a Virginia treasury warrant describing land surveyed in 1795 by Andrew Johnson for William Wilson and Benjamin Martin.[2] According to local histories, Edwards filed ejectment suits against the occupants of the land he claimed, but "a few days before a suit to evict, Edwards would go and offer to compromise with people" or just get the mineral rights. Page upon page of the Clay County deed books record these conveyances from Edwards to farmers "to settle conflicting claims."[3]

The local histories differ on the name of Edwards's firm and the dates of its operation, but Edwards was not the first entrepreneur to attempt to develop the region. Before the formation of Clay County, Virginia chartered the West Virginia Iron Mining and Manufacturing Company, to do business on "two tracts of land in patents to Benjamin Martin and William Wilson." The charter specified that "the privileges hereby granted shall in no way impair the rights of any other persons who may have claims upon the . . . tracts of land."[4] That firm apparently failed, and Edwards's family purchased the land, "sight unseen," from the estate of New Yorker Charles O. Handy in 1849.[5] Edwards was an incorporator of the Paint Creek Coal and Iron Mining and Manufacturing Company and the Henry Mining Company as well.[6] The charters of these firms contained no admonition concerning the rights of occupants of the land; the deeds in the Clay County records show that Edwards wasted no time in asserting control. Such threats, coming so soon after the county was partitioned from Kanawha, Nicholas, and Braxton counties, were surely disheartening to locals who had assumed that a nearby courthouse would bring convenience, not challenges to their landholdings.

These examples of overlapping claims and conflicts between owners illustrate one method that was used to develop a legal challenge of ownership. Faced with the expense of an ejectment suit, many of Edwards's perplexed adversaries accepted his offer; they compromised their titles with him. His claims were registered in the Richmond land office as well as the Kanawha County Courthouse, and these deeds were superior, in the eyes of the courts, to the locally maintained records.

The Nicholas County Circuit Court ordered the sheriff to sell the entire 105,000-acre tract of land to pay back taxes in 1854. Edwards redeemed the parcel for $1,250, according to an 1866 sheriff's deed. Occasionally Edwards lost his bid to dispossess a farmer. In 1868 John Duffield was awarded lands by the court system.[7] Important to the study at hand is the clear evidence that land controversies in Clay County began in the 1850s, not the 1880s. Although the challenges to farmers' deeds continued throughout the post–Civil War era, it appears that title controversies were well resolved before industrialization began in earnest. Edwards sold the land, or some rights to it, to the heirs of Alan Caperton in 1882.[8]

Similarly, in Greenbrier County, at midcentury, the Richard Parker Foulke family was attempting to establish a new county, a new county seat, or a railroad line to enhance the value of their speculative lands along Meadow River. William Parker Foulke sought legal advice from attorney and landowner Samuel Price of Lewisburg regarding the best way to establish control over a tract of land patented to George Anderson and Oliver Toles and subsequently claimed by Hamilton Wade and Mary Wade. In his letter, Foulke also asked for tax advice concerning ten parcels of uncontested Foulke land. He urged Price to retain his letter for future reference.[9]

To his father in Philadelphia, Foulke wrote that he was discovering conflicts with family surveys: "Jacob Amick survey conflicts with our No. 9, from the middle of it to Anglin's Creek." Suspicious local residents were a substantial concern for Foulke: "The people here are so quick that a suspicion of my design [to control the river] would suffice to thwart me." Efforts for the new county seat were going poorly as well. "The bill . . . does not pass at this session by reason of informality in the proceedings here." Even so, young Foulke was determined to pursue his plan. "With a county seat near us and a railroad within ten miles, land must rise," he told his father. Predicting that one or both events would be realized in a moderate length of time, he encouraged family patience: "At all events, with such light taxes, the land we have is worth a little nursing."[10]

The separate interests of commercial agriculture were expanding within the transmontane in the first half of the nineteenth century as well. Farmers were imitating the Shenandoah Valley experience, as the western economy began to diversify and require internal improvements. The development was politically divisive for Virginia. Slavery was threatened by the taxation required to fund highways, bridges, and navigation systems.[11] Western commerce was growing rapidly. Mountain agriculture, which did not depend on slave labor, was becoming too independent. Farmers' rising numbers threatened the eastern planters' political and economic dominance of the state.

Western economic independence also threatened to slow any industrial transformation within the region, because a class of wageworkers was unlikely to arise from independent farmers. Slaves, because they were owned by others, could not be used as labor for an industrial transformation either. They were too costly. Therefore, the desire of the East to preserve its hegemony and the desire of the absentee industrialists for a labor supply recast the region's history as a struggle for control of one of the factors of production.[12] In essence, the landed planter of eastern Virginia was struggling against the absentee capitalist for control (or creation) of labor supplies.[13] Increasingly, absentee landowners, New England industrialists, and Tidewater elites became bound by their mutual need to dominate the West. This short-lived alliance became increasingly more visible in the rising numbers of absentee-dominated corporate charters issued by Virginia just before the Civil War.

Other links between the planter elite and the industrialists were prevalent also. Southern planters frequently found comfort in social and political ties outside the South.[14] It seems plausible that the issue of securing a labor supply for the second industrial revolution ultimately played a role in bringing the North and the South to civil war. Slaves, as one factor of production, stood out of reach of the industrialists, and this issue ultimately divided planters from the industrialists. Slaves were the most available source of labor, which, according to Barrington Moore, Jr., was essential to northern capitalists: "Here was a serious sticking point. Free land to the west tended to draw off laborers, or at least many people thought so."[15] The Civil War, at some level, may have been a struggle between powerful capitalist groups for control of a great portion of the nation's labor supply. After the Panic of 1857, the price of cotton declined, while the price of slaves continued the increase begun in 1807 after the ban on the slave trade. If free laborers truly were moving to the West, away from the factories of the North, then the captive labor supplies of the South would have offered a lucrative field for merchant capitalists. Virginia's failure to find a way to abolish slavery, that is, to generate a supply of wage labor, and to colonize blacks outside the South without economic ruin probably was the greatest barrier to an economic alliance between industrialists and Virginia planters.[16] New England and lowland Virginia can be seen as sparring with each other for control of the West; this interpretation is enhanced by the fact of the Civil War.

Shadows of this triangular political arrangement that allied Tidewater planters, speculators, and absentee landowners against the western farmers and businessmen fall darkly upon the history of Virginia, the transmontane, and the state of West Virginia. Out of this liaison emerged the political activity and economic realities that defined the region's industrial era (1880–1920). By the time industrialization arrived in 1880, the southern states provided most of the land and many of the workers that were essential to the northern-led economic transformation.[17]

Extractive industries developed quite apart from the interests of the transmontane populace and in apparent disregard for their interests. Yet control of the fixed land supply was necessary to both industry and agriculture. The farmers with whom the industrialists were competing were able, but no match for well-trained, highly paid corporate lawyers. Corporate representatives were successful when they challenged local farmers over deeds to property. This pressure for land, over time, altered the social organization of the region. Farmers were not ignorant of their rights, nor were they willing to yield easily to outside pressure, but they were outmatched in the courtrooms. The cost of sufficient legal talent prevented a great many farmers from fighting their adversaries more aggressively.

The fact that Virginia's western population was increasing while the eastern population was slowly declining added to the friction between the two regions. The population of Virginia's transmontane increased and became ever more vocal between 1820 and 1840.[18] The new residents took advantage of panic-stricken speculators' rush to raise cash, purchasing lands that absentee owners were selling. More available land at more attractive prices in these decades brought at least a 51-percent increase in population to the transmontane area. The growth was sufficient to trigger the creation of several new counties. Pocahontas County was formed in 1821; the census of 1830 reported its population at more than two thousand persons. Western Virginia's population continued to grow. By 1840 Logan, Morgan, and Nicholas counties had been formed. The new counties represented new political organizations and, in time, additional opposition to eastern-dominated state and federal governmental policies. Like every other newcomer to the Monongahela region, these farmers found that their land claims were at risk of being challenged from outside. Their political influence would be eroded as well.

Representing Virginia in Congress in the first decades of the nineteenth century was a group who devoted themselves to restoring what they perceived to be Virginia's "fallen prestige," rather than confronting the issues presented by the changing West.[19] These leaders longed for the deference and grandeur of the lush plantation days of the past, when the planter elite led the state without challenge. They were not sympathetic to national or state plans for western economic development.

Traditional Virginians were unsettled by Kentuckian Henry Clay and his economic ideas. Senator Clay's American Plan found favor in western Virginia in 1828. The scheme would have raised taxes and tariffs to support development of the West with federally funded internal improvements. Clay believed that American strength required economic independence and military might. These concepts formed the foundations of his American Plan, which meshed nicely with the ideas of Virginia's proponents of internal improvements. Yet Virginia's voice in Congress spoke only for the fading cavalier and the declining planter elite, not for the bustling western population that produced neither tobacco nor slaves.[20]

A similar array of interests dominated the Virginia statehouse, where the East maintained a tight grip on political power, despite the growing population in the West. This political distribution consequently placed the interests of absentee landowners ahead of those of western residents, with the inevitable result of inferior political status for the West. Neither eastern planters nor northern industrialists could accommodate the needs of the West without undermining their own security. Collaboration was possible between planters and yeomen when yeomen were insulated from "mercantile intrusions," but conflict was inevitable when planters allied with "captains of economic development." Neither the planter elite nor the merchant capitalists of New England could risk the consequences of political success for the West, which would almost certainly bring higher taxes and, ultimately, the demise of slavery, since taxes would make the system unaffordable.[21] New England capitalists eschewed overt political interference, preferring a passive role. Never a force for change, "merchant capitalists fed off existing modes of production, no matter how backward." Absentee investors were financiers and, as such, "adjusted their interests to those of the prevailing ruling classes and resisted all attempts to introduce revolutionary transformations into the economy, into politics, into class relations."[22] Even though absentee participation in the economy of Virginia's transmontane was passive in this era, it was significant; the North could have changed the fortunes of the West, but it chose to respect and accept the planter elite's social order. Ultimately, the northern capitalists would compete with the southern planter elite and by the tool of war would successfully impose the priorities of northern merchant capital upon the region's economy, at the expense of the entire South.

Grumbling about representational reform in the western reaches of Virginia prompted the state to commence constitutional revisions. Despite western population growth, however, changes rejected western interests. Revision of the Virginia state constitution was undertaken in 1830 and again in 1851. The 1829–30 revision brought no relief to the West. Generally, the changes protected the interests of Tidewater planters, even in decline, and did not enhance or implement any part of the proposals of mountain farmers and Virginia manufacturers. Protected, too, were the interests of absentee land companies, speculators, and industrialists. Personal property and livestock taxes remained high, while land taxes were kept low. Slaves were taxed at a rate lower than land, and state-funded internal improvements were voted down.[23]

Generous terms and confusing rules for redeeming lands for back taxes gave leeway to absentees who may have found Virginia's taxes burdensome. Historically, land agents and absentees went years without paying taxes, and they ultimately were able to negotiate an amicable and less burdensome tax compromise with county assessors. Francis and William Deakins in 1836 struck such a deal with the sheriff of Randolph County. The Deakinses' records indicate they paid taxes and penalties on 4,130 acres of land for the years 1832–36 that totaled $1.06.[24] Wealthy landowners avoided taxes even as they strengthened their political positions.

Remembered predominantly as the instrument that slammed the door on the hopes of slaves because it outlawed manumission and tightened black codes, the Virginia constitution of 1831 also derailed the interests of the western Virginia inhabitants in favor of absentee owners and the eastern planters. Conservatives such as Abel Upshur, the fervent advocate of the mixed-basis representational scheme, argued successfully at the Richmond convention that the term *majority* could reflect interests other than numerical superiority.

The statesman successfully contended that the holders of the most property have the greatest stake in the nature of the government. Universal white male suffrage, he believed, had been demonstrated a failure by the French Revolution. Upshur's plan gave the East a twenty-eight-vote majority in the new assembly.[25]

In order to win western support, the East promised to reapportion the legislature within ten years. Despite that assurance, western delegates to the convention accounted for all but one of the forty votes against the new constitution. It was adopted over western objections.[26] Without fair representation in the statehouse, western Virginians were again disappointed in their quest for improved transportation and communication links.

Possessing only one major internal improvement, the 1818 Cumberland-to-Wheeling National Road, western Virginians were anxious for state policies that would enable them fully to tap the economic potentials of their homeland.[27] The taxes necessary to fund development of resources would have made speculation in lands prohibitively expensive and would have made painful dents in planter resources. But a tax increase would have given western Virginians a more equitable role in directing the state's economic and political course. The political control, though not the political majority, resided with the planters, who decided to tax livestock and personal property more vigorously than land or slaves.[28] Thus, internal improvements were never funded by the state.

Lawmakers succeeded in denying tax aid to western development, but they did not halt internal improvements. The legislature did not oppose the privately financed ventures that accompanied western growth. Early industrial activities and privately funded internal improvements in the Monongahela country were routinely licensed by the state. Charters were issued for several projects in the region, and older charters were revised. In 1824 the Cheat River Bridge Company charter of 1805 was amended to revise the amount of stock the firm could issue.[29] Among their goals, westerners wanted navigational improvements on the Kanawha to facilitate shipments of such products as David Ruffner's salt and John P. Turner's coal.[30] They also sought bridges, stream channel improvements, and, always, roads.

Without the political strength that would come from a one-man, one-vote constitution, the West could never achieve economic growth. The 1841 reapportionment did not materialize despite the promises made in the 1830 convention, and the West remained politically weak while overtaking the East in population. Steady population growth accounted for the formation of twenty-seven new counties between 1800 and 1849.

Even without state assistance, determined private sector efforts continued to open up the interior of Virginia to economic development. Roads and other transportation improvements were the focus of the western entrepreneurs. Later on, the costs of mineral exploration and development required larger amounts of capital than transmontane entrepreneurs could amass, and outside investors became more prevalent in the region. Absentee control of Virginia's western regions was so common by 1855 that Virginia's native entrepreneurs were beginning to despair. Edward Kenna lamented that the Kanawha coalfields were managed by non-Virginians. John P. Turner, who began mining in 1817, was a New Yorker. Virginia lawmakers increasingly recognized that the West was dominated by investment groups from New England and other non-Virginia areas. University of Virginia professor William B. Rogers reported to the Virginia General Assembly on coal in the Kanawha Valley in this era. His report "marked the end of wholly local ownership of coal mines" in the Kanawha.[31] Virginia's lawmakers were even more determined not to tax themselves to support an absentee endeavor.

The corporate charters of the period reflect a strong desire on the part of western Virginians for more and better transportation networks. Activities that were located in or near the Monongahela region had been authorized by Virginia's legislature earlier and initially represented Virginian-led pursuits. In 1832 the state approved a lottery to raise funds to construct a road from Moorefield to Franklin. That same year, the state chartered a turnpike company based in Romney. A dam on the South Branch of the Potomac was authorized on March 20, 1832.[32]

The rise of railroad building, and planter objections to the costs of the project, ultimately forced the shelving of the James River and Kanawha Canal through the interior. The resulting lag in economic development deepened the rift between East and West. As a consequence of this retreat from political discourse, power drifted to the most conservative of the state's leaders, who, since American independence, increasingly had been allied politically and economically with the New England industrialists.[33] The wisdom of Jefferson was no longer available to agrarian or commercial Virginians; their old intellectual had died in 1826.

As the West-East rift deepened, fears of the dismemberment of Virginia were being expressed and were being taken seriously. At least one delegate, W.B. Giles, linked rending Virginia with similar breaches in other southern states, and ultimately the Union. More talk suggested the possibility of redrawing boundaries between Virginia and Maryland to give Maryland more western land and consequently to induce a westward push of the Baltimore and Ohio Railroad to Parkersburg. The newspapers of Winchester, Charleston, and Wheeling began to recommend severing the West from Virginia.[34]

The West had expected the assembly to reapportion representation after 1841, equalizing the region's influence in state affairs. Throughout the 1840s, disgruntled westerners had called repeatedly for reform and constitutional revision and occasionally for separation of West from East.[35] An 1851 attempt to patch up relations in the form of a new constitution gave the West more representation but did not fully resolve inequities. Disharmony among westerners weakened their ability to deal more effectively with the East, but by 1850 they succeeded in their call for a convention. Unable to defeat the planters' insistence upon a mixed-basis apportionment, the more populous West was consoled with a House majority, while the East controlled the state senate and excepted slave property from equitable taxation.

The West was awarded by that convention 83 of 152 House of Delegates seats and 20 of 50 senate seats. Representation at the reform convention was apportioned to assure eastern supremacy in the outcome. Only 59 delegates came from the West, while the East sent 76. Had representation at the convention been based upon the white-basis plan of the West, that section would have received a majority of representatives, leaving the eastern portion of Virginia a minority, with 61 convention seats to the West's 74.[36] Such a shift in the composition of the constitutional convention would have produced a document that reflected western concerns. Probably it would have also seriously eroded the constitutional protection of slavery in Virginia by the hand of equitable taxation, an untenable proposition for the Tidewater planters.

Never totally committed to slavery, Virginians always struggled with the institution because it worked economic hardship on most Virginians, as demonstrated by the continuing East-West debates. Because the threat to the institution was grounded in rational economic interests, it was a serious problem for the survival of the planter elites. Western Virginians were not proemancipation, nor did they oppose slavery per se; they opposed exempting slave property from fair taxation, and they opposed using slaves as a basis for representation.[37] Changes in taxation were designed to ease the burden on slave owners but not mountain farmers. Farmers paid taxes on land and livestock, while slaves were taxed at a fixed value of only three hundred dollars each.

The potential ramifications of a rising population in the West and a declining population in the East likely engendered an additional proposed reform that prohibited the formation of counties smaller than six hundred square miles.[38] Such a restriction on county size posed hardships for westerners. Rugged terrain and the absence of roads, canals, or navigable rivers slowed the development of commerce that had characterized the settlements of the Valley of Virginia in the late 1700s. A further limit on the creation of counties compounded the challenge to commerce in the West by limiting the rise of new communities.

Along with the population, land transactions and mineral

extraction companies increased in the western reaches of Virginia before the Civil War. The state's records indicate that a steadily increasing number of charters for mining companies were granted by lawmakers. Beginning in counties that lay to the east of the Blue Ridge, mineral exploration moved westward quickly. Generally these firms were financed, at least partly, by eastern or absentee capital. These corporations were limited by law to a specific locale, and they were legally restricted to ownership of a maximum acreage of land.[39] Maximum permissible landholdings varied, and in some cases, holdings were vast indeed. Supplementing an earlier charter of the Berkeley Coal Mining and Railroad Company, the legislature in 1836–37 authorized "any quantity of land included in or in the vicinity of the coal region" up to a limit of ten thousand acres. Furthermore, the firm was given permission to dam the Potomac River. On April 2, 1838, Virginia incorporated the Virginia Mining and Manufacturing Company and also granted incorporators John and Jacob Shariff of Morgan and Berkeley counties permission to purchase and hold ten thousand acres of land upon which to construct railroads.[40]

As the number of charters for mining firms increased, so did the amount of land claimed by industrialists. Before long the supply of land became insufficient to satisfy the claims of all potential owners. It quickly became apparent that the farmers of the transmontane and the industrialists were heading for confrontations over titles to the land. The manner in which these conflicting claims were resolved effectively disestablished a large portion of the traditional mountain farming culture and set in motion a process of industrialization that brought negative changes to the Monongahela region.

Many of the new corporations were businesses located in or near the Monongahela.[41] At least fifty-two thousand acres of land in a four-county area of the Monongahela region were targeted by industry before 1840. The future link between industry and state government was forged in this era. In the transmontane, as the Civil War loomed, business leaders took the lead in West Virginia's statehood movement, particularly

Francis H. Pierpont and Arthur I. Boreman, both coal company investors. Pierpont headed the restored government of
Virginia, which gave permission for the formation of West
Virginia, and Boreman served as the first governor of the new
state.[42] Peter G. VanWinkle, one of the first two U.S. senators
from West Virginia, was linked by marriage to the Rathbone
Oil firm of New Jersey, which had interests in Wirt County.

Over time, firms incorporated in other states also began
operating within the transmontane. Aside from the Virginia
charters recorded in the Acts of the General Assembly, little
evidence of their number is available. Other organizations
are mentioned in land records, deeds, court transactions, and
local histories, and thus we can establish a minimum number
of entrepreneurs. The actual, surely greater, number is elu-
sive. Local histories tell of John Taylor who in 1845 built a
mill on the Cheat River, served in the Virginia legislature,
and owned six hundred acres of land on the west side of Cheat
River bottom. W.J. Mason around 1850 constructed a water-
powered sawmill near Leadmine. Abraham Parsons, a de-
scendant of an original settler and a member of the local
gentry, built a lumber and grist mill on the slough of the
Cheat River at about the same time. His mill, which was destroyed by a flood in 1857 and then rebuilt, occupied a very
important site along the Cheat during the next fifty years,
when the industrial activity of the region increased drastically. Parsons sold the mill in 1872 to Abraham Currence, another local resident. The mill was later moved down the
slough far enough to allow for the construction of a railroad
siding for the West Virginia Central and Pittsburg Railroad.
In 1933 local resident John W. Minear purchased the old fa-
cility, dismantled the equipment, and tore down the
building.[43]

Not all the companies doing business in the region were as
long-lived as Abraham Parsons's mill, but many were organized in the same decade as his business commenced. As
businesses increased in the region, many charters for corporations were issued by secretaries of state or by acts of the
legislature. Other businesses, however, were not corporate
entities.

The temperament of the Virginia legislature grew more sympathetic to privately financed western development in the 1840s and 1850s. Transmontane businesses were among these early corporations, but by 1860 the majority of Virginia's coal and timber concerns were chartered in Virginia by eastern Virginians or New Englanders. About 15 percent of the land that eventually constituted the Monongahela National Forest was controlled by industrialists during the antebellum period, and the percentage continued to increase. In 1841 two firms alone controlled 74,300 acres of transmontane territory. These two firms were owned by three persons: Evan T. Ellicott, Andrew Ellicott, and Charles Carter Lee. Their holdings brought to at least 126,300 acres the amount of land controlled by industrialists before 1842.[44] A subsequent act of the legislature stipulated that Lee's private property could not be seized for payment of the corporation's debts.[45] The figure of 126,300 acres is conservative, because it accounts only for permits granted by the legislature. Foreign, out-of-state, or unincorporated firms probably held more land still.

Resident mountain businessmen continued their efforts for improved transportation systems in the region, hopeful that they could also share in the bounty of economic development. Navigational improvements on the Cheat River were the focus of the 1844 charter of the Preston Navigation and Manufacturing Company. The incorporators were local citizens John Ambler, Gustavus Cresap, H.G. Ambler, James Averill, D.C. Ambler, and Buckner Fairfax. The firm was empowered to improve navigation on the Cheat from Horseshoe Bottom in present Tucker County to Ice's Ferry in Monongalia County. The resident entrepreneurs were limited to one thousand acres of land, a sharp contrast to the generous allowances given to eastern or absentee-controlled mining and manufacturing companies in the same era.[46]

Occasionally the legislature acted to end controversies over landownership. On February 23, 1854, the assembly granted title to twenty thousand acres of land in Lewis County to Gideon P. Camden, R.P. Camden, and Minter Bailey. The legislation effectively eradicated any prior claim to the land, whether held by resident farmers or absentee owners. The act probably resolved some sort of controversy over absentee claims, because a year earlier the legislature had chartered the Lewis County Mining and Manufacturing Company, and Bailey was among the incorporators. The others included David S. Peterson, Albert A. Lewis, and George W. Jackson.[47]

Increasingly, absentee entrepreneurs in the 1850s continued to look to the region. Absentees chartered the Hampshire Coal and Iron Company on March 14, 1853. Incorporators included Victor DeLaunay, Reuben Johnson, Thomas C. Atkinson, Jerry Cowles, and Rodman Joyce, of Romney and New York. Capitalized at two million dollars, the firm was permitted to hold ten thousand acres of land.[48]

The Monongahela Mining and Manufacturing Company was chartered on April 8, 1853, by Francis H. Pierpont, James (J.O.) Watson, E.L. Boydston, J.S. Barnes, Jr., Austin Merrill, James Neeson, and Benjamin Fleming of Marion County and at least four unidentified others. This very important organization was the precursor of the absentee-owned Consolidation Coal Company.[49] The incorporators were leaders in the West Virginia statehood movement and the coal industry.

Parkersburg native Pierpont was a Whig politician and manufacturer who opposed the power of the eastern slavocracy and publicly condemned the 1860 Virginia state income tax. "The slaveholder will break up every establishment in the state," he warned. Because the slavocracy controlled Virginia politics, it would wield the power of government. Pierpont warned westerners that the East would tax "your labor in a way that will surely starve your families."[50] The Fleming family was prominent in the coal industry and in politics, sending a son, A.B. Fleming, to the governor's mansion in 1890. Watson, with his son Clarence and son-in-law A.B. Fleming, built railroads and a coal empire in the Fairmont coalfield.

Between 1850 and 1863, Virginia chartered corporations to do business in several Monongahela counties, including Randolph, Pocahontas, and Tucker. Permission was granted for these firms to control approximately 107,000 acres of land in the immediate region, which accounted for a substantial proportion of the territory within the Monongahela.[51] Combining this acreage with the 126,300 acres noted previously, a minimum of 233,300 acres of land was in the sights, if not the control, of industrial organizations by the eve of the Civil War. That amount of land accounts for territory the size of a small West Virginia county and is sufficient to have drastically influenced the way of life of resident mountain farmers, whose economy and culture relied upon an affordable supply of farmland. Presumably the early charter restrictions on landholdings were designed to deter speculation, but they were not effective, and in time the restrictions were dropped from the acts of incorporation.

Despite a rising population in the West during the first decades of the nineteenth century, political equality with the East was not forthcoming. Mountain farmers and western entrepreneurs remained in the majority in these years before the Civil War, but their political influence never blossomed. Absentees shared a common interest with the eastern establishment. In the form of investment capital supplied by merchants located elsewhere, absentees seemed benign until the war. At that time, they turned to the development of timber and coal in the Appalachian transmontane. The friction between West and East grew sharper. Because the political and economic objectives of the two sections were mutually exclusive, an accommodation satisfactory to both could not be reached. The East continued its dominance of state affairs by refusing to allow the West equal representation in the legislature. Astute absentees cast their support with the eastern-led political majority because the higher taxes desired by the West threatened the profitability of speculation in land, the vehicle necessary to speed industrialization to the mountains.

Industrialization could not have succeeded without control of a great amount of land within the region. The significance of acquiring and controlling that land is a critical, but untold, chapter of the history of the Appalachian mountain region. On the eve of war, Virginians could not devote their full attention to the motives of industrialists, yet the sectional strife that tore the nation asunder provided the cloak that profiteers and entrepreneurs needed to engineer profound change within the mountains. The tactics employed by absentees and easterners destabilized the land-dependent mountain farming society and brought economic distress and social change that accelerated and exacerbated negative changes during the industrial transformation that lay ahead.

5

Pufferbilly Politics
Coal Dust, Sawdust, and Cinders on the Farmland

Political defeat of the West in 1830 and 1851 created a nurturing environment in which wealthy and ambitious men could direct the industrial development within Virginia's mountains. The influence of industry increased rapidly between 1850 and 1860. Traditional mountain farm society yielded political and economic leadership to absentee capitalists who in prior decades had successfully claimed the natural resources of the mountains. Timbering and mining proved to be incompatible with farming, and the political influence of the farming culture declined as industrialization advanced. The traditional economic activity was displaced, and new ways supplanted the old. By 1920 farmers had become a minority in the region; their political power was inconsequential.

Although the western Virginians sought internal improvements to encourage commercial development and local industry, they were neither aware of the true nature of the transformation that was taking place nor equipped to influence the ultimate direction of that transition. Industrial development came about when absentee owners, not local gentry, so thoroughly controlled the government and society that local participation in the prosperity was confined to very modest levels. The voices of the 1830s and 1840s in western Virginia, which had demanded political equality and state participation in industrial development, were silenced by political defeat before the Civil War.

Two attempts at representational reform had failed. In the midst of civil war, Virginia was severed largely for Union strategic interests, but logically also to keep the mountain wealth of northern investors within the borders of the Union. Many leaders of the statehood movement, though not all, had economic ties to the Northeast. After 1865 the burgeoning industrial activity was mistaken by West Virginians as the arrival of those internal improvements that had been so long in coming. What happened, in fact, was that the economic and political leaders who had subjugated western interests before the war were, in the postwar years, able to manipulate western development in order to reserve the benefits for themselves.

Although iron and coal industries were organized and working within the Monongahela region as early as 1722, their ranks grew slowly during the eighteenth century.[1] In the early nineteenth century, small local industries increased in number throughout the western areas of Virginia; by 1860 many industries were poised to commence mining and timbering activities. The magnitude of the changes that accompanied industrial growth, however, was completely obscured by the cataclysm of civil war. West Virginia's experience in these years lends much credence to the theory that the foundations of the modern industrial state were laid during the Civil War.[2]

Earlier developments were significant too. In the case of West Virginia, the previous century of speculation in land had equipped industrialists to move swiftly into production of coal and timber. Little time was wasted on land acquisition after the war's close. The political careers of U.S. senators Stephen B. Elkins and Henry Gassaway Davis of West Virginia meshed with their business ambitions: their careers provide nearly perfect behavioral portraits of Gilded Age industrialists.[3] Politically loyal to the interests of big business, Davis, Elkins, and their colleagues secured hegemony in federal and state leadership that underscored the increasingly influential role of industry in the affairs of West Virginia.[4] Barely perceptible before southern secession or during the war, this influence had been growing for nearly a century before hostilities erupted between North and South.

The postwar infusion of capital into the region was gigantic in its proportions, but it did not enhance the economy of the new state of West Virginia. The industrial development largely enhanced only the fortunes of those investors who owned mineral-rich timberlands in the region. These and other businessmen-politicians dominated the new state by ensuring a sympathetic state government. Governor Arthur I. Boreman, the state's first, was a stockholder in at least two coal companies. Senator Peter G. VanWinkle was linked to the oil industry. These and other leaders guided West Virginia's polity to suit the needs of their industries. They served in the state legislature and the U.S. Senate and as party political bosses. Native West Virginian agrarian and redeemer politicians occasionally succeeded in tempering the fervor of the industrialists, but not in defeating their interests.[5]

By the time Lee surrendered at Appomattox, the government of West Virginia already had written a constitution devoted to industrial development. In the first decade of statehood, Henry Gassaway Davis, with the help of his son-in-law Stephen B. Elkins, Nathan Bay Scott, and J.N. Camden, bent resource-rich West Virginia to the industrialists' will. Each of these men represented the state in the U.S. Senate, although Davis and Elkins were tied to West Virginia more as entrepreneurs than as residents with a personal stake in the state's future. Civil War railroading brought Davis to West Virginia; later his daughter Hallie captured Elkins's heart. They resided in the state only to satisfy residency requirements for their U.S. Senate seats. Davis, Elkins, and their industrial associates were the source of campaign dollars and political power that paved the way for later successful political careers of many of their lieutenants and that ensured the continued concern of state government for the needs of extractive industry.

The first postwar acts of the state legislature enhanced business within the Monongahela region by chartering railroad construction, regulating timbering companies, and revising corporate charters in ways that improved business opportunities. As with industrial growth throughout the nation, no concomitant legislative effort occurred to moderate industrial activity or to protect smallholders from industrial excesses. The second industrial revolution brought to the Monongahela region a tremendous influx of mudsill-class industrial jobs and temporary industrial activity, but local citizens reaped no lasting prosperity. For the state and the region, the lasting impact of industrial domination would be felt in future years. The regressive land tax structure that had favored extractive industry haunted efforts to trigger other forms of economic growth in the state.

Gaining access to the state's treasure of resources was the first industrial priority. West Virginia's legislature on March 2, 1864, incorporated the West Virginia Central Railway Company and granted it broad, unregulated powers to connect regions of the state by rail. Among the railroad incorporators were Simon Cameron, who had served as U.S. secretary of war under Abraham Lincoln, and Francis H. Pierpont, who had served as head of Virginia's pro-Union, or "restored" government, which in 1861 gave state approval for the creation of West Virginia.[6] The state board of public works paid cash for stock in the corporation, demonstrating the new state's interest in participating in the nation's industrial boom. The West Virginia Central proposed to build a railroad from the Pennsylvania line in Preston County through Taylor County to Buckhannon, Charleston, and on to the mouth of the Sandy River in Wayne County. The line would connect the major coalfields and timber regions in West Virginia to the northeastern industrial corridor.

Two years later, Davis, who was sitting in the state legislature, proposed to build his own railroad through the Monongahela forest area. His project, the Potomac and Piedmont Coal and Railway Company, was partly an out-of-state venture. Incorporators were Henry Gassaway Davis, Thomas B. Davis, W.R. Davis, and W.R. Armstrong of West Virginia; J. Philip Roman of Cumberland, Maryland; and Baltimore residents James Boyce and R.G. Reiman. The charter enabled the firm to operate and construct railroads in Mineral, Grant, Tucker, Randolph, Pocahontas, and Greenbrier counties, along the waters of the North Branch of the Potomac River and the Cheat, Tygart, and Greenbrier rivers.[7]

Under the provisions of the charter and chapters 42 and 52 of the *West Virginia Code,* the company was given the power to condemn land. Nearly every railroad project in the nation was similarly chartered, and excesses occurred everywhere. West Virginia, however, suffered exceedingly because the court system and politics were structured to stifle legitimate objections to railroad conduct. Railroad foes were vilified as enemies of progress. Before long, the railroads owned the coal- and timber-rich land through which their trains ran, giving rise to a small but very powerful group of entrepreneurs, guided by Henry Gassaway Davis. The tool of condemnation was a powerful boost to the railroad builders as well as a heady inducement for landowners to negotiate land sales. Multitudes of property transactions enhanced the well-being of the local legal profession. Generally these lawyers conducted farm sales for a fee, customarily 5 percent of the sale price. Commissions became important sources of income for attorneys, whose presence in the region became more and more pronounced. Grafton attorney John Thomas McGraw was actively involved in obtaining land for the industrialists, even while he served as a retainer for the Baltimore and Ohio Railroad, as a federal tax collector, and as Democratic party boss for the district. In Pocahontas County, W.G. Bratton and C.F. Moore were active in land acquisitions for industrial organizations, particularly the West Virginia Pulp and Paper Company. In nearby Pendleton County, B.H. Hiner and Wilbur F. Dyer assisted the industrialists.

Davis sat in the state legislature that approved measures of vital interest to him. Elected to the House of Delegates in 1866, he was an outspoken "Union conservative." Davis periodically served in government to facilitate the exploitation of the state's resources. He was a state legislator (1866), a state senator (1869), and a U.S. senator (1871). Throughout the Civil War he flourished as a supplier to the Union army, despite Confederate depredations in Hampshire County. His business skills brought wartime profits, and in peacetime he turned to politics to protect his investments. From his first term in the legislature, Davis devoted his public career to pampering railroads and coal, the sources of his own fortunes.[8]

The son of a prominent Baltimore merchant who lost everything in the Panic of 1837, young Henry Gassaway Davis worked as a foreman-superintendent on Waverly Plantation until he was twenty years old. Then he left to seek his fortune in the new industry of railroading. Qualified by physical strength for the position of brakeman, Davis was assigned to the Cumberland, Maryland, outpost of the Baltimore and Ohio Railroad Company in 1842. He advanced quickly to the position of conductor, developed a friendship with the president of the railroad, and became acquainted with national leaders of the time.[9]

When the railroad expanded westward in 1853, Davis went with it as station agent at Piedmont, to take advantage of the opportunities that would come from the development of the timber and coal in the region. He used his wife's inheritance the following year to finance his first investment in land, coal, and timber. He acquired his first parcel of land as the result of a mortgage default. By 1858 Davis had become so successful he was the moving force behind the creation of the Piedmont Savings Bank.[10]

During the Civil War, Davis supplied timber and coal to the Union army, via rail. His ability to anticipate and meet military requisitions resulted in handsome rewards. Even though Hampshire County was quite often under Confederate control, Davis remained staunchly pro-Union and prorailroad. Ultimately he supported statehood for West Virginia, although he had taken no part in prewar politics. After the war, Davis was a "protection Democrat," favoring tariff reduction on most articles but a high tariff on bituminous coal, in which he had important interests.[11]

Civil War hostilities had complicated, but not stopped, land transactions in the region, forcing state government to make adjustments when local governments were not organized. Civil government was not functional in Hampshire and Hardy counties in 1862, and the restored government passed legislation to allow one land title controversy to be moved to

Preston County, where the dispute could continue.[12] At issue was title to sixteen thousand acres of land. Parties to the dispute were Angus W. McDonald of Hampshire County and the Potomac and Allegheny Coal and Iron Manufacturing Company. McDonald was a partner in another coal company, the Hampshire Coal and Iron Company.[13] Several other mining companies were at work in Hampshire County during this time, which suggests the likelihood of increasing conflicts over land.[14] The McDonald case illustrates one way in which the war contributed to confusion over land claims. The suit, the verdict, and any changes in ownership of the Hampshire land were recorded in another county's records and are, excepting serendipitous discoveries, lost to history. Other transactions probably were similarly handled during the war; likewise, records of them are difficult to find and evaluate. This war-related difficulty provided a window of opportunity for those who sought to amass landholdings in the region, but the McDonald litigation shows that not even war could suspend the land controversies. Land matters were important in the transmontane, and they received the full attention of state government.

After the war, Davis bought one thousand acres of Deakins land in the Cheat River country, at the summit of the Alleghenies, paying fifty cents an acre.[15] Much of the land, which lay in West Virginia and Maryland, was formerly part of the Fairfax estate. Davis's railroad carried the resources of the mountains to locations elsewhere for manufacture. He was liberally rewarded for his enterprise in locating, extracting, and exporting West Virginia's natural resources.

Davis's political career enhanced his railroading successes. He was a member of the powerful state legislative committees on taxation and finance, roads, and internal navigation, each of which oversaw aspects of his business enterprises. Davis's role in the state legislature included the successful bid to create Mineral County. His brother Thomas B. Davis, representing the new county, and George W. Washington, representing Hampshire County, were named by the legislature to run the line that partitioned Mineral County from

Hampshire.[16] Keyser, seat of the new county, was a mere stone's throw from Davis's Piedmont businesses.

Because the state government was controlled by industrialists like Davis, local ventures also were molded, with great finesse, to industry's purpose. In 1868 the legislature chartered the Horseshoe and Backbone Turnpike Company, to make an internal improvement sought by Tucker County citizens.[17] The project reflected the ardent desire for roads and improvements that had been of critical importance to residents of the transmontane since its settlement. Davis also had much to gain from the turnpike, because he owned seventy thousand acres of land and a fourteen-foot seam of coal, whose products the road would carry out of the region.[18] Unlike the West Virginia Central Railroad, the turnpike company received no state dollars.

The Tucker County turnpike project was led by local leaders William R. Parsons, Arnold Bonnifield, Jesse Parsons, Rufus Maxwell, and David Closs, who opened the corporate books on the project, which was designed to build a road across Backbone Mountain to get coal out to the Cheat River. These five incorporators were natives of the region who could trace their ties to the Horseshoe's original settlers. They represented families who controlled thousands of acres of prime bottomland in Tucker County, and they also dominated local politics. Bonnifield was the first clerk of the county. Maxwell settled in the area before 1854, owned nearly one thousand acres of land, and was the first prosecuting attorney for Tucker County.[19] Jesse Parsons had been district constable before the county was formed and was logically chosen its first sheriff. Descended from the original settlers, the Parsons clan alone controlled several thousand acres of land. William R. Parsons was one of the first county commissioners.

Presumably to keep participation in the venture available to cash-poor local farmers, the turnpike company charter allowed subscriptions to be taken out in labor after the company was organized. A roadway twelve feet wide, with a grade of five degrees or less, was stipulated by lawmakers, who also granted the businessmen the right to charge and collect the tolls allowed by law. The legislature fixed tolls at 1.5 cents per bushel of coal, 0.5 cent per bushel of lime, and 1.0 cent per cubic foot of round or hewn timber.[20] The actual fees that the legislature set are not as important as the fact that the lawmakers set some. The legislature was regulating local entrepreneurial behavior to the benefit of industrialists like Davis, who owned large amounts of timber and coal in the region. Transportation costs were a critical concern to timber and coal developers, and the Horseshoe and Backbone charter provided a way to control some business expenses.

As a state senator, Davis in 1869 was appointed to committees on finance and claims, internal improvements and navigation, and auditing accounts. He continued his probusiness efforts that characterized his tenure in the House of Delegates.[21]

There was little public scrutiny of industry-related legislation. Public concern among ordinary West Virginians was focused on political allegiances and loyalties that lingered from the Civil War. Restoring civil rights to former Confederates and extending civil rights to newly freed blacks worried many West Virginians. Residents of the new state were very fearful of allowing ex-rebels to participate in government and skeptical about racial equality. The Senate Education Committee, for example, struggled for months over a proposal to charter integrated Storer College in Harper's Ferry before Senator Joseph T. Hoke of Martinsburg successfully maneuvered the legislation past the objections of his colleagues.[22]

Revision of the state constitution in 1872 brought changes that made it easier for industrialists to get control of land, but the new document was so hopelessly confusing that only lawyers claimed to understand it. Redeemers who wrote the revised constitution "were lawyers and specialists in the complex system of land registry." They provided for West Virginia the same revision of land law that had earlier enabled them and "their predecessors" to benefit themselves.[23] The land provisions guaranteed legal work for decades. The new constitution barred railroad officials from serving in the legislature, reflecting growing state resentment of the Baltimore and Ohio Railroad. The provision may have been an attempt at railroad reform, but its success was dubious. Davis was by then in the U.S. Senate, so the proviso only affected his competitors. Critics assert that the section on land titles made litigation the chief business of the state.[24] Popular support of the document reflected hopes that all West Virginians, not just the industrialists, would realize economic prosperity.

Among the changes was the same self-garroting law that Kentucky had passed in 1794, recognizing titles to land that were obtained under Virginia jurisdiction; the new West Virginia constitution also recognized titles obtained under the previous state constitution. This great leap backward was among the land clauses that later gave rise to so many lawsuits and strengthened the grip of absentees on the land, the law, and the resources of the mountains. The state's industrial development proceeded quite rapidly after 1872, but growth "took place in the context of a political economy that allowed men like Davis to identify their private interest with the public welfare, and to pursue it successfully by political means."[25]

Senator Davis, in his capacity as a protection Democrat, continued to use his political skills to enhance industrialization and to protect American industry, particularly coal mining. His efforts were so fervent that in 1883 Davis came under fire from his Senate colleagues for voting in his own self-interest, apparently with a determination that exceeded even the generous ethical limits of the Gilded Age. Reminding his colleagues that he voted faithfully for their interests, he staunchly demanded similar consideration. Davis opposed lowering the coal tariff and vociferously defended his right to pursue his interest as a coal miner in this issue.[26]

After two terms in the Senate, Davis did not seek reelection, returning instead to his coal mines, land, and railroads in West Virginia. By 1884 the old Potomac and Piedmont Coal and Railway Company had grown substantially and was rechartered as the West Virginia Central and Pittsburg Railway Company.[27] With Davis at the head of the corporation, it successfully challenged the monopoly of the Baltimore and Ohio Railroad by introducing a competing connecting rail line into the coalfields. This competition aided both Davis and other industrialists of the region because customers could bid down haulage rates and negotiate special deals with carriers.[28]

The behavior of Davis and other men like him contributed to a failure of the state to develop a mature industrial economy. Some scholars believe an overreliance on primary industry created a colonial and dependent economy. According to John Alexander Williams, West Virginia "remained in the industrial age the backwater it had been in preindustrial times."[29] West Virginia actually was not a stagnant "backwater" but a fledgling commercial and agricultural region firmly engaged in developing its own capitalist identity. Gavin Wright has written that colonialism can be seen as a distinct economy "located within the political jurisdiction of a larger country, subject to laws, markets, policies, and technologies that it would not have chosen had it been independent."[30] In the Monongahela region during the industrializing period, rugged individualists were working for personal fortunes. There was no oversight. There was no regulation. Therefore, many abuses occurred. During the fifty years of industrial activity within the region, more and more land, political power, and money gravitated to the control of fewer and fewer people, upward and away from local control and local benefit. The rapid influx of industrial workers in the thrall of industry further destabilized the political balance, because local political leaders worked diligently to direct when and how these workers voted.[31]

Explained another way, by dominating the political structure of the state and controlling land and taxation, the industrialists were able to ensure their personal financial success. This was not at all the same thing as ensuring the economic dominance of a mother country. Nor did these changes encourage diverse economic growth. Industrial intrusion derailed a capitalist transformation that was following traditional Virginian paths of agriculture and commerce. The economic changes that came to the Monongahela with the captains of industry served the interest of individual and personal gain. So ruthlessly devoted to profit were the developers of the mountains that when the market for coal was depressed, the industrialists kept making a profit by recapturing wages in company stores and through rents on company houses.[32]

These individual entrepreneurs interrupted the developing agricultural economy of the region and brought negative changes to its citizens. The local commercial agriculture and small-scale economic developments that had been proceeding since settlement were supplanted by absentee interests and speculation. The disruptions of industrialization could not have taken place on such a broad scale if industry had not already secured control of the politics and the land decades before.

This undemocratic system was led and controlled completely by the small industrial brotherhood of Henry Gassaway Davis, Stephen B. Elkins, Nathan Bay Scott, and J.N. Camden. Neither the political nor the economic atmosphere was particularly hospitable to the "reform surge" that characterized the late nineteenth century. As elsewhere in the South, democracy was subverted in the mountains, which weakened capitalism.[33] In the acute phase of the industrial transformation, the undemocratic political control exercised by men like Davis quickly facilitated the rise of industrial interests, at the expense of the agricultural pursuits that had characterized the local economy.

Not just a railroader, Davis was the premier industrialist in the region's timbering era. The North Branch Lumber and Boom Company was chartered in 1867 by T.W. Davis, Henry Gassaway Davis, J. Philip Roman, and Basil Gartlett to construct a log boom on the Potomac River at Cumberland, Maryland. Booms effectively block the use of the river for other navigational purposes, because they hold logs in one location until, swollen with spring rains, the streams are at flood stage and can carry the timber downstream to a mill or rail siding. Davis's charter forbade land speculating and limited the firm's landholdings. Such restrictions, however, did not restrain Davis's business activities in West Virginia.[34]

Throughout the early postwar period in the Monongahela, the indigenous elites of the region continued to seek road construction. Jesse Parsons, the local turnpike builder, was involved in a second road project in 1869. He, David Blackman, Archibald Wilmoth, Elam Hart, Jacob Long, David Hart, William Evans, William Ewin, A.D. Weils, Summers Mc-Crum, and Isaac Startzman, representing local leaders of Tucker, Randolph, and Preston counties, incorporated a turn-pike company to build a road from New Interest in Randolph County to Holly Meadows in Tucker County and then to West Union or Chisholm's Mills in Preston County.[35] This second effort at road building emphasizes the importance local people placed on lessening, not preserving, their isolation.

Many local residents also aspired to success in the industrial arena, beginning with timbering their lands. Several factors made this a rational decision. Through timbering, farmers could have their lands cleared at little expense to themselves. The pressure on the real estate market made farm expansion otherwise unaffordable. The additional input of cash allowed farmers to improve their operations or to get ahead financially. Unfortunately, other conditions negated these considerations. Challenges to deeds were common. Many farmers who sold their timber were never fully paid when companies went bankrupt. Also, the lure of wages in the mills and mines of the region drew family members away from the farm.

Increasingly, farming confronted a new set of difficult challenges. Keeping in mind the findings of Ronald D Eller, that a local middle class facilitated the early economic development of the mountains of Appalachia and then waned in influence, the experience of the Monongahela gentry is understandable. The transmontane middle class, unlike its counterpart in other American industrial districts, never developed into an independent and powerful segment of the new industry-based economy. Absentee-owned extractive industries such as timbering and mining did not generate capital for investment in local businesses.[36] Instead, these industries created closed and self-reliant communities that had their own housing, currency, recreation, and work. Future study may confirm that cooperation with the industrialists was as unavoidable for the resident middle class of the region as it became for those who turned to industry for jobs. Local

leaders may have hoped to change and survive in a new economic climate, but their cooperation with the industrialists
helped to stifle independent economic and political activity,
which led to the demise of an independent middle class.

Certificates of incorporation for firms doing business in
West Virginia that bore only the names of absentees give credence to this observation. By the time of full industrialization of the region, local desires for internal improvements
were subverted by Davis and other industrialists, who did not
concern themselves with the conditions of roads or schools or
utilities and who did not relish paying the taxes required to
establish and maintain them.

Throughout the post–Civil War period, West Virginia state
government kept watch for developments that might have a
negative influence on the state's industries. Sometimes the
state took action to aid industry. Tariff reforms were particularly troublesome. Joint Resolution number 4 urged the U.S.
Congress in 1870 not to lower the tariff on coal. At the same
time, state lawmakers issued Resolution number 16, creating
a commission to investigate abuses by the Chesapeake and
Ohio Railroad in West Virginia. The commission was granted
subpoena power to facilitate its investigation. The legislature
was, apparently, attempting to enhance the competitive position of other railroads or to prevent the Chesapeake and
Ohio from capricious rate-setting that was so characteristic
of the period.[37]

Labor shortages were anticipated by the leaders of industry, and the state responded with immigration programs.
Governor Boreman in 1867 addressed industrial needs with
his approval of and participation in one of many immigration
companies that were created to bring European immigrants
to the West Virginia coal mines, timber operations, and railroad companies.[38] The corporation may have been formed to
capitalize upon a request of John Williams, a general agent
representing the American Emigration Company of New
York. Williams wrote Boreman in January 1867, seeking information on possible sites in West Virginia where immigrants might settle. The state also issued a charter to the
International Real Estate Society, to procure immigrants

from Switzerland, Germany, and eastern Europe.[39] Both the state and private industries were involved in bringing immigrants to the region. Davis and the Baltimore and Ohio Railroad also endeavored to increase the immigrant workforce. West Virginia appointed its own immigration agent, Joseph H. Diss Debar. Debar designed the Great Seal of West Virginia and sketched scenes from rural life, but his contributions to industrial development were problematic, and his motives questionable. He died in 1876 while imprisoned in New York, serving a sentence for his conviction as a confidence man.[40]

With a staunch and sympathetic state government in place, the Davis brothers continued to expand their holdings in the mountain region. In 1870 they created the Cheat River Boom and Lumber Company. Stockholders were Henry Gassaway Davis, Charles M. Bishop, Thomas B. Davis, Charles Hooten, and W.R. Davis. Under the act of incorporation, the firm had the authority to deal in lumber, construct tramways, hold lands, and erect wharves. The legislation defined the Cheat River as a public waterway and specifically absolved the corporation from liabilities for damage of fire or flood caused by "any person not in their employ." The act also protected a preexisting Cheat River firm. The Rowlesburg Lumber and Iron Company was not prevented from constructing its own boom as well, the legislation said.[41]

The Monongahela Gas Company, another Davis enterprise, was chartered in 1873. Holding 500 shares apiece were Baltimore residents Alexander Shaw, George Appold, William Larrabee, Thomas Gemmell, Charles J. Baker, Edward Roberts, Alexander Robinson, James Hewlett, and John A. Hambleton. Davis held 95,500 shares of stock in the firm. Other absentee-led firms organized to do business in the region before 1870 included the New York–financed Peytona Cannel Coal Company, which was incorporated on March 7, 1866, by Aspin Wall, Henry Pierrepont, H. Dubois, D.L. Suydam, W.A. White, A.A. Low, Peter Cornell, Francis Vinton, John Howell, and Edgar S. VanWinkle. Kingwood Gas, Coal and Iron Company incorporators were from York and Philadelphia, Pennsylvania. The Boreman Oil Company was formed on July 26,

1866, and the act of incorporation listed incorporators as A.I. Boreman, F.P. Pierpont, J.C. Hupp, J.H. Charnock, and Jos. Snider.[42]

The ranks of the corporate leaders included millionaire absentees, West Virginia politicians, senators from many states, and entrepreneurs of every description. Only a few of these business leaders were locally grown, and their task was to encourage local support of the industrial pursuits. The lure of wagework brought only temporary satisfaction to the local population, which was manifestly unable to provide the thousands of workers the industrialization required. The pressures to sell their lands changed the farmers' way of life in the Monongahela. Heightened demand for land pushed the price beyond the farmers' resources, and agricultural expansion became more and more difficult. Even though the stresses on traditional landownership patterns were severe, the cultural changes that came with rapid industrialization also produced difficult challenges for the region's traditional residents.

6

Farmer Politics
Life and Work with and without Coal, with and without Absentees

A few counties in West Virginia did not industrialize and were not coveted by absentees. The farmers of Monroe County retained control of the land and the local government, with the result that traditional agriculture characterized the region through the twentieth century. A gentry class evolved that paid most of the taxes and held most of the political power. Like the Monongahela region, Monroe County was settled early in Virginia's history; the county itself was carved from Greenbrier and Botetourt counties in 1799. Agrarian since its settlement, Monroe County fared much better economically than the counties in West Virginia that were industrialized in the Gilded Age.

Similar in size and terrain to Clay County and Tucker County, Monroe differs significantly from them because it has no recoverable coal. Another important characteristic of Monroe County is that early enough in its history it had a courthouse within a day's ride of most residents. Securing deeds was not the monumental task for Monroe citizens that it was for Clay and Tucker residents. Although settled between 1760 and 1805, these two counties were not incorporated until land acquisition by absentees was in full swing. If the rhythms of settlement and growth had been uninterrupted in Tucker and Clay counties, the economic character of those areas probably would be very similar to that of Monroe County. The same frontier culture affected the settlement of each of the three counties.

Settlement of Monroe County took place during the era of

the French and Indian War. The earliest recorded settlement occurred about 1760. Despite the speculative land ventures that were sweeping the nation in the years after the Revolution, very few of Monroe's earliest settlers claimed vast holdings, a fact that rests at the foundation of the county's history.[1] Most of the earliest settlers in the county claimed farmland of less than three hundred acres. A few of them owned small numbers of slaves. Mostly, Monroe County settlers fit the classic definition of southern "plain folks," or "yeomen." In the first fifty years of the county's settlement, 1,324 land grants were recorded. By 1860 the population had grown to 10,757, and in 1910 Monroe County's population reached 13,055. It has wavered little since then.[2]

Although most settlers claimed small farms, some claimed larger estates. But unlike the land companies, speculators, and agents who were rushing to grab vast amounts of the western territories after the American Revolution, Monroe's wealthiest settlers appear to have moved into the region and assumed their duties as gentry in the traditional Virginia ways. There was no coal to lure industrialists into the region. It was agricultural. Because of a multitude of healing springs in the county, it was an early resort area as well. Between 1800 and 1820, thirty-one grantees claimed parcels of land greater than three hundred acres, but they remained in the county and pursued their fortunes as farmers, much as the Bonnifield, Parsons, Maxwell, and Fansler families of the Horseshoe district did.

Monroe County's landowners remained on the land, settled along the fertile bottomland, and established farms of various kinds and sizes. They became the political and social leaders of the county. Their land and tax records could not have been easily impeached by absentees. Well into the twentieth century, Monroe County lands remained available to private ownership and farming. Presently, the federal government is the only significant absentee landowner in Monroe County, controlling the lands most likely to become the focus of any future extractive industry. The Thomas Jefferson National Forest includes the southeastern edge of the county and holds recoverable but undeveloped iron ore deposits.[3]

The extent of farming activity and farm size remained relatively stable in Monroe County. In 1880 there were 682 farms between one hundred and five hundred acres in area. This yeoman farm group increased in number through the end of the century. The population density of Monroe County grew slowly over the same period. In 1850 the county had 22.32 persons per square mile. By 1920 the population density had increased gradually to 28.75 persons per square mile, still a sparse population. In 1894 the West Virginia State Board of Agriculture reported that approximately 60 percent of Monroe County land had been cleared for farming. Farmers controlled 60 percent of the wealth in the county and paid 80 percent of the taxes. Farming and grazing were the largest sources of income for residents.[4] The pattern of landownership in Monroe County is clear: the land remained in the hands of local residents throughout the period. The tenacity of sparse settlement and self-sufficiency suggests that independent farming in Monroe County was successful. The population has varied by only about two thousand persons since 1870. These persistent self-sufficient farmers fared better in hard times because they owned enough land to feed themselves. Independent of layoffs, strikes, industrial disasters, and market swings, the farmers of Monroe County preserved their traditional culture and honed their traditional skills.

Despite the rigors of farming, Monroe County citizens remained self-sufficient throughout the industrial age. The low welfare payments in modern Monroe County suggest that citizens there have not become economically dependent, as many have in Clay County, where industry acquired nearly all of the farmland during the years preceding the industrial development of coal. In fiscal year 1975, for example, the state reported that welfare payments for Monroe County's 11,272 residents totaled $833,682.49. That same year, Clay County's 9,330 residents received $1,760,635.03.[5] Even though the two counties were economically similar in 1870, their fortunes later diverged drastically. The only important difference between the two counties is that one industrialized and one did not. Unlike the residents of Monroe County, Clay residents lost control of the land and had nothing to fall back on in hard times. Monroe County farmers were able to resist what historian Robert Brenner calls an irrational decision to give up their means of reproduction, because the land enabled them to support, or "reproduce," themselves, independent of outside economic pressures. They remained in control of their economic destinies.[6]

The social upheaval that was wrought when industrial activity deprived farmers of their land was exacerbated by the rapid changes that followed. In Clay County, the first serious blow to the residents was the loss of their lands. The only recourse for many of these dispossessed farmers was to accept work in the timber and coal industries, becoming, therefore, dependent upon another for their means of support in the form of wages. This dependence was the second hard blow to the region, because when the coal boom ended in the twentieth century, there were no more wages, no other jobs, and no land upon which to return to farming. There were a few government jobs, but for most, welfare dependence was the economic reality for twentieth-century Clay County. Many of Clay County's farmers were dispossessed before the Civil War, at the direction of one industrial developer, William H. Edwards.

Modern economic distress in Virginia's former West is rooted in the successful prewar challenge to property rights of self-sufficient farmers and the rapid immigration of thousands of industrial workers. Economic dependence upon the coal and timber industries was thrust upon newly landless mountain Virginians and was secured by thousands of equally dependent immigrant workers who were brought to the region from Europe by industry-financed immigration companies. In the industrial counties, these exploited workers became the political majority, and they voted at industry's behest as soon as they were naturalized. Naturalization costs were often underwritten by the political machinery.[7]

Indigenous western Virginians became economically dependent upon coal mining and timbering precisely because they lost control of the political process and the land. The record of so many mountain Virginians' being defeated by deed challenges brought by absentees in the 1840s and 1850s represents a loss of the means of reproduction. Theoreticians observe that this is rarely a voluntary step.[8]

Persistent self-sufficient farmers in Virginia's transmontane fared better because they were more independent of the boom-and-bust cycles than those who lived in the industrial regions. A 1916 local history of Monroe County hinted at disappointment that industrialization passed up the region, but the writer was sufficiently prescient to recognize that the county's "lack of great mineral wealth tends to keep at a distance the demoralization observable in the coal and oil districts."[9]

The Caperton family of Monroe County once tried to interest William H. Edwards in a speculative land venture in their county, but he spurned the twenty-one thousand acres offered by agent Henry O. Middleton because "Monroe County was fit only for goats." Edwards, however, subsequently sold some of his Clay County holdings to the Capertons.[10]

Virginians whose land rested atop coal deposits had no independent means to resist the changes that industry wrought. Clay County's experience differed from Monroe County's because coal was present and the landowners were successfully challenged by absentee claimants. As a result, despite early farmer settlement of the region, its transformation from agriculture to industry came quickly and relentlessly shortly after the Civil War.

A decline in farm size and a decrease in farm population is often cited as evidence that farming was in decline, independent of industrialization, in Clay County. Census records indicate that average farm sizes in transmontane counties decreased between 1850 and 1900, leading analysts to conclude by 1935 that farming was becoming a less successful economic venture. "Probably more than half the mountain farms are less than fifty acres," the U.S. Department of Agriculture reported.[11] But this statistic could instead point to an increase in agricultural activity, that is, more people farming smaller acreage. Actually, dissecting average farm size statistics reveals a tremendous upheaval in land use in the industrializing regions.

Farm Sizes in Clay County, West Virginia, 1870–1910

Acreage	1870	1880	1890	1900	1910
1,000+	0	3	2	2	0
500–999	11	13	11	4	10
100–499	3	177	233	207	258
50–99	36	126	200	303	348
20–49	127	69	114	244	297
10–19	87	58	30	102	82
1–9	111	53	25	98	104
Total	375	499	615	960	1,099

Sources: U.S. Department of the Interior, Census Office, *Ninth Census, 1870* (Washington, D.C.: GPO, 1872) 1:71 idem, *Tenth Census, 1880* (Washington, D.C.: GPO, 1883), 13:3:98; idem, *Eleventh Census, 1890*, (Washington, D.C.: GPO, 1894), 5:196; idem, *Twelfth Census, 1900* (Washington, D.C.: GPO, 1902), 5:136–8; idem, *Thirteenth Census, 1910* (Washington, D.C.: GPO, 1913), 7:5541.

Throughout the period of industrialization in Clay County, the numbers of farms that fit the yeoman category, one hundred to five hundred acres, actually increased, from 177 in 1880 to 258 in 1910. As a percentage of total farms, however, this group declined in influence. This suggests that there were many new farmers. Many of them, perhaps, were part-time farmers. For Clay County, 485 new farms were reported between 1880 and 1910. In the same period, 12,408 acres of land were added to farming.[12] This acreage probably came from newly cleared forest; it does not seem likely that the land was from the redistribution of larger farms. Sons of farmers could choose between working in industrial jobs and remaining on the farm, effectively lessening the demand for the subdivision of family-owned land. Assuming that preexisting, and presumably successful, farms were not declining in size (the logical assumption given the net increase in available farmland), then the new acreage yielded farms of an average 25.58 acres each. These new farms would not have been large enough to support a family; they probably represented efforts of coal mining families to supplement miners' wages.

It is likely that some of the farmers who withstood Edwards's threats of ejectment, or who bought farms before

1880, kept their lands intact and did not sell or subdivide them after 1880, leaving the 485 "new farms" to make do with the 12,408 "new" acres of farmland. Of the 485 new farms reported between 1880 and 1910, 483 of them were smaller than 50 acres each. Of that number, 186 farms were smaller than 20 acres each. In 1890 there were 169 Clay farms smaller than 50 acres, and of that number, 55 were smaller than 20 acres. By 1900, 200 of Clay County's 960 farms were smaller than 20 acres.[13] Population statistics explain the change. The population of Clay County rose from 2,196 in 1870 to 13,125 in 1930, reflecting timbering and mining activity in the region.

The increasing numbers of smaller farms between 1880 and 1900 suggest an increase in the amount of part-time farming. Traditional farmers in the region were fairly stable. Miners' wages in this period varied considerably, but they were not adequate to support a family. Thus, gardening and farming were essential. By 1922 the bituminous coal industry reported that a coal cutter in the Kanawha fields was paid ten cents per ton and a coal loader was paid forty-three cents per ton, for an average daily wage of $4.20–$4.40. Union miners earned about two dollars a day more. On average, miners worked 180 days, or less, per year.[14]

The wage was not sufficient to support a family, but if a small portion was used to purchase cheap land, the family could grow food on a smallholding and thereby subsidize the mining wages. Clay County's hillside land was priced between four and nine dollars per acre in 1893–94.[15] It was a price a coal miner's family could afford if they were desperate to augment the mining wage. Such coping strategies are well documented in studies of coal mining communities elsewhere. Coal industry representatives also remarked on the prevalence of such activity. "The native American is not so much interested in the saving and satisfaction which comes from garden-making," observed one, "but the foreigner often introduces the European intensive method of farming and seems to utilize every inch of space around his small house." West Virginia, Kentucky, and Alabama miners also raised some sort of livestock, usually hogs.[16]

Applying the same analysis to the changing farm sizes in Monroe County during the same years reveals a modest increase in the number of small farms, generally accounted for by the loss of a few large farms. In Monroe County, land— therefore wealth—was being redistributed among more persons according to pressures not associated with industrialization. There was a net gain of 397 new Monroe County farms between 1890 and 1910, but there was a net loss to farming of 6,079 acres. As there was no employment alternative for farmers' sons, the land for the 397 new farms probably came from the redistribution of larger farms. Monroe County's population was 11,124 in 1870; it rose only to 13,141 by 1930.

In 1890 the census reported that 8.94 percent of Clay County farms and 9.58 percent of Monroe County farms were smaller than twenty acres. But Monroe County did not show a dramatic rise in the numbers of small farms by 1900, when only 10.69 percent of the farms were reported smaller than twenty acres, compared with 20.83 percent of Clay County farms. This reinterpretation of the census data suggests a stress on the supply of farmland in Clay County, no doubt traceable to a 77-percent increase in the population between 1890 and 1900. By 1910 Clay County had experienced a further population increase of 24.1 percent; by 1920 the population had increased another 12.2 percent.

These statistics also suggest that outside influences, not culture or rural mentality, accounted for the economic disarray in the mineral-rich mountainous regions of West Virginia. One group of traditional mountain farmers remained moderately successful and independent over a great span of time, while other similar groups of farmers declined in their ability to influence their society. Clay County yeoman farmers maintained their absolute numbers during the industrializing era, but they soon became a political minority. In time, Clay County lost its identity as an agricultural area, and farming skills were lost. Younger residents chose mining or timbering over farming. Thus disestablished, the traditional culture of Clay County regressed, and workers had little but dependence as an economic alternative when the mines shut down.

Coal was the locus of change in Clay County, but similar destabilizing events were also occurring in the Monongahela region at the behest of those who sought timber and, later, coal. In the late 1860s and early 1870s, lumber and boom companies followed the railroads into the Monongahela.[17] These economic pursuits required workers in numbers the region could not supply, and immigrants were brought in to fill the gap. The vast immigration to the region introduced perplexing new cultural and social ways to the indigenous population. Mostly from Italy and eastern Europe, thousands upon thousands of temporary workers changed the way of life for the culturally homogeneous farmers of the Monongahela. Until the immigrants arrived, the white Monongahela residents recognized the community of freed slaves as the only significantly different ethnic group among them.

These blacks constituted the only ethnic diversity in the region before industrialization.[18] For Pocahontas County, the number of "free colored" residents in 1870 was 259 persons, up from only 20 in 1860. Randolph's "free colored" population in 1870 was 183 persons, a jump from 14 in the 1860 report. Tucker County indicated 27 "free colored" persons in 1870 and 16 in 1860. In 1870 Clay County listed 4 free blacks, and Monroe County reported 1,003. While each county contained some foreign-born citizens and some whose parents were foreign-born, the preponderance of the residents were born within the region.[19] Of those residents who reported foreign parentage, their background was northern European. Church affiliations were overwhelmingly Protestant and overwhelmingly similar from county to county. Methodist and Presbyterian were the only church affiliations reported for Pocahontas County in 1870. Randolph County reported Baptist, Methodist, Presbyterian, Roman Catholic, and United Brethren in Christ congregations. Tucker County reported Baptist and Methodist churches. Monroe County reported Baptist, Christian, Methodist, Presbyterian, and Roman Catholic churches. Clay County reported Baptist and Methodist churches.[20]

Before industry came to the mountains, Tucker, Randolph, Pocahontas, Clay, and Monroe counties contained a fairly even division between men and women, strongly suggesting that a stable, monogamous family structure underpinned the social system.[21] Thousands of new workers changed this family-focused region. The populations of four of these five counties grew astronomically in fifty years, and the complexity of cultural background of the residents increased. The great growth in the numbers of single males so far outweighed the increases in the number of women that it is very unlikely that the population increases were accompanied by a stable growth of families in the region. Profound cultural and religious diversity arose in the region as well. By 1910 the Monongahela counties had a large Jewish population and a synagogue, an Italian language newspaper, and several Catholic priests. Lebanese merchants introduced Middle Eastern culture.

Traditional social diversions changed as well. Family and church-based social activities were challenged by nickelodeons, opera houses, saloons, and traveling salesmen.[22] New social customs also evidenced a rapidly diversifying culture. For example, in 1913 the *Davis News* reported that several "Polanders on Blackwater Avenue were engaged in a drunken free-for-all fight." Eight of the miscreants were "locked up and one was treated for a gash on his forehead." Fined seventy dollars for their disruptions, they explained they got carried away by a "pre-nuptial event."[23] The incident made the front page. Such accounts hint that cultural clashes were increasingly becoming a part of life in the Monongahela region.

Indeed, life there was much different in 1910 than it had been in 1870, when 1,077 landowners claimed ownership of a total of 443,095 acres of unimproved farmland. Jacob Arbogast of Pocahontas County claimed the most—39,880 acres. Unimproved acres provided the trees the lumber barons sought. The total population of Pocahontas, Randolph, and Tucker counties in 1870 was 11,539. By 1910 the total population would rise to 59,443, which would include members of only 3,882 farm families.

Having dominated politics and government on the state and federal level and having secured their claims to most of the land they needed, the industrialists were by 1880 poised to harvest profits of a magnitude that could scarcely be imagined by the now-displaced mountain farming society.

7

Champagne Politics
Scrambling for Every Tree, Crushing Every Foe

During the 1880s, industrialists tightened their grip on the timber and mineral resources of the Monongahela. The ensuing frenzy of mining and timbering in the years before the First World War forever changed life in the mountains. Participating wholeheartedly in the transition, the government of West Virginia issued increasing numbers of charters of incorporation to resource extraction companies. Hundreds upon hundreds of deeds for land and timber were registered in courthouses throughout the region. These activities foreshadowed the rapid disappearance of the forest and the final transition of the region from agriculture to industry. By 1890, nearly all the land of the Monongahela region was under the control of timber or mineral companies. A few farmers remained, although their tenuous grip on the land was weakening. Farming in the midst of the industrialization was fraught with difficulty. Expenses rose because animals and crops were at risk from new dangers. Fences were costly burdens for graziers, who bore alone the responsibility of barricading their animals from logging trains or steam machines. An increasing population of nonagricultural workers began to change the Monongahela region in many ways.

Corporations merged. Larger firms devoured smaller ones. The businesses were ruthlessly efficient. The era was characterized by fewer but larger companies whose headquarters were far away. Through the last two decades of the nineteenth century, the industrialists vied among themselves for control of the ever-diminishing supply of land and timber. Except in election years, the communities where their enterprises were located became less and less important to them.

Despite the social and economic turmoil that the industries brought, local leaders still believed that internal improvements were finally making their way into the mountains and would bring lasting prosperity to West Virginia. Although the arrival of industrial giants brought a temporary interruption of the region's isolation, only an unbalanced economic surge accompanied it. The industrialists did not reinvest in the broader local economy. After decades of futile struggle with Virginia's eastern elites over the issue of internal improvements, the railroads that finally penetrated the remote western regions were, like the jobs, only temporary. When the timber barons left, they pulled up their rails.

Between 1866 and 1915, West Virginia's industrial giants Henry Gassaway Davis and Stephen B. Elkins dominated the economic and political affairs of the Monongahela. They were unconstrained by any regulatory oversight or competing economic interests.[1] For the most part, they absorbed opponents and competitors into their operations or eliminated them through the ruthless business practices that everywhere distinguished the Gilded Age. Weakened opposing interests presented no threat to the industrialists' designs. West Virginia's mountain farmers were unable to resist the transformation at hand. The great monolith of devotion to industry absorbed the state's other economic and political leaders.

The ranks of Davis's Democratic party were filled with local leaders who supported and encouraged the industrial transformation. They employed some local people in a middle role in their operations, signaling to the citizenry, however speciously, that everyone could profit from the development of the region's resources.[2] James Parsons served Davis as an engineer, and A.B. Parsons was an attorney and a member of the Democratic party machine in Tucker County. But no local leader achieved the status and success that accrued to Davis himself. Locals who were economically and politically successful owed their success to cooperation with Davis and Elkins and, later, with Samuel E. Slaymaker of the West Virginia Pulp and Paper Company.

It is difficult to take precise measure of the extent of Davis's and Elkins's business and political activities, but the record left by those who dealt with them does offer some insight into how they operated.[3] The relationship between the J.L. Rumbarger Lumber Company, the Dry Fork Lumber Company, the West Virginia Spruce Lumber Company, the R.L. Whitmer Company, and the Condon-Lane Boom and Lumber Company illustrates the business practices in this West Virginia timber region during the industrial era. These organizations, all led by entrepreneurs from outside the region, were successful, in varying degrees, in the intensely competitive Monongahela lumbering industry. Their success partly resulted from the thoroughgoing domination of the timber industry over every other aspect of the region's economy and politics. As the enterprises flourished and grew, other smaller ventures of the same type arose. Hopeful investors, large and small, came to the mountains in the 1880s to participate in the economic windfall. Local entrepreneurs at first perceived a common interest with these industrialists.

As the more powerful members of this group controlled more and more of the local and state government and resources, the locals could not keep up with the outsiders. The pace of development quickened. The momentum of the transformation could not be stopped, nor could it be redirected. In the 1860s and 1870s, government had been shaped to enhance industry, so no regulation of industry or tax reforms were forthcoming in the 1880s.

Of the multitude of corporations that were chartered to do business in the Monongahela, those dominated by Davis and Elkins were undoubtedly the most successful. Davis's name appears on no fewer than fourteen corporate charters issued before 1892.[4] Sometimes the names of the firms belie their ownership. The experience of the J.L. Rumbarger Lumber Company, located in the town of Davis, illustrates how a small local enterprise could be helpless to protect itself from the ambitions of stronger, wealthier organizations. Just as industrialists had used devious legal maneuvering to acquire farmlands in West Virginia in the preceding years, they used similarly shabby legal tactics against their smaller competitors within the region. The Rumbarger Company began as a family venture but ultimately was gobbled up by a larger organization, which in turn was absorbed by the next larger firm. This process went on and on, until there was no lumber left in the region. After the first round of outsider involvement, Rumbarger's headquarters were moved out of the forest region and into the Philadelphia business district.

J.L. Rumbarger began operations in St. George, West Virginia, in 1884. An Indiana native, Rumbarger served his company as president. His family members were officers in the firm. S.T. Rumbarger was secretary-treasurer, R.R. Rumbarger was superintendent of the team and log cutters, W.R. Chase was traveling salesman, and D.C. VanBuskirk was superintendent in the Canaan Valley area of operations. In 1885, with Chase investing ten thousand dollars, the firm moved its main office to Davis, West Virginia. It opened a branch office at Dobbin and discontinued the St. George branch. In 1887 Margaret Rumbarger was elected to the board, and the firm purchased the "Elk Garden" tract of land. The mortgage on this large parcel of timberland was held by G.W. Dobbin, a Baltimore financier who maintained a hunting lodge and weekend retreat near the town of Davis. (In 1857 G.W. Dobbin and W.B. Dobbin had received a 27,188.5-acre grant of land from the state of Virginia.) In February 1888 Rumbarger Lumber Company sold off its booms, dams, logs, and mill on the Blackwater River to Albert Thompson, R.B. Currier, and L.H. Hamilton. By 1907 this organization had evolved into the Pittsburgh-based Babcock Lumber Company, through a succession of owners and transactions. The Rumbarger acquisition was named the Blackwater Boom and Lumber Company, renamed the Thompson Lumber Company, and finally called the Babcock Lumber Company.[5]

In what was the beginning of the end of Mr. Rumbarger's control of the firm he founded, the organization voted in November 1888 to allow board members to be nonresidents of West Virginia, and the corporate headquarters was moved to the town of Dobbin.[6] Within a few years, Henry Gassaway Davis acquired the Rumbarger lands, including the Elk Garden parcel, via a progression of leadership changes within the

Rumbarger organization. Rumbarger in 1896 acquired the Harper and Welton tracts of timberland, which included more than ten thousand acres of land in the Dry Fork region of Tucker County.

Purchase of these tracts may have represented the absorption of the Clover and Horseshoe Boom, Land, and Lumber Company of St. George. Ezekiel Harper, a partner in the Clover firm, had declared ownership of more than 7,000 acres of land in the 1870 census. Clover's incorporators were members of the local gentry, and they owned a lot of land. Harper was joined by Rufus Maxwell, who owned 1,000 acres, Peter Wilt, with 170 acres, and Robert Phillips, with 195 acres. The other incorporator was T.J. Varner.

As Rumbarger's business became more complicated, the firm appointed F.T. Rumbarger as attorney to keep the company in compliance with West Virginia law. The directors' meeting held in Piedmont, West Virginia, on April 2, 1897, involved a change of corporate membership. Chase and VanBuskirk transferred their stock to the Rumbargers; the minutes do not disclose what payment they received. The Rumbargers canceled Chase's one hundred shares and reduced the stock from seventy thousand dollars to sixty thousand. The directors then adjourned. Later that day, the stockholders of the Rumbarger firm convened their annual stockholders' meeting, whereupon the following changes took place: Margaret Rumbarger resigned as a director of the firm, and Robert F. Whitmer was elected; J.L. Rumbarger resigned as a director of the firm, and Martin Lane was elected. Whitmer was elected president of the company, and Lane was elected treasurer.[7]

Less than a year later, on January 17, 1898, William Whitmer and Sons, another lumber company doing business in Tucker County, appointed Martin Lane to vote its proxy at the next meeting of the Rumbarger Lumber Company. Lane was instructed to vote for himself, Robert F. Whitmer, and Samuel E. Slaymaker on the board of directors of Rumbarger Lumber.[8]

In March Lane attended the meeting of the Rumbarger board, which by this time had moved its center of operations to the Girard Trust Company building in Philadelphia's financial district. There was a confrontation: F.T. Rumbarger attended and vigorously protested the meeting. He took exception to the ratification of minutes of a January 18, 1898, meeting at which he was removed from the chairmanship of the company. His objections were overruled. The directors next passed a resolution acknowledging that the Rumbarger firm was indebted to the Davis Coal and Coke Company for three hundred thousand dollars. To settle the matter, the directors voted to transfer 2,400 acres of land in West Virginia and Maryland to the Davis interests "to forestall creditors." They noted that twenty-five thousand dollars and an extension of time on their debts could keep Davis from calling in his notes against the Rumbarger Company.[9] In this way, the hand of Henry Gassaway Davis touched the affairs of his competition within the Monongahela timbering region.

A counteroffer advanced by the Rumbargers, unexplained in the minutes, was rejected, but their protests were duly noted. The two founders of Rumbarger Lumber threatened to sue Whitmer, Lane, and Slaymaker under the laws of West Virginia. Rumbarger protested that the sale of land to Davis was unnecessary, and in any case the land in question was worth a great deal more than twenty-five thousand dollars. His counteroffer of thirty-eight thousand was apparently declined. It is the last time the Rumbarger name appears in the minutes of the J.L. Rumbarger Lumber Company.

In 1909 the Rumbarger firm accepted the offer of the Parsons Pulp and Paper Company, later known as the Condon-Lane Boom and Lumber Company, to sell out for six hundred thousand dollars or four thousand shares of stock in the paper company and two thousand shares of stock in the Whitmer firm.[10]

In the meantime, the Dry Fork Lumber Company was busily gathering timberlands as well. Also a Whitmer enterprise, the Dry Fork firm purchased 400 acres of land on Red Creek from L. Hansford and the timber on 250 acres from Wilson Thompson, the timber on the "Babb Place" from the Red Creek Lumber Company, and timber covering 16,947 acres from Robert Bridges and his wife, of Baltimore. The directors of the Dry Fork Lumber Company—Martin Lane, R.M. Whitmer, Thomas Coale, and Thomas Russell—in 1910 sold the company's assets, surrendered its charter, and went out of business. Robert Bridges ultimately sold his timbered acreage to the federal government.[11]

The blending of political power and economic dominance in West Virginia with the national political machinery is revealed in one of Davis's partnerships. In a letter to his friend and partner R.C. Kerens of St. Louis, the industrialist outlined the ownership interests in twelve thousand acres of land as follows: A.S. Hewitt, John A. Hambleton, Augustus Schell's heirs, R.C. Kerens, James G. Blaine, J.N. Camden, Thomas F. Bayard, J.B. Chaffee, and J.R. McPherson, one-twelfth each; and Stephen B. Elkins and Henry Gassaway Davis, "three-twelfths jointly, making twelve twelfths, or the whole."[12] New Jersey senator McPherson responded to Davis, suggesting that their land company obtain its charter in New Jersey, "as West Virginia law may not permit a corporation to hold that amount of land." New Jersey had liberal corporation laws. McPherson promised, "I can easily obtain you a charter in New Jersey if you desire it." The note was written on letterhead from the U.S. Senate.[13] Five of Davis's associates in this venture were present or former senators. James G. Blaine had been involved in questionable railroading activities and was rejected by the Republicans as a presidential candidate in 1876. Many Americans considered Blaine the epitome of seamy politics and responded to his 1884 presidential nomination, which was engineered by Elkins, with a taunting cry of "Continental Liar from the State of Maine." Nevertheless, Blaine, who had served as U.S. secretary of state in 1881 under James Garfield and Chester A. Arthur, was appointed again in 1889 by Benjamin Harrison. After the turn of the century, Davis's nephew was president of the Blaine Mining Company.[14]

Henry Gassaway Davis's enterprises and the West Virginia Pulp and Paper Company remained two of the most highly visible timbering ventures in the Monongahela. Sometimes benevolent to his competition, sometimes ruthless, Davis dominated the industrial activity within the region and proved astute in national economic affairs as well. At first his interests were limited to railroads and coal mining, but soon Davis explored investments in pulpwood. In 1880, while he was still serving in the Senate, his son-in-law Elkins investigated the merits of entering the business, reporting in a letter to Davis that he knew of Philadelphia proprietors who were interested in the enterprise and would facilitate learning all of the details of the business. Elkins recommended that their agent investigate so Davis could judge whether merely to sell the timber to the pulp industry or to establish works of their own.[15]

In the same long letter, Elkins also advised Davis that he had made "connections" that would provide much valuable information about another proposed Davis railroad enterprise. He recommended retaining an engineer to review the line and make recommendations. James Parsons, Elkins said, "as you of course know is a leading engineer and what he would say would be entitled to consideration." Elkins relayed an account of a meeting he held with the president of the Richmond and Allegheny Railroad, who had expansion plans that involved Davis and West Virginia. "He made some hints that he would like to make a combination so as to get the benefit of our charter and your influence. I have sent him down the charter today so he may look at it," Elkins wrote.[16]

Liaisons and partnerships such as Elkins was detailing seemed to characterize business within the West Virginia mountains. There, as in other industrial regions and banking centers throughout the nation, big business was getting bigger. The Gilded Age was nearing full flower.

Within the timbering regions of West Virginia, an ever-decreasing number of absentee elites and entrepreneurs increased their power and wealth, and an ever-widening sea of poorly paid industrial workers was fortunate to end each working day alive and unhurt. Industrial hegemony was nearly complete. Farming declined as the challenges to agriculture and husbandry multiplied. The small, nonagricultural middle class of doctors, teachers, builders, storekeepers, journalists, mechanics, journeymen, and service workers remained dependent upon the new industries for their economic survival, because miners and lumbermen and their families were the only source of patients, students, customers, patrons, and clients. These middle-class citizens were no longer independent enough to tax their interlopers in ways that would diversify the course of their region's economic development. These local residents constituted a dependent and subordinate middle class that survived by meeting the needs generated by industrialization. They possessed no political tools to trigger investments in the broader local economy. They were facilitators of the transition. They were of fleeting importance, soon redundant, and never strong enough to be independent of the industrialists.[17]

The local political system protected the economic system because the industrialists thoroughly controlled state and national politics. As participation in the democracy declined, so did the diversity of economic activity. When individuals competed for resources, the industrialists prevailed. West Virginia's fencing laws illustrate the point. Grazing of livestock, the major economic activity of the indigenous farmers, became financially difficult in the era of railroads and timbering, because the 1867 laws placed the burden of fence costs on the shoulders of farmers and livestock owners. Railroaders and loggers, who controlled the legislature, were exonerated from damages caused to any livestock that wandered into a work area. Before arrival of the industries, expensive fence construction was not necessary, and farmers pegged their profitability to the availability of free range for their animals. To make matters worse, the law held farmers responsible for damage their animals caused to industry workers and to machinery and other equipment.[18] Such lopsided laws came from a government of one mind and one priority. Once the political majority in West Virginia, the farmers were declining in numbers and consequently also in political influence. As the old mountain gentry dwindled, so too did the quality of the democracy within the region. Their minority voice was all but ignored. This pattern has been identified in other regions. Similarly delayed economic growth in other parts of the American South also has been linked to the demise of democracy and has been a major theme in other works on Appalachia.[19]

Capitalizing on a tax structure that since the 1830s had turned away from land, the industrialists paid only minimal taxes on their real estate. The more recently legislated tax exemption of coal and timber further spared the industrialists from public obligations. Davis controlled the Democratic political machine in West Virginia, especially the Second Congressional District, thus assuring that his businesses would not be burdened by costly taxes. The low land taxes in West Virginia did not allow for construction and maintenance of roads, schools, and utility systems of the caliber that would have attracted additional businesses to the region, thus broadening its economic base. The resources were exploited, not developed.[20]

Some surviving corporate records reveal the control over land that Davis maintained in the Monongahela region of West Virginia. In the Roaring Creek district of Randolph County, as of June 17, 1892, he had options on the coal rights to 11,577 acres of land, which were to expire in 1891.[21] Also in 1892, Davis organized the Jefferson Coal Company, to mine 3,150 acres in Maryland and 1,300 acres in West Virginia.[22] The December 31, 1892, statement of profit for the H.G. Davis Coal Company indicated a total profit "to date" of $127,878.84. Owners of that firm were Davis, his brother Thomas B. Davis, R.M.G. Brown of Kingwood, F.S. Landstreet, Harry Buxton, and Robert Bopst.[23] Davis's list of assets in 1893 reveals that he had absorbed the lands of many of the region's local elites. The January statement of assets for the firm shows about 8,724.5 acres of land that Davis had acquired from local owners.[24] These lands had passed between speculator and absentee for almost two hundred years. Modest-sized tracts were acquired from local residents between 1880 and 1910.

The names of the people from whom Davis acquired these lands represented those local entrepreneurs who in 1870 had attempted to bring internal improvements to their region. But most important, they were the local political leaders.

With their lands in Davis's control and their political support behind him, the rest of the citizens followed suit, as the region's land books demonstrate. These holdings, vast as they were, represented only one of Davis's many firms. Ten years before, Davis and Elkins had acquired more than fifty-five thousand acres of land upon which they built the town of Davis, and they purchased the ninety-thousand-acre Caperton tract to the south of the Monongahela region. The supply of land for sale seemed almost endless.

Agents wrote continually to Davis's organization, claiming to represent willing sellers of prime land. These proposals overwhelmingly came from lawyers and real estate agents. In the Monongahela, land agents, not landowners, negotiated between buyers or sellers and Davis. For example, on July 26, 1900, lawyers James A. Bent, the mayor of Elkins, and Wilson B. Maxwell, also of Elkins, invited Davis to sell his "Stalnaker tract" of land in Randolph County, near Millcreek. The plot contained 2,284 acres.[25] B.H. Hiner, an attorney from Franklin, in Pendleton County, wrote to Davis in March 1901, offering to sell two tracts of land. One he priced at five dollars per acre; the other he offered as a mineral purchase only, for three dollars per acre. "The surface is owned by rural farmers," the lawyer wrote.[26] Parsons resident and Democratic Executive Committee member L. Hansford wrote Davis in reference to "the Elliot lands on Red Creek," where Davis ultimately owned a coal mine. The tract contained "634 acres of a 1,080 acre tract free from lap or other encumbrance"; it was also adjacent to a tract that contained proven coal reserves.[27]

Earlier, William W. Croghan, of Richmond, had offered to sell Davis two hundred thousand acres in Randolph and Tucker counties. These lands, originally owned by one William Dewers, were reportedly located on the headwaters of the Cheat River. Croghan said the title was good, being "recorded in Richmond." No such original deed has been found in either county's deed books or in the archives of the U.S. Forest Service. Croghan apparently was a latter-day victim of overlapping land claims.[28] It is unlikely that his parcel of land existed, because such a vast amount of land would account for almost all of the area of Tucker County, which encompasses 270,080 acres. Farmers in Tucker County had claimed almost 150,000 acres themselves, as reported in the 1870 census.

Another early offer sent to Davis in 1885 from B.L. Butcher, a lawyer and real estate agent in Randolph County, offered for sale "two tracts in Randolph County, one 5,500 acres or more, and one of 6,000 acres." Butcher represented the lands as being located on the headwaters of Middle Fork, Buckhannon, Buck Fork of Elk, and Sugar creeks. It was, he said, covered with native forest, including cherry, and underlain by Elk Run coal. Butcher said he was looking for buyers of the land, at two dollars per acre, "here or in Europe."[29] Butcher's letter is characteristic of the letters from lawyer-agents in the region at the time. A 5-percent commission or finder's fee generally was suggested by the writers of such letters as a fair remuneration for locating the lands for Davis's enterprises. Lawyers in Pocahontas, Randolph, and Tucker counties were active participants in the industrialization of the region, but these local entrepreneurs were, in the end, only pawns in a much larger enterprise.

Much less frequently did actual landowners contact Davis. Farmers sometimes wrote Davis asking to purchase modest-sized parcels of land, but the record is silent concerning his compliance. Tucker County deed books do show many conveyances of home sites and town parcels in Davis. The record so far is also silent about how agents acquired their listings.

The historical record would seem to imply that landowners were willing to sell out to industries. The transactions revealed in the land books of Tucker, Randolph, and Pocahontas counties and the numbers of agents within the region indicate a brisk land market. But such an assumption must also consider the difficulties that accompany such a drastic change in lifestyle. If farmers were abandoning old ways, to what were they turning? Where would they live? How would they acquire skills to earn a livelihood if they were landless? Because southern cultural ways equated landownership with respectability, it is more likely that some negative changes occurred that encouraged farmers to reconsider their options.

The records of industrializing Clay County suggest how pressures could be brought against farmers in this period. Clay County farmers have left generous and unequivocal evidence that they were coerced to sell or compromise their holdings. The records of the Davis companies and the West Virginia Pulp and Paper Company indicate that sometimes industries resorted to ejectment tactics when they desired land.[30]

Many conditions that could adversely affect the quality of farming prevailed in the region. Rising land prices limited a farmer's potential to expand, sounding a death knell for market-sensitive commercial farming. Industrial surroundings would have had a negative influence on agriculture. Polluted runoff from denuded hillsides fouled supplies of drinking water. Soil erosion, downstream flooding, and forest fires caused constant tribulations. Fencing, to keep livestock clear of trains and machines, seriously strained a farmer's resources, but West Virginia law placed the burdens of fencing on owners of livestock.[31]

The influx of immigrant workers changed the nature of the community in ways that may have been perplexing to indigenous farm families. The relatively large number of young single men in the timbering and mining regions brought increasing crime and drunkenness. New languages, new customs, and new religions were not always greeted with a welcoming curiosity. The continuing danger from disease, accident, and confrontation with industrial competitors were bewildering developments that discouraged farming.

Farmers often cooperated with lumber barons to clear more farmland, but this sometimes brought disastrous results. In at least one area timber contracts proved ruinous for farmers who were not protected from the possibility of the lumbermen's business failure. Thirty-eight Randolph County farmers sustained varying losses in 1893 when the Buckhannon River Lumber Company defaulted on its debts. Negotiating timber deeds with the farmers, the company paid $1.25 per thousand board feet of good lumber. The lumber company recorded all thirty-eight deeds in the Randolph County deed books.[32] A $25.00 down payment, with the balance due on or before June 1893, was the most common arrangement. The firm was in default by that time, and large creditors and local banks attached the timber to lessen their losses. All of the timber purchases were named in the foreclosure suits filed by banks, railroads, and powerful individuals.[33] Nearly all of the plaintiffs were powerful industrialists. Farmers lost their timber without remuneration. Apparently they were without legal remedy.

8

Reform Politics
Tariff Woes and West Virginia's Backwoods Campaign

No local character with the wealth and the stature of Kentucky tycoon John C.C. Mayo emerged from the Monongahela, but local leaders were essential to the success of industrialization within the region.[1] John Thomas McGraw of Grafton succeeded as an agent of the industrialists, primarily because he could deliver votes, but he never approached the wealth of Mayo or the power of Henry Gassaway Davis. McGraw was a corporate attorney for the Baltimore and Ohio Railroad and also served as internal revenue collector and chairman of the Democratic Executive Committee of West Virginia's Second Congressional District, which encompassed Davis's industrial region. By 1910 McGraw was president of the West Virginia Midland Railroad Company, headquartered in Grafton.

McGraw's contacts throughout the state political networks, press, and regulatory agencies were thorough and effective. The records of his political conduct in election years illustrates the close relationship of politics and business in West Virginia. During the congressional campaign of 1894, the Democrats found a rich, dollar-sensitive voter resource within the lumber camps of Tucker and Randolph counties, and their political machinery was sufficiently disciplined by McGraw to deliver crucial votes. McGraw was the campaign manager for Congressman William L. Wilson, who was seeking reelection. Wilson was a Davis protégé turned political foe. He advocated modest tariff reform and was therefore opposed by Davis, who enjoyed the protection his businesses received from high tariffs. McGraw and Davis were friends and political allies. Therefore, party loyalty silenced Davis's opposition to Wilson, but he did withhold active support of Wilson's candidacy.[2]

Through his many industrial activities and his legal practice, McGraw enjoyed political leadership in the Second District. Despite his friendships with Davis, Stephen B. Elkins, J.N. Camden, and Nathan Bay Scott, McGraw was loyal to Wilson and the Democratic party machine. In his district, he ruled this machine absolutely. McGraw's ability to deliver votes protected his position as a vital actor in the industrialization of the region. Although his 1894 efforts for Wilson failed, the energy he expended to bring Democratic voters to heel demonstrates the political tactics that have been commonplace, and usually effective, in West Virginia.

One of the party's responsibilities was directing how and when newly arrived industrial workers voted. During the 1894 campaign, the Democrats focused efforts to win votes within immigrant communities. New citizens, unfamiliar with the voting process, acquiesced. McGraw's disciplined political machinery delivered needed votes from coal miners and lumber workers. No industrial village within the mountains was too small or too remote to escape his notice; party disciples relentlessly pursued every voter.

E.D. Talbott, committeeman from Beverly, wrote McGraw on Democratic Committee letterhead, to explain that there were "about 300 voters in this county that vote the way the dollar points and we will have them to keep in line, as by that means two years ago, we increased our majority more than 200 votes." He urged McGraw to send two hundred dollars immediately and as much more later as might be possible, because "we will have use for every dollar we can get." He further instructed McGraw to have the postmaster general affix Congressman Wilson's postal frank on campaign literature: "We have had that done here frequently."[3]

Reporting on the "political atmosphere" in Randolph County, Talbott told McGraw that five Democrats in Mingo Flats would not vote to reelect Wilson, but he assured McGraw that he would "get their names and have them looked after." Talbott promised to deliver the full vote in Dry Fork but noted that it would be hard to get every voter out to the polls. In Middle Fork, Wilson was expected to increase his strength, but so was his opposition. The vote in the Elkins district was uncertain, but Talbott proposed to make a house-to-house canvass "with funds."[4]

Charles H. Straub, president of the Pickens, West Virginia, Tariff Reform Club, informed his colleague William L. Key in Washington that "we are badly in need of campaign funds as there are quite a number of voters here who are on the doubtful list." Straub wanted the funds for incidental expenses and the costs of transporting voters to the polls. He also explained that he would need to transport ten or twelve foreigners to file their naturalization papers in Beverly. "Chairman Kittle has agreed to help us as much as possible, but I do not think that he will be able to do us justice as a great deal of money will have to be spent in the Roaring Creek District," Straub continued. He further advised Key that a forceful speaker, fluent in German, would be helpful.[5]

Committeeman Charles Powell of Fairmont wrote McGraw, taking exception to criticism of his Marion County efforts on behalf of Wilson. He declared that the committee had done everything asked by McGraw: "All printed matter has been promptly sent out, Wilson's pictures delivered, lists made for papers, hacks furnished to bring people into town to hear speeches." He suggested that McGraw and the B and O Railroad arrange free transportation for potential voters to hear Wilson speak in Fairmont: "We feel sure that by these excursions an immense crowd can be gotten here." Later he warned McGraw that there was bitter feeling toward the candidate in some Marion County circles and in every district there was some opposition to him. Talbott, in Beverly, wrote McGraw again to advise him that he had agreed to fund the naturalization costs of "the Dutch that [Straub] wants naturalized and to pay for their papers."[6]

These political efforts were, for McGraw and Wilson, unsuccessful. But the candidate's loss reflected the interests at work behind the scenes. At least one historian has concluded that Wilson lost the election simply because he was outspent by the Republicans, who were equally well organized.[7]

Tariff reform, the only issue of any concern to the powerful leaders of West Virginia, was an uncomfortable subject for the Democrats, particularly Davis, who opposed reform and did not actively support his party's candidate. Nor did he publicly oppose him. Party politics and the maintenance of a well-disciplined machine were important considerations for the industrialists in West Virginia. It was preferable to them to retain proindustry leaders, however, even if it meant yielding a governmental seat to the opposing party. Davis and J.N. Camden were Democrats; Elkins and Nathan Bay Scott were Republicans. The four were also friends who kept their politics in perspective: they sought a government sympathetic to their economic interests. Which party led it was less important to them.[8]

It is questionable whether the average West Virginia voter in 1894 would have identified tariff reform as a topic of vital concern. Certainly other things bore more significance for the average citizen. Roads, schools, higher wages, and shorter working days were issues that might have generated voter participation without much cost to either political party machine. These issues, however, were not on the political agendas of the men who led the mountain industries.

Almost no voices were raised to criticize the industrialists or their political behavior. The state press as thoroughly supported the industrialization mania and partisan politics as the legislature did. Romney newspaper editor J.J. Cornwell became governor of West Virginia by virtue of his loyal service to the industrial views of taxation espoused by Davis and Elkins.[9]

The only cautionary advice was by this time ten years old, and it had come from the West Virginia Tax Commission. In 1884 that agency had objected to the systematic removal of assets from the state and the widening embrace of absentee control of West Virginia's resources. At the behest of the legislature, the commission sought to "collect and report whatever information [would] enable the legislature to legislate intelligently and with safety upon subjects calculated to advance the development of the state." The commission criticized absentee roles in West Virginia. A state, the report said, is prosperous if property is owned by its citizens.[10] The report alleged that the many industrialists within the state had concealed their true objectives and were instead pursuing goals that would work to the state's detriment. The tax commissioners' argument echoed the pleas advanced at the turn of the nineteenth century by Kentucky's founders, who had argued unsuccessfully before the Supreme Court in 1821 that the interests of the state are superior to individual rights to own property. Like Kentucky, West Virginia would be "doubly unprosperous when property is rapidly passing from her present population or home people into the hands of non-residents."[11]

Perhaps the magnitude of absentee control of the state was just becoming evident to them, but the commissioners were somewhat inaccurate in their perceptions. If the patterns within the Monongahela region matched those in the state as a whole, then the amount of land actually passing to out-of-state control in the 1880s was minuscule when compared with the amount of land that had been in absentee hands since the region was settled but just then was being brought into production. Second, the local control the commission cited was nonexistent. By 1884 the role of indigenous citizens was irrelevant to the direction in which state government and industry were steering the state. The industrial forces within government were accurately identified by the tax commissioners, but their admonitions to the people went unheeded. The commission correctly reported that those who controlled the state's government also controlled its economy and, therefore, were guided by the profit motive.[12]

Although the commissioners identified many interlocking relationships that have since become illegal and widely accepted as detrimental, as agrarian reformers they limited their opprobrium to railroads. Rate-fixing and kickbacks were common railroad practices that frightened away honest capital. Another tactic the commissioners criticized was the selling of stock to unwary local investors who were later "frozen out" of the business by the original investors. Their admonition brings the unfortunate Rumbarger family to mind. Perhaps concerned state residents interpreted the report as just one more partisan foray into the railroad rate wars that dominated West Virginia business at the time. Perhaps the commissioners were echoing the national frustration with the railroad industry that was so prevalent in the period. The absence of criticism of other industries probably weakened the case for railroad regulation in the 1880s, but in such a staunchly proindustry arena as West Virginia politics, the commission's call for reform had no impact on public policy. Nor were J.M. Mason, E.A. Bennett, and Joseph Bell, the commissioners, in complete agreement. In signing their call for remedial legislation, Bennett and Bell indicated that they were not in accord with all parts of the report.[13]

Despite the warnings, railroading, timbering, and mining continued unabated in West Virginia. Federal regulations ultimately brought some relief to rail customers in the mountains. Reform legislation sponsored by Senator Elkins and others established standard railroad rates during the Progressive Era. Paradoxically, these federal regulations grew out of industry frustration with the high costs associated with various states' differing regulation of railroads and the rate wars such as those that dogged the lumbermen in Randolph, Pocahontas, and Tucker counties.

In Pocahontas County, the West Virginia Pulp and Paper Company carefully structured its links to the Pocahontas County leadership but kept its business considerations uppermost in political decisions. Samuel E. Slaymaker and the WVPPC controlled at least 200,000 acres of the Monongahela directly, and later, with the cooperation and blessing of Davis and Elkins, they controlled more. A Philadelphia native, Slaymaker focused his endeavors on the town of Cass, in Pocahontas County, which took its name from WVPPC vice president Joseph K. Cass. Slaymaker was one of the first lumbermen to see the red spruce and northern hardwood stands on the headwaters of Shavers Fork of the Cheat River. Undaunted by the lack of means to get the logs out, he set about forming a timber firm of his own.[14] He secured a tract of 173,000 acres under the name S.E. Slaymaker and Company and went to work timbering in the Monongahela. Soon renamed the West Virginia Spruce Lumber Company, Slaymaker's enterprise ultimately became a subsidiary of the WVPPC.[15] His early associates variously included Robert F. Whitmer, Martin Lane, Levi Condon, J.L. Rumbarger, and other Tucker County timber executives. Slaymaker built the Greenbrier Cheat and Elk Railroad, which ultimately connected with Davis's Western Maryland Railroad in Webster County.[16] Surviving records of these early firms, when woven together, portray the methods and motives of the men who industrialized the Monongahela.

By 1900 Slaymaker and his firm were incorporated into the WVPPC empire. Slaymaker was assured by the Luke family, which owned the company, that his financial interests were fully protected: "In making our deal with you, the intention was to be perfectly frank and we have held nothing in reserve. It seems to us the original agreement fully protects you when we agree to take back your stock at any time."[17]

Slaymaker's service to the Lukes came after his long association with other lumber companies in the Monongahela region. The minutes of the Whitmer lumber companies show interlocking ownership among lumber and rail companies, and Slaymaker was an officer in more than one organization. Inevitably, the control of these organizations moved toward more and more powerful individuals and away from any local influence. Successively larger concerns moved in. Bigger businesses in Philadelphia and New York, led by men like Slaymaker and the Lukes, cooperating with Davis and Elkins, controlled more and more of the diminishing forest acreage.

Insecure claims to land, extending into the past as far as original settlement, enabled these individuals to engineer the successful land transactions that accompanied the rise of industrial activity in West Virginia. Timber experts like Slaymaker, land agents like L.A. Rheaume, and dozens of skilled local attorneys were invaluable to the companies that utilized their services. Knowledgeable in land, timber, and railroading, they rose steadily in the regional industrial hierarchy to become critically important to the success of the resource extraction within the Monongahela region.

In the 1890s, several of the companies operating in the forest were acquired by the Condon-Lane Boom and Lumber Company. The deeds reveal a pattern of land acquisition reaching back at least twenty years. Absentee agent Rheaume of Baltimore painstakingly reconstructed portions of a Federalist era land grant to Levi Hollingsworth. The grant spanned the Allegheny Mountains of Pendleton, Pocahontas, and Randolph counties in West Virginia and Highland County in Virginia. Hollingsworth was a Philadelphia speculator who owned vast lands in the mountains—more than 137,245 acres of land in Pendleton County alone before 1800. In the early federal period the land was deemed worthless for any purpose but timbering.[18] In 1832, before roads had penetrated the region and before coal was discovered in the Monongahela, Hollingsworth's heir was advised to review the land from the back of a horse or from a balloon, because the nearest road was forty miles away.[19] In 1892 most of that century-old original Virginia land survey remained intact, owned by out-of-state residents, but some parcels had been surveyed off. A few overlapping claims of local farmers also had to be considered. By tracing the deeds backward, this pattern of absentee land acquisition becomes evident.

Levi and Emily Condon sold to the Condon-Lane Company all their considerable landholdings in West Virginia, as described in a lengthy deed that was recorded in several counties. The largest Condon parcel was a tract astride the Allegheny Mountains in Pocahontas and Pendleton counties, West Virginia, and Highland County, Virginia, containing about 28,352 acres. There were two exceptions totaling 3,000 acres, which had been "sold by McClung and Anderson to various parties prior to the partition of the Hollingsworth Survey."[20] These deed "exceptions" were often the lands of local farmers. The Condons had purchased the land from Wilbur F. and Lou Dyer of Grant County in November 1889.[21] Dyer, an attorney, had been actively involved in land transactions during the 1880s boom.

Included in the Condon-Lane deed was a tract of land that Maria A. Shaw unsuccessfully sued to recover in 1890 from the Randolph West Virginia Boom Company, as well as all the other property of the Randolph Company, which approached 33,200 acres.[22] Maria Shaw, a widow, wished to keep her husband's land for her own use, but the lumbermen defeated her. The suit is evidence of the treachery that accompanied business dealings in this region. The deed to Condon-Lane then listed several parcels, some quite large by mountain farming standards, that had been acquired from local residents by Rheaume for the Randolph Company. Two such parcels may account for the excepted 3,000 acres noted in the Hollingsworth survey. The Hoffman lands consisting of about 1,800 acres were conveyed to L.A. Rheaume by W.B. and Carrie H. Maxwell on October 27, 1888. The 1,200-acre Sponagle tract located on Gandy Creek in Randolph County cornered on the Maxwell tract. According to the deed, it was conveyed to Rheaume by land lawyers James A. Bent, W.B. Maxwell, and others on November 17, 1888, and was then conveyed by Rheaume to the Randolph West Virginia Boom Company.[23]

Throughout the region, several small tracts of land were acquired by Rheaume. In the Black Fork district of Tucker County, a small parcel of five and one-half acres showed the same pattern in title: local owner to agent to lumber company. Beginning in 1887, the land was transferred from Jacob H. Long and his wife, Lucinda, to Rheaume, and then to the Randolph West Virginia Boom Company. The Longs also conveyed another two and one-half acres that ended up in the same deed.[24] Presumably these small tracts were strategically important to the lumber company, or Jacob Long's cooperation was essential in other ways.

Additional small parcels were also included in the Condon-Lane deed: a 2-acre tract, first sold by residents David and Ruth Long in October 1888; a 0.5-acre tract sold by W.D. Goff in 1880 to Rheaume and later sold to the Randolph Company; and finally a 0.5-acre tract sold in 1888 by L.E. Goff to Rheaume, then to Randolph, to Condon, and to the Condon-Lane Company.[25] Five and one-half more acres, originally belonging to Mary Jane and Jesse Pennington, ended up in the same industrial package. The Penningtons also conveyed a parcel containing 2.94 acres of land in November 1888. A 12-acre parcel, owned originally by George W. White and sold in

December 1888, was included, as was a 5-acre parcel belonging originally to Silas R. Blackman. Fourteen more acres were acquired by Rheaume by written contract from Jacob H. Long and his wife, conveyed to the Condon-Lane Company, by the Longs' deed dated May 22, 1890. The Longs' contract is not otherwise recorded in the Condon-Lane document. The absence of a deed citation or date in this transaction is troubling, because the 14 acres comprised a valuable island in the Cheat River (probably Bretz Island). Transferred also were 2,721 acres of merchantable saw timber on land owned by G.W. Yokum.[26]

This convoluted and lengthy deed reveals the chain of title that transferred ownership of the mountain land from the occupants to the timber companies, but none of the deeds carry information about the families who occupied the land for one hundred years after the Virginia conveyance. Were their titles insecure? Did they, like the Clay County farmers, face threats of ejectment? From these land records, it is possible to conclude that absentee owners of lands within the Monongahela and speculators passed large portions of land among themselves, dealing when necessary with farmers who resided on relatively small portions of the territory. White, Long, Blackman, Goff, and Pennington are the surnames of those first families who settled within the region in the late eighteenth and early nineteenth centuries before there were courthouses in which to record deeds. Those surnames also appear in the 1870 manuscript census of agriculture. Because these names appear again on deeds of sale in the 1880s, it is necessary to consider the possibility of a forced conveyance of land such as occurred in Clay County and elsewhere during the industrialization of the Appalachian Mountains.

The eighteenth-century experience of original Cheat Valley settlers Salathiel Goff, Noah Haden, David Minear, James Parsons, Thomas Parsons, and William Parsons whispers from the past. Among them they registered claims in Morgantown to more than 8,000 acres of land along the Cheat River. Most of their claims were unpatented and languished, lost, for more than a century in Monongalia County's records.[27] Some of these claims constituted the lands partitioned off the

large parcels of land that absentees and land agents were attempting to recapture. In the Federalist era, challenges to
their claims could sometimes be turned back. No such protection existed in the Gilded Age. John Thomas Goff turned
back a challenge from the Deakins family in 1790 after
William McCleery, a Morgan's Town (Morgantown) attorney
and land agent, advised the Deakinses that Goff could prevail
in a challenge to his 240-acre claim made in 1781.[28]

By 1890 Monongahela residents no longer enjoyed the protection Virginia law had given to their settler ancestors. They
faced powerful opposition if they were reluctant to sell their
lands. Even if a settlement claim could have been advanced
by one of these farmers, it could not have been defended successfully, because West Virginia law and U.S. Supreme Court
rulings unequivocally supported the kind of claims that the
industrialists and land agents could defend. Armed with this
legal arsenal as well as the personal talents of timbermen like
Whitmer and Slaymaker and politicians like Davis and Elkins, powerful men with ruthless determination could flourish within the mountains. Farmers were nearly helpless to
stop the transitions that were beginning.

9

Pulp and Paper Politics
Swashbuckling through the Forest and Poaching the Game

Samuel E. Slaymaker was one of the most successful timber-men in the Monongahela region. His successes on his own and his later associations with the Whitmer companies and Condon and Lane inevitably drew him to the top. By 1900 his affiliation with the West Virginia Pulp and Paper Company allowed him to capitalize on his broad experience and expertise. From his Philadelphia office he kept close ties with William, John G., David L., and Adam K. Luke, who owned the firm. The WVPPC had mills in Piedmont and Davis, West Virginia; Luke, Maryland, just across the river from Piedmont; and Covington, Virginia. Corporate headquarters were located on Broadway Avenue in New York City. With the addition of Slaymaker's personal timber holdings, the Luke enterprise expanded southward through the Monongahela, toward the forks of the Greenbrier River.

As the business grew, haulage rates were ever more important aspects of the Lukes' profitability. By the turn of the century, it was time, they believed, to contact Henry Gassaway Davis and arrange rail rates on hauling pulpwood out of the Monongahela to their mills. They were acting on Davis's announced plans to expand the West Virginia Central Railroad south from Elkins to the Forks of the Greenbrier River. Even as Pocahontas County attorney C.F. Moore, who rose quickly to a position of trust within the Luke organization, was negotiating a rate schedule with Davis's railroad, the paper company was planning to capture an additional advantage in negotiating rail rates. Apparently playing one railroad against the other, David Luke told Slaymaker that the Chesapeake and Ohio Railroad rate quote was not satisfactory and advised him that since the West Virginia Central rates had not advanced, "it will be necessary for the C and O to make us better rates than they named." The very next week, WVPPC was confronted with the possibility that the negotiations with the railroads would reverse. Luke assured Slaymaker that the C and O would respond appropriately in the matter of freight rates: "I do not think there is any danger of the West Va. Central being able to cut us off although, as you suggest, it might be better if we were so fixed that we could ship over both roads." To that end, he requested that Slaymaker report the best rates available from Davis's railroad.[1]

Supplying pulpwood to the mills was another concern to the Lukes, who told Slaymaker that "it seems to be impossible to count on our friends [and Slaymaker's old firm], the Condon-Lane Boom and Lumber Co." Despite price-fixing deals between lumber and paper companies, troubles arose. Condon-Lane repudiated a five-year pricing agreement that Whitmer had made on pulpwood, but the Lukes were prepared to seek legal action "to hold them up to the agreement."[2]

Supplies of pulpwood remained uncertain in the winter of 1900. Two other Davis firms, Beaver Creek Lumber and Otter Creek Lumber, had agreed to supply hemlock pulpwood at four dollars per cord. Pulpwood supplies continued to challenge the leadership of the WVPPC, and Slaymaker was unable to negotiate a contract with Monongahela timber firms that would guarantee a reliable supply. Company treasurer John G. Luke responded, "It is, we take it, impossible to make any kind of an agreement or contract that will fully provide for all contingencies." He reminded Slaymaker that the pulp lands were bought primarily as a protection for company pulp mills, and "we want to have it clearly understood that the question of pulp wood supply is of the first importance." Railroad rates were clearly a second priority. In the same letter, Luke rejected quotes from the B and O and proposed to secure a more satisfactory rate from the West Virginia Central.[3]

Twenty years of frenzied industrialization had nearly depleted the timber reserves in the Monongahela. By 1900 pulpwood sources were diminishing, and the paper company was forced to locate sources of raw materials elsewhere. Slaymaker was dispatched to explore sawmill sites in New Hampshire and Florida. Although the company was thinking beyond West Virginia, considerable land in the Monongahela remained under its control. Because the organization owned so much land, the few persisting Pocahontas County farmers were beginning to recognize Slaymaker as the man to contact if they wished to purchase land.

Despite the region's shift from farming to industry, not every farmer was willing to sell out to the timber interests. A few still wished to expand their farms. John F. Wooddell sent a letter to Slaymaker in Philadelphia, offering to purchase land. "I Under stand that the Jacob Sheets farm belongs to you. If it does and you want to Sell it I would like to buy it of you if you dont want to[o] much for it." Wooddell was frustrated in his attempts to find Slaymaker in person at Cass, and he further promised that "your pay will be good."[4] Slaymaker's records do not indicate whether he met with Wooddell or not, nor do they indicate whether a sale occurred.

The pace of timbering quickened, while the number of trees and privately held farms in the region diminished. Prominent industrialists sometimes found themselves in competition. One such incident found Senator Davis, Slaymaker, and the heirs of Senator J.N. Camden all contending for the same lands, even as a fourth party was attempting to purchase the land, perhaps redeeming it for back taxes. E.D. Talbott, the attorney and Democratic committeeman, wrote to Slaymaker in June 1900 to advise him that back taxes were due on the land along the Cheat Valley. Davis, who held a mortgage for would-be purchaser J.B. Ward's taxes on the parcel, had not taken any of the land, although Ward could not repay the two thousand dollars he had borrowed from Davis. Ward planned to purchase all the Camden lands on Cheat River and Cheat Mountain. Owing to an adverse claim held by John G. Luke on part of the tract, Davis declined the land except that part not claimed by Luke. Ward did not want Davis to have only the clear title; it was to be all or nothing, but he did not have sufficient funds to return Davis's advance for taxes and thus keep the land. "Davis wants to pick out all the land not in dispute, but Ward and the Camden heirs don't want to let him have it that way if they can prevent it," Talbott wrote.[5]

The back taxes were considerable for 1900, and former senator Davis expected repayment of his two-thousand-dollar loan. Hence, the lawyer advised Slaymaker that Luke could probably count on acquiring "all the Camden Land in Cheat Valley, if it is taken in time. Davis informed me last week that he did not want any of the land to which there was an adverse claim."[6]

Luke later complained to Slaymaker that the Ward lands contained unheard-of exceptions and limitations and urged his agent to keep himself fully informed. Luke directed Slaymaker to find a disinterested expert (a timber cruiser) to evaluate several smaller tracts the pulp company had purchased. He expressed concern that the firm might suffer some losses through those purchases.[7] Although they were well equipped to unravel the legalities of landownership in West Virginia, the Lukes and other industrialists were not exempt from the anxieties of conflicting titles, overlapping claims, or ejectment suits against them. Land claims required ever-vigilant management for the paper company.

Politics in the election of 1900 was another crucial arena for Slaymaker and the Luke family. By 1900 populist appeal was perceived as a political threat to the local industrial order, and the firm redoubled efforts to preserve the influence of Stephen B. Elkins in the Senate. Reelection of President William McKinley was important as well, for his opponent, William Jennings Bryan, threatened to inflate the economy with free coinage of silver. Essentially a class struggle, the issue of silver or gold as a basis for currency was taken seriously by the industrialists, who preferred the deflationary gold standard, which limited the supply of money. Populists preferred the inflationary silver. All industrialists strove to maintain their control of politics to avoid economic losses that would come from a Bryan victory: lowering of the tariff, silver coinage, and labor unionism.

In West Virginia, Elkins's supporters had distinct ways of achieving his successful return to Washington. In this era before direct election of senators, the Lukes and Slaymaker worked hard to ensure the election of Pocahontas County delegates to the state senate who would remember the importance of Elkins to the paper company and Pocahontas County. In this spirit, one candidate forwarded to them a bill for $697, presumably for campaign expenses. The statement from Daniel O'Connell, a woods contractor, astonished the Luke brothers, who avowed in a letter to Slaymaker that they did "not know anything about this." Expanding their comments on the election, they told Slaymaker that the West Virginia Pulp and Paper Company desired harmonious relations with O'Connell and would not want any friction or trouble, at least until after the election. "We want to do what we can to elect him, and after that time will see if we cannot make some arrangement that will be more satisfactory to all concerned," John Luke wrote.[8]

As the 1900 election drew nearer, David Luke sent his frank political concerns to Slaymaker, expressing the firm's ardent wish for O'Connell's election: "In the first place, it will be a very good way of side-tracking O'Connell, and in the second place, we are very anxious to have Mr. Elkins returned to the Senate." The Lukes were convinced that Elkins "is going to have a pretty hard pull to get through and will need every possible vote." The emerging Progressive party influence would be nipped easily by West Virginia industrialists, but the lumber barons took the threat seriously.[9]

The Luke organization placed a high value on Elkins's approval of their efforts. Lamenting that being "newcomers" in Pocahontas County placed the leaders of the paper company at a political disadvantage, David Luke observed that if "we do everything that can possibly be done, it is at least evidence to Elkins of our good faith." The senator expected solidarity from his colleagues in industry. The Lukes spent on the election "two or three thousand dollars, which we will not begrudge if we can only get results." Concern surrounded the political conduct of the Pocahontas County Republican chairman, N.C. McNeil, who was "not acting straight, and some of the other prominent Republicans doing no better, which is very unfortunate, and which means that so much more work will have to be done through Democratic sources" to have O'Connell elected.[10] McNeil had nominated Nathan Bay Scott of Ohio County for the Senate in 1899, which annoyed the Lukes. Although Republican in official allegiance, the Lukes retained sufficient Democratic ties to subvert the political process for business purposes if it was necessary. McNeil, however, was reelected.

The Lukes soundly denied to Slaymaker that they had sent him a telegram advocating the election of O'Connell, about which the Pocahontas County press was ruminating. "By the way," John Luke wrote in a second note to Slaymaker that day, "I have a letter... which says the local Democrat papers in Pocahontas County are making considerable capital out of a telegram which it is alleged was sent from the New York office." Luke conveyed public reports contending that because the message was telephoned, it was public property. "Did you receive such a telegram? We have no recollection of having sent anything from here."[11]

The election of Elkins to the Senate came after a long battle among West Virginia Republicans, who were divided on the focus of the party. Idealistic leaders of the state, defenders of the Union, and leading blacks—all Progressives—were chary of Elkins's iron-fisted industrial devotion, but they were unable to stop him. After consolidating his hold on West Virginia Republicanism, Elkins was never seriously challenged again, even though Progressive ideology was more and more evident among members of the party. After 1900 all Republicans acknowledged Elkins as their leader. His later sponsorship of modest reform legislation neutralized his critics. Davis, the Democrat, worked diligently for his party in the state that year too, with the result that West Virginia political leaders, no matter what their party affiliations, actually supported the platform of industrialization.[12] The Lukes need not have feared either way. Elkins's return to Washington was assured, their lingering concerns about the "loyalty" of O'Connell aside.

Party loyalty was secondary to industrial loyalty. In a cavalier note to former governor A.B. Fleming, former senator J.N. Camden, a Democrat, said the compensation for the party's "overwhelming defeat is that we ought to make lots of money."[13] In West Virginia politics, the significant political differences were between reformers and industrialists. The Progressive minority was never able to wrest control of either the Republican or the Democratic party. The leaders of both parties were first and foremost industrial colleagues, and other political objectives were of secondary importance to their overarching economic interests.[14]

With President McKinley returned to the White House and Elkins to the Senate, in early 1901 the WVPPC leadership returned its attention to business. The expansion and development of its own railroad, a personal triumph for Slaymaker, was nearing completion. The concern to maintain a steady supply of pulpwood was ever increasing in the lucrative business conditions that followed the Republican sweep of the year before. Under the direction of Slaymaker, the railroad construction proceeded apace, and the Lukes praised their administrator profusely for his skills as a railroad builder.[15]

The pulp company continued to grow. The need for workers was unrelenting. Efforts to secure a labor supply resulted in a tremendous influx of European immigrants. Company superintendent E.P. Shaffer reported to Slaymaker on the daily business in the woods, while Slaymaker searched for still more sources of timber for the firm. An ever-growing labor force was required to fell the trees that were milled daily. The local population had long since exhausted its ability to supply sufficient workers for the railroads and lumber mills.

References to such matters as the labor force, however, were brief, when they occurred at all, in the correspondence between Slaymaker and the Lukes. Slaymaker's efforts increasingly were focused upon timber and land acquisition, leaving conduct of the mills and camps to Shaffer, in Cass. The workers who were crowded into the lumber camps remained anonymous. Their payroll records were kept by nationality and number, as were their work assignments. In 1900 Shaffer wrote Slaymaker: "Have the promise of fifteen Italians to go to work tomorrow, will start them in on the upper end... the Austrian Crew are working... above the place we got the tomatoes the day you was up there."[16]

Shaffer relayed a request from the West Virginia Central Railroad to rent some of Slaymaker's unused timber camps along the rail line. He urged the executive to send a veterinary handbook, since distemper was threatening the logging horses. "The roan has it now and if we had a good book we might get some better idea about treating them," he said. Colic, too, thinned the animals' ranks.[17]

By December 1900 the New York office learned of smallpox in the West Virginia lumber camps and briefly expressed hopes that the company's lumbermen would be spared. Vaccination efforts and quarantine measures were immediately instituted. They would prove futile. At the time, treasurer John Luke was more impressed with the gift of West Virginia's wild game that Slaymaker had made to him: "Thanking you very much for the wild turkeys... I am greatly obliged to you for wishing to send along the deer as a present, but I... will be better satisfied if you will send me a bill for both." A scornful Luke added, "With reference to the violation of the game laws, the writer is not likely to lose any sleep about it."[18]

The new year brought another encounter with Slaymaker's old colleague Robert F. Whitmer. Allies when threatened as a class, the barons of industry in West Virginia were nevertheless willing to compete fiercely against one another in their own arena. From William Whitmer and Sons came the message that the firm had purchased two-thirds interest in five thousand acres of land that the Lukes also partly owned. Pressing for a quick, cheap sale, Whitmer threatened to have the land partitioned as John Luke reported, "If you are not disposed to sell we will then have to make some arrangement for a division, as we are cognizant of the fact that this timber must be taken off at once or we will get nothing."[19]

C.F. Moore counseled the paper company to be skeptical of the Whitmer proposal, especially the allegations of low prices paid for the parcel known as the Kinport tract. Moore recommended that the firm call Whitmer's bluff and encourage him to go ahead and partition the land so the paper company could retrieve the timber from its third as well. John Luke, in recounting the offer to Slaymaker, said, "We would, however, be afraid to make a deal with Whitmer unless we were sure we would get our money."[20]

Within the year, Whitmer was flexing his muscle with the Davis enterprises, and their local manager sought senatorial advice. A letter from the Davis-owned Beaver Creek Lumber Company of Davis to Senator Elkins in Washington contended that the company's attempts to purchase timber along the Red Creek line of the Dry Fork Railroad had been thwarted. Whitmer was threatening to block Beaver Creek's access to rail cars to haul out the lumber even if the company successfully negotiated for the lands. "We of course do not intend to get into a war with Mr. Whitmer, but in order to know what we are about," Superintendent I.A. Allen wrote, "I write to ask whether you and Senator Davis cannot see that we are supplied with cars in case we purchase the timber and operate a mill along the Dry Fork road." Elkins circumspectly deferred the matter to Davis's judgment.[21]

As the struggle over the rail cars continued, other troubles loomed. Disease had not spared the Luke enterprise. Smallpox struck the West Virginia lumber camps in November 1901. Well insulated in New York, however, the Lukes could be philosophical about the illness within their camps. Slaymaker, who was then visiting at Cass, received a sympathetic but detached comment in a note of thanks for another West Virginia wild turkey: "We are very sorry indeed to hear that you have smallpox in your camp, and trust that it will not be long before you can have it stamped out." Assigning blame to the natural requirements of timbering, Thomas Luke added, "It must be a pretty tough proposition to have small pox in a camp where men are herded together as they must be in a lumber camp." No concern about numbers of cases, or deaths, or actions taken to corral the disease were included in this communiqué from Thomas Luke, who added, "Mrs. Luke will be very glad indeed to have a pair of deer horns.... Do not go to too much pains in the matter, however, as we know you have troubles of your own while you are in the woods."[22]

With those few words, the Lukes turned again to the matters of acquiring additional land. Their correspondence dealt no further with workers' health and welfare. Descriptions of five additional tracts of land in the Monongahela region were forwarded to Slaymaker by Shaffer in this time period, as the appetite for the waning timber in the region continually forced the companies into ever more strenuous efforts to gain land. If anything, the Lukes' skills of acquisition were sharpened by legal expertise and determination in the face of diminishing reserves of timber.

Fights over land continued, even between these old friends and associates. Moore advised Slaymaker that the paper company was bringing legal action against his old firm, the Condon-Lane Company, and Kinport, owner of the land that Whitmer mentioned. The lands were probably portions of the Levi Hollingsworth tract that had been packaged by L.A. Rheaume for Condon-Lane in 1890. By the turn of the twentieth century, the timber value was considerable, and the lands were once again subject to disputes between absentee claimants and occasional residents. "I am of the opinion that when the suit is instituted we may be able to deal with them to good advantage," Moore said. He advised Slaymaker to act quickly to protect the company's interest in another tract of land lest heirs attempt to regain ownership. Using familiar old loopholes in the holdover Virginia land system, Moore urged Slaymaker to demonstrate settlement and use of the land. "It is important that we arrange at once to take actual possession of the McVeigh lands," he wrote. Slaymaker was instructed to "see that some one is put on the land as a tenant even if a cheap house has to be built... it may be important for us to have possession in case... the McVeigh heirs [try] to get hold of it."[23]

The fight for the land continued into the following year, 1902, when Moore again urged Slaymaker to put tenants on the land: "Have this done as quickly as possible as it will go far toward establishing our title." Moore said the firm wanted a tenant put in actual possession of that portion of the McVeigh land lying in Pocahontas County and another in possession of the part that the firm claimed in Randolph County. "Please have cabins built at once and parties put in possession."[24] Such a step would obligate the other parties in the legal fray to initiate a suit to evict, placing the West Virginia Pulp and Paper Company in the enviable position of being a defendant, not a plaintiff, in a civil action to eject.

Quite aside from any dispute over title to the ever-scarcer timber in the Monongahela, the lumbermen, as an interest group, were willing to fix prices and markets. Speaking for "our Association," Albert Thompson of Philadelphia, representing the Blackwater Boom and Lumber Company of Davis, warmly responded to a query from Slaymaker: "I have your... price list of West Virginia spruce, and, so far as I am able to judge, it is substantially the same as that adopted by our Association." Thompson indicated to Slaymaker that the other West Virginia lumber companies were willing to set prices together. The industrialists were hastening to take advantage of labor and weather problems that were troubling their New England competitors.[25]

Through the rest of the decade, Slaymaker and his compatriots searched widely for more timber. The once seemingly endless supply of Appalachian hardwoods, spruce, and hemlock was nearly gone. While he negotiated for a few large tracts remaining in the Monongahela—Henry Gassaway Davis still owned at least thirty thousand acres of timber—Slaymaker also turned his attention to Florida, Maine, South America, and elsewhere for sources of pulpwood. The West Virginia Pulp and Paper Company operated in Cass until 1942. WestVaCo is the modern successor to the firm and continues operations in the region. By 1974 the company was the sixth largest landholder in West Virginia.[26]

The death of Henry Gassaway Davis in 1915 signaled the passage of West Virginia's Gilded Age. In a gentlemanly fashion, his will remembered loyal and loving family and associates. To the region he deforested, he bestowed a hospital, a children's home, several churches, a cemetery, and a college.

In Kanawha County, he arranged for the building of a children's shelter and a park. West Virginia sent his likeness to the U.S. Capitol, as one of the state's two. Davis's heirs have carried on many aspects of the coal and timber business, but from New York and Washington, not the denuded mountains of West Virginia.[27]

10

Federal Politics
Conservation, Reforestation, and Economic Gridlock

The influence of absentee landowners and industrialists is a poorly explored chapter in the long history of the mountains of the Virginias. A further perplexing aspect of the region's history is its ultimate transfer to the public domain as the Monongahela National Forest. The accounts of the great land companies and their stockholders do not discuss the fate of the residents who were dispossessed by the quest for timber and coal and land. The federal role in the dispossession of the mountain culture is poorly understood as well. Merchant capitalists held the original speculator claims in much of the region, enabling absentee influence and control to overtake the western regions of Virginia early in the eighteenth century. The history of the transmontane must therefore reflect the lasting influence of these crucially important early years.

Few of the early western Virginia settlers survived the deed challenges brought by absentees. Consequently their cultural requirement of land could not be met, and in the unfolding of time, the mountain farming culture declined. By the early twentieth century, the creation of the Monongahela National Forest sealed the farmers' fate by foreclosing their options for growth and development. In response, indigenous residents chose to make such accommodation as their reason and resources allowed.

Absentee landowners remained quietly at work throughout this time, inexorably steering the Monongahela region into a new era of industrial development that transformed the agricultural area into an industrial one. Between 1880 and 1920, farms and forests gave way to sawmills, coal mines, and railroads. Simultaneously rural and industrial, the region met a future that unfolded in perplexing and unfamiliar directions. The pattern did not resemble the changes that accompanied industrialization within cities. Nor did the transformation reflect artists' conceptions of harmony between nature and industry. Popular paintings of the late Victorian era portrayed steam engines chugging benignly past unperturbed farm animals as they grazed in the foreground, but the realities of the matter were far different than such artistic license suggested. Livestock ran terrified in all directions at the approach of the locomotives. Clouds of smoke blocked the sunlight. Ashes smothered the meadows—where they still existed. Timber camps rose in former hillside pastures, while stumpage, or slash, or fires, or any combination of those things sullied the surrounding hills. Once crystal clear, the streams ran brown with mud. Tree stumps covered thousands of mountainsides, a reminder and a measure of the wealth in hardwood and red spruce that was being taken out of the region.

Land sales in Pocahontas, Randolph, and Tucker counties continued until the timber was gone. Oral tradition maintains that not one mature tree stood in Randolph County by 1910. After the enabling legislation was passed in 1911, the federal government purchased thousands of acres of mostly denuded and ruined land. Between 1915 and 1932, the Forest Service acquired 261,986 acres of land in the Monongahela. Over the ensuing decades, the forest grew to a potential purchase area of 1,644,240 acres.[1]

Federal absentee ownership of the forest region appeared to bring a measure of stability to the mountains in the 1920s. It also preserved enough of the records of land transfers to make it possible for researchers to investigate the influence of absentee landowners in the Appalachian Mountains. Federal records of the acquisition process identify those persons who sold land to the government as well as those individuals who received the initial conveyances from the Virginia land office. These records contain evidence of the prolonged and overwhelming importance of absentee landowners within Appalachia.

Lands purchased by the Forest Service were first recommended by the National Forest Reservation Commission, which was directed to report annually to Congress. The commission was composed of the secretary of the army, the secretary of the interior, the secretary of agriculture, two members of the Senate selected by the president of the Senate, and two members of the House appointed by the Speaker.[2] The composition of this committee made politicization of its function almost inevitable, given the political and industrial activity of national leaders at the turn of the century.

For example, among the first lands purchased in 1915 were the properties of Henry Gassaway Davis and his subsidiary firm, the Otter Creek Boom and Lumber Company. Absentee owner Wilbur Bridges, who earlier had sold his timber to William Whitmer and Sons, sold his land to the Forest Service, after seeking advice from Davis on the matter.[3]

The government worked in "purchase units," acquiring at least 100,000 acres at a time. Sometimes the purchase was for even larger amounts. Lands that bounded the mountain headwaters of navigable streams were the first chosen by the service. These locations are precisely where the timber companies had focused their activities. The Cherry River Boom and Lumber Company holdings of 153,000 acres were conveyed to the government in the early years of expansion, as were the lands of many other local lumbering operations.[4]

As the government began the process of acquiring the land, the sum of eleven million dollars originally set aside for purchases of lands was increased. The government paid fairly well because sellers were taking some risks in waiting for the federal bureaucracy, with its laborious surveys, to take action. Unlike the land sales of the 1880s and 1890s, in the federal acquisitions the role of local lawyers and realtors was muted. Land agents were excluded from the government's transactions; officials believed that such participation would unreasonably inflate prices and enrich some persons unfairly.[5]

Although condemnation was a method available to the government, foresters only rarely resorted to the tactic when boundaries could not be determined or title could not be established precisely.[6]

In October 1913 the Forest Service crews began survey work on twenty-two thousand acres of land belonging to the Davis-owned Otter Creek Boom and Lumber Company. The work continued through December; presumably because of the harsh winter weather, surveying was then suspended until March 1914. The survey was completed by May. Also that month, the survey crews completed 85 percent of the survey on a twelve-hundred-acre tract of land being conveyed by the Davis Land Company. Surveys of a one-hundred-acre tract and a two-hundred-acre tract also were included.[7]

June 1914 brought completion of the survey of the Davis tract, and the Bridges estate of 16,000 acres was half surveyed. Also surveyed for the Monongahela Forest that year were 6,000 acres belonging to the Raine Andrew Lumber Company. A second, smaller tract of 218 acres owned by the Otter Creek firm was surveyed by November 1914. Other survey work in the Monongahela followed later. Within three years of passage of the Weeks Act, establishing the national forest system, about half of an initial purchase area had been surveyed.[8]

Farmers also sold to the government, but most of the land the government bought was absentee-owned, or the domain of West Virginia's own industrialists, senators Henry Gassaway Davis and Stephen B. Elkins. Conveying the land to the public domain enriched the sellers of the ruined land. Yet removing the acreage from local tax rolls permanently reduced the region's tax base. Generally, "the public domain" refers to land whose original owner is the government, but the eastern forests that were placed under federal control were acquired from the private sector. This is a sharp contrast to the vast public domain in the western United States that has been given away or sold cheaply to the public.

Lands in the public domain were used to populate the western United States by encouraging settlers to move to the region. In the East, public interest required the local land supply to be constricted, effectively discouraging population growth. Eastern land was a controversial issue, and many disagreements over ownership were settled in the courts. These records document settlement patterns because they identify individuals and locations that were important during frontier as well as industrial times.

The history of the Monongahela National Forest is further different from that of other federal reserves because as the land moved from private to public ownership, many permanent changes were made that affected the future well-being of the region. The government paid generous prices for the land, even after the ravages of industrialization had rendered it nearly worthless. Frequently the government did not obtain mineral rights, which would raise troubles later in the twentieth century, when environmental concerns became ever more worrisome public policy questions.

Private industry deforested the region, leaving it economically prostrate. No permanent growth had occurred. The wealthy men who brought the industrial transformation, feeding local hopes of permanent economic growth, departed as suddenly as they had come. In exchange for fifty years of false hopes and social upheaval, most of the region was left impoverished and almost bereft of resources for recovery. Instead of vast industrial ownership of the lands within their borders, Tucker, Pocahontas, Greenbrier, and Randolph counties experienced the new trend of federal domination. The government purchased the barren, timbered land and ultimately created the Monongahela National Forest in the interests of flood control and reforestation.

After the upheavals of industrialization, the federal government in 1915 became the final, permanent absentee owner of more than 25 percent of Randolph County, about 35 percent of Tucker County, and about 46 percent of Pocahontas County. The Monongahela region was by that time a lifeless wasteland that most lumbermen were anxious to sell. Purchase of these areas quickly followed the passage of the Weeks Act of 1911. In waves of appropriations, the government increased the federal holdings from 261,986 acres in 1932 to 665,900 acres by 1933.[9]

The federal government has been involved in forestry since 1878, but acquisition of eastern federal forest lands began with the 1911 law. Active campaigning for an eastern forest reserve commenced in 1899.[10] Supported by conservationists, including Theodore Roosevelt, the legislation also received enthusiastic backing from the lumber industry. The Monongahela was among the first forests established.

The timber barons who previously controlled the Monongahela held vast political power that enabled them to exploit a growing desire for conservation efforts and preservation of America's rapidly dwindling forest reserves. Many of them were senators or former senators or were closely allied with lawmakers. Rather than undertake a costly reforestation project on its own, the timber industry quickly realized that federally directed reforestation would place the financial responsibilities for such a project on the shoulders of the public. Two national lumbering associations began as early as 1902 to lobby for federal acquisition. The National Hardwood Lumber Association and the National Lumber Manufacturers Association worked hard for passage of the Weeks Act.[11]

President Theodore Roosevelt's 1902 message to Congress asserting that natural resource conservation was imperative encouraged supporters of the forestry plan. The president was appalled at reports he received that testified to wasteful and dangerous timbering practices. Citing the absentee landowners of the mountains, Roosevelt told Congress, "The home and permanent interests of the lumberman are generally in another state or region, and his interests in these mountains begins and ends with the hope of profit."[12]

Owners of the lands in the Monongahela were quite willing to sell to the government. Mined out, timbered, and burned over, the useless lands were a financial drain, hardly worth the modest taxes that would continue to be levied on them. Had the government not purchased the lands, it is likely they would have been abandoned.

The denuded forest lands were acquired by the federal government to protect stream flow and prevent fire and erosion. Devastating downstream flooding was linked to timbering practices in the years before. This relationship between forest cover and flooding downstream was only an untested conservationists' theory in the first decade of the twentieth century. Experts and politicians raged in debate over the matter. A new group of scientists, foresters trained in Europe, were caught up in the debates. From European perspectives and training, these experts, led by Carl A. Schenk, were able to recommend ways to avoid deforesting the United States by the device of a federally managed forest reserve.[13] The earliest interest in creating a national forest was sparked by public desires for a national park in the Great Smoky Mountains to provide recreational outlets.[14] Quickly, though, many Americans perceived that conservation and reforestation were equally desirable federal activities. So, with a blended desire for recreation, preservation, and conservation, the nation turned to capturing the eastern Appalachian Mountains and placing them within the public domain.

The issue of whether this land acquisition may have constituted an incredibly expensive industrial subsidy apparently did not arise. Given the political and economic attitudes of the time, that is not surprising. Most Americans fervently believed that what was good for business was good for America. The forest was purchased, from the perspective of conservationists and industrialists, to protect and provide a continued and renewable source of timber for the nation. In response to appeals by leading conservationists, vast portions of the Appalachians, stretching from the White Mountains of New England to southern Georgia, were targeted for federal acquisition.

Passage of the enabling legislation, however, did not come easily. Reluctant lawmakers did not believe the project important to any but the districts where the forests would be located. While the Weeks Act was before the Congress, timber baron Stephen B. Elkins and glass tycoon Nathan Bay Scott were West Virginia's senators.[15] Incessant lobbying, damaging floods on the Monongahela and Ohio rivers, and vast, devastating forest fires in the western United States convinced Congress that federal control of the watersheds of the East was necessary. Dire warnings that the United States could end up like the deforested nations of Europe also helped to bend the Congress to a more enthusiastic stance.[16]

As the law was implemented and land purchases were begun, federal title attorneys struggled to determine who were the rightful owners of land targeted for government purchase.[17] This toil continued for years. The trail of absentee ownership was noted by federal lawyers, who were careful to recommend land for purchase that was clear of encumbrances and title challenges. Government regulations required that boundaries close, based upon federally conducted surveys. This groundwork proved frustratingly slow and difficult. The inadequacy of the metes and bounds system of survey and the few geological markers available confounded the survey teams even in the twentieth century. Most of the old eighteenth-century surveys relied on the Fairfax Stone, the Cheat River, and the Deakins Line. All of these had been altered through human and natural disturbance during the ensuing two hundred years.

Where records existed, the earliest land grants were traced forward by the federal agents, and chains of title were established. Where that was not possible, the government occasionally preferred to use condemnation proceedings. Landowners, large and small, who were anxious to sell, grew impatient with the government. The process was agonizingly slow for many sellers. Davis, who was selling a thousand Tucker County acres to the government, was unused to waiting for federal bureaucratic delays, and he had a letter sent to the government, saying as much. Davis's long years in government had made him confident that his titles would not be challenged; only boundary details and acreage adjustments might be necessary. C.M. Hendley, secretary of the Davis Land Company, complained to William L. Hall, the assistant forester of the U.S. Department of Agriculture, about the delays. The letter, on Davis's letterhead, stated that in May 1911, at the request of the Forest Service, the Davis Land Company had offered the department, "at five dollars an acre, among other parcels two tracts of land on Shavers Fork of Cheat River, a parcel of 1125 acres . . . and the other, 75 acres." The company, Hendley continued, agreed to a price of four dollars per acre, cooperated with the federal agency, and still lacked a definitive arrangement. He suggested bringing the deal to a swift conclusion or "abrogating the agreement of sale." The company, Hendley explained, had sold land of similar value within the previous year for six dollars per acre. He added that a private sale could be completed in a week or two from the time negotiations were begun, "and the purchasers, knowing the conditions here, are not exacting as to acreage and title."[18]

Hendley's letter prompted the immediate attention of the assistant forester. But it is likely that Hendley was bluffing. Industrial activity in the Monongahela was beginning to decline, and land sales were less and less likely for the years ahead. Even though Davis and his secretary were impatient, the land acquisition policies of the Forest Service required that land be purchased on a per-surveyed-acre basis, not by parcel, as had been the practice during the industrial period. Davis had to wait nearly another year before the sale was completed.

Records of the government's title attorney suggest that there were many purchases from smallholders within the area designated for the forest, but most of the land that the government acquired was sold by timber companies, absentee landowners, or other industrial organizations. Small parcels owned by local residents were purchased if the owner so requested, or to make boundaries even. Many smallholders were anxious to sell out. Population was declining, erosion was worsening, and by 1910 the timber was gone. Some dwelling in the forest area occurred as well, but unlike later responses to the federal government's eastern forest purchases, residents of the Monongahela offered almost no opposition.

The cooperation citizens of the Monongahela gave the Forest Service is a surprising contrast to the resistance that the state and federal governments encountered in Cades Cove, Tennessee, before the establishment of the Great Smoky Mountains National Park.[19] Most Monongahela residents wanted cash from the sale of their land. Farming had become nearly impossible. The Forest Service archives contain many complaints from citizens that focused on governmental paperwork. These sellers declared that the government was taking too long to consummate the transactions.

Thomas Cover, at age seventy-two, wrote to complain of delays in the completion of his sale. Cover informed the government that some sellers wanted him to "finance a fight against the Government for justice with the people" who were upset with delays in the fulfillment of their transactions. "I feel the government is setting a terrible example in failing to carry out their contracts and taking advantage of poor mountain people," Cover wrote.[20]

The government, however, would not be pushed in Cover's case. Francis G. Caffey, solicitor for the U.S. Department of Agriculture, advised the agency of the possibility of overlapping claims, and the matter was referred to the Department of Justice to determine "if Cover is attempting to convey lands to which he has no title."[21] Cover was offering 2,076 acres to the government.

The lack of local opposition to the national forest project may have resulted from the residents' many years of experience with large, powerful corporations that could bend the law to suit themselves. Davis's railroad charter had given him the authority to condemn land if needed, and no doubt it was. Mountain dwellers would remember the power an absentee could wield when the government arrived to survey its forest purchases. These farmers well knew that large landholders could direct vast resources toward forcing public policy to suit their personal purposes.[22]

Over the next few decades after the passage of the Weeks Act, the federal government acquired title to most of the previously timbered land in the region and allowed the forest slowly to reestablish itself. A nursery was organized in 1919, and the first red spruce seedlings were transplanted to the forest in 1921.[23] Federal purchase of the wasted region and the conservation efforts that began soon thereafter are responsible for the existence of the national forest today. Nevertheless, it must be remembered that the federal government is no less an absentee owner than Lord Fairfax, Francis and

William Deakins, George Croghan, George Washington, Levi Hollingsworth, Henry Gassaway Davis, Stephen B. Elkins, Samuel Slaymaker, or Robert F. Whitmer, each of whom controlled land within the region.

Whether or not the federal government would be as difficult an absentee owner as the timber barons had been probably was not a question that local leaders pondered at the time. The arrangements for payments in lieu of taxes were apparently acceptable to the counties affected by the forest purchases. In the preindustrial and industrial times, absentee owners and corporations were notorious in their lassitude toward paying taxes. A steady federal check, even though smaller than assessed taxes, probably appeared to be an attractive alternative to the timeworn struggle of assessors and sheriffs, who constantly dogged absentee owners to recover delinquent property taxes.[24]

Of Randolph County's total 669,657.6 acres, 177,524.6 acres are owned by the Forest Service, according to 1974 figures. Ten corporations or individuals control another 179,959.0 acres, for a total of 357,483.6 acres owned by absentees, including the government.[25] Thus, 53 percent of Randolph County is owned by eleven individuals or organizations. Tucker County is even more heavily dominated by industrial owners. Of a total county area of 269,868.8 acres, approximately 93,837.8 acres are owned by the federal government, and 94,083.0 acres are owned by nine other absentee owners.[26] So ten owners control 188,020.8 acres, or 70 percent of the land within the county. Still fewer owners dominate Pocahontas County, which contains a total of 603,270.4 acres. Of that number, approximately 279,983.4 acres are contained in the Monongahela National Forest, and 176,732.0 acres are owned by five other corporations.[27] Total acreage owned by industry and government in Pocahontas County is 456,715.4 acres, or 76 percent of the county's land mass.

It is additionally significant that the absentee owners are sometimes the same in each county. Apart from the Forest Service, Island Creek Coal owned in 1974 a total of 23,586 acres in the three counties. In Pocahontas and Randolph counties, Georgia Pacific owned 11,810 acres of land, and Mower Lumber Company owned 113,236 acres.[28]

Twenty-seven percent of the real estate tax base of Randolph County is owned by the Forest Service. Forty-six percent of Pocahontas County is owned by the government, and 35 percent of Tucker County is federally owned as well. Additional private absentee ownership compounds the difficulties inherent in concentrated ownership of so large a percentage of the land in the region.[29]

These economic realities exist in Clay County as well, where eight absentee owners control 103,411 acres of the county's total 221,702 acres. Those owners, none of whom are governmental agencies, control 47 percent of the land and, therefore, most of the tax base. Less than 25 percent of the land in Monroe County is in concentrated ownership.[30]

The combined influence of private absentee owners and the federal government in these counties, whose economies now rely on tourism, is greater than absentee influence in coal-producing counties. The "degree of control of land in the tourist counties by all of the absentee, government, corporate and large individual owners" is in some cases 60 percent of the total county land surface, according to the Appalachian Land Use Task Force.[31] For Randolph County, the total is 53 percent, for Tucker, 70 percent, and for Pocahontas, 76 percent. Absentee influence is overwhelming, yet absentee interests are not shared by the people who live within the region.

The land for the Monongahela National Forest largely came from the body of absentee-owned territory that had been changing hands since the days of Lord Fairfax and the Deakins brothers. Local farms that were absorbed into the forest, though numerous, constituted a relatively small proportion of the total forest area.

Because of absentee and federal ownership of so much of the land, residents of these counties do not control the wealth there, nor can they tax it to provide continuing public services. The federal and state governments do not tax each other's holdings—a sacred tenet in the treaty between the states and the national government. Likewise, the counties involved can tax neither state nor federal holdings. Instead, the counties must be content with small donations. Federal gifts in lieu of taxes augment meager revenues from a system of land taxes that unfairly burdens resident landowners and rewards those whose land is not productive.

One obvious consequence of federal absentee ownership is that the potential tax income of the local government has been significantly reduced. Although the federal government makes payments to these counties, those revenues traditionally are based on actual forest production and generally have been less than land tax would be.[32]

In 1974 VISTA worker Si Kahn raised the issue of whether local governments could function properly in the face of their federally weakened local tax bases. The policy, he contended in his polemic, titled *The Forest Service and Appalachia*, unfairly increased the tax burden on residents.[33] At that time, the Forest Service gave the local governments about seventy-five cents per acre per year.

It is an open question whether the benefits associated with tourism and reestablished timbering replace those lost tax revenues or the lost opportunities of more diverse economic activities. Since the 1960s, federal law has required that the forest be maintained to satisfy the interests of all its users. The "multiple use sustained yield" approach guides Forest Service policy in making compromises among the multitudes of forest users.[34] The Forest Service believes its primary task "is to provide advice and guidance and coordinate plans for the interaction of land uses and management actions on wildlife."[35] The Forest Service further believes that managed timbering and development of recreation and tourism potentials of these federal reserves are superior to private absentee ownership. Residents of absentee-dominated regions increasingly suspect that all powerful absentees influence their regions in ways that detract from their economic well-being. A constricted supply of available land retards diversified economic development. Public lands encourage certain developments, such as recreational facilities and second homes, and discourage other developments, such as industry or mining, "the consequences of which are valued by some and opposed by others."[36] Private absentee owners generally pay somewhat more taxes than the government payments bring to county governments, but local residents pay the most.[37]

The government reservations, however, do not place nearly as great a demand on local infrastructure as an industrial activity does. With little land available for purchase in the mountains, there is limited potential for population growth in these areas. Consequently, there will be little future demand for larger schools, or roads, or more public utilities. This in turn discourages what modest growth might be afforded by the existing land supply. The true difficulty arises with the realization that the existing tax base cannot satisfactorily support the modest infrastructure already in place. Although the present number of schools, roads, towns, and utilities may be adequate for the size of the area and its population, the tax base is still inadequate to maintain, improve, and replace these developmental necessities. Nor will tax revenues from an aging population keep pace with changing standards and new developments. This gridlock of frustrating economic limits goes to the heart of the mountain residents' historic plea for state assistance in internal improvements.

A depression-era investigation of the grave economic difficulties of the southern Appalachian farmers identified isolation and limited roads as exacerbating economic problems in the region. But the region's system of taxing land also engendered much federal discussion. The region's isolation and its land tax structure were cited as compelling sources of woe for the poor farmers. The U.S. Department of Agriculture's 1935 study noted that low land values were caused by topography and low fertility, "though no small part reflects the combined effect of meager resources and inaccessibility to large markets."[38]

This interpretation of conditions within the mountains ultimately proved as damaging as the conditions themselves, for it has guided development efforts, despite their demonstrated ineffectiveness. The constricted supply of land available to local use was not addressed by the 1935 study. Anterior to nearly all of the region's economic difficulties are the contradictory philosophies about land and public finance that have characterized politics within the mountains for all of their settled years. Landownership issues, because they so directly influence public finance issues, have troubled the region's occupants for as long as they have assembled to select their representatives to their legislatures.

11

Ptolemaic Politics
Copernican Thinking and Changing the Political Paradigms

Since the eighteenth century, the majority of landowners in the Monongahela region have favored higher taxes to fund improvements, but the region's powerful absentee owners have succeeded in keeping property taxes low.[1] Absentees remain singularly important in influencing the affairs of the region. They profit from a long-standing, carefully tended land tax system that discourages growth and development within the mountains.

Philadelphia; New York; Washington, D.C.; Portland, Oregon; Roanoke, Virginia; and Baltimore, Maryland, are the homes of those who wielded power and influence over the fortunes of the region's occupants during the great industrial transformation. Their influence continues and is frequently enhanced by federal forest policies. Like the interests of planters and northerners of a century and a half ago, interests of absentee landowners remain well served by the conditions that historically have caused hardship within the West Virginia mountains.

Controlling land taxes has been a priority of absentee owners despite the fact that the region depends on these sparse revenues to fund most government services and public education. By some estimates, the state's regressive tax structure has cost West Virginia's schools more than $150 million annually since the 1970s.[2] At the same time, West Virginia's tax system retains the preference historically given to owners of vast lands, which proves burdensome for resident property owners with small incomes.

Farmers and other residents pay more per acre under the state's classified system of land taxes than they would if they paid flat per-acre taxes. They pay more taxes per acre of land than absentees do. Owners of nonresidential land have been relatively lightly taxed on a per-acre basis, although in West Virginia their tax classification is assessed at a higher rate per one hundred dollars in valuation. These procedures apply very little pressure to owners to improve land into higher tax categories or to sell it, freeing up land for additional population growth and economic development. The system continues to shelter the wealth of the absentee and resident owners of corporate nonfarm land and encourages subversion of the process of revenue gathering. It "invites any class or group of property owners to . . . exert political pressure . . . to shift the tax burden to others by seeking a downward reclassification."[3]

This property classification approach to revenue gathering has adversely affected the economically stressed Monongahela region of West Virginia. Because of a constricted supply of land, the population cannot increase in ways that would increase property tax revenues. The entire revenue question has failed to address issues beyond the relative value of improvements upon land. Sharper legal distinctions would have separated the inherent value of all land from the relative values of specific parcels and the nature of production generated on the land.

Taxation has influenced many land use choices. West Virginia tax policy historically has ignored the idea of land as inherently valuable regardless of improvement or productivity. Land has not been taxed in the context of its scarcity for all purposes, and thus its importance in the generation of revenue has been tragically undervalued. While tax reforms, demanded by some as long ago as the early 1800s, would have increased state revenues and available land supply, neither Virginia nor West Virginia ever exported the property tax burden to place it upon the shoulders of those who own the land.

The state's history is replete with evidence of outside domination and wholesale shifting of taxes to residents. The disputes between Virginians concerning the matter of public finance were sufficiently bitter to sire the state of West Virginia. The continuing difficulties in public finance bring into question whether absentee landownership can continue to be completely unregulated.

The matter is an ethical as well as a financial issue. The Monongahela region's history indicates that the present concept of property rights will face increasing challenge in years ahead, responding as it always has to reflect changing social needs. Property rights in the United States have served as a method of organizing the social system. Property rights reduce conflict among members of society because they provide some order to the process of gathering and distributing wealth. They ration scarce resources. They provide for future use. Property rights provide incentives to individuals to increase or improve the output available from their land. Property rights also give society a mechanism for reducing public burdens by placing them upon the shoulders of interested individuals. The experience of West Virginia suggests, however, that there should be some important limits upon how land can be used. Only when property rights increase the productivity of resources "and society gets part of the gain, [does] creation of private property in resources leave all members of society better off than they would be otherwise."[4]

Obviously, the system of exclusive property rights is profoundly ingrained in modern society. So too is the ongoing struggle to determine what is the public's fair share of private property. This deeply politicized public responsibility has prompted review of the whole idea of property rights. Some ethicists suspect that the concept of unrestrained rights in property is nearing obsolescence. They foresee a time when the idea of complete ownership will supplant the present adherence to absolute ownership. The difference lies only in the latitudes of land use choices.

One philosopher has predicted a "Copernican revolution" in land law. The struggle of early astronomy to defend the views of Ptolemy against the (correct) philosophy of Copernicus represents the magnitude of challenge that awaits government tax authorities and legislatures. This Ptolemaic astronomy model provides philosopher Ramsey Martin with his argument that any belief systems, whether they concern the solar system or landownership, can become obsolete. Ancient scientists chafed under the theory of astronomy offered by Ptolemy. His view that the sun revolved around the earth did not explain all of the observations made by his scientific colleagues. They were forced to make exception after exception to his geocentric theories. Yet every one of these ad hoc limits upon the astronomy of Ptolemy forced scientists to contend with a weakness in his theory. Copernicus explained all the new observations, but his theories were forbidden by clerical authority. The church viewed as heresy the possibility that the earth revolved around the sun, preferring instead to insist on the reverse. Copernicus himself was forced to recant his theories. Ultimately, however, Ptolemy's astronomy was rejected because it failed. The heresies of Copernicus were accepted as truth. So then, Martin reasons, as society makes ad hoc reductions to the idea of unrestrained rights in land, society acknowledges a weakness in the fundamental idea that land can be absolutely owned. Another paradigm will become necessary.[5]

Within the Monongahela's history of trouble and exploitation, a similar Copernican perspective has awakened: it is not people who own the land; it is land that exists as the locus of success for all. At some level, therefore, unrestrained rights in land must be tempered, as evidenced by their historical failure to provide for the common good. The quests for empire within the Monongahela, in all their forms, have relied on the well-defended privilege of landownership. Speculation in land, timbering, coal mining, and railroading have been ill managed and have failed in their promise to the citizenry. Repeatedly the public burdens of the region have been shoved upon the shoulders of those least able to afford them, even as the burdens become more and more expensive. As public policy makers look for new revenue resources to provide for increasingly costly public services, pressures upon a fixed land supply will regenerate the old, old political questions that are shrouded, but unresolved, in the history of the Monongahela.

This is the message of the region's experience. Property rights, political power, and taxation remain unfairly distributed because they were undemocratically acquired by many powerful interests. One class of landowner has been more responsible for public revenues than other classes. Absentee landowners have avoided equal responsibilities to the public good because of the ways they chose to use taxable resources.

Absent landowners may prefer low taxes that do not support enhanced sanitation services, schools, or recreational facilities that they would readily demand in their places of residence. They continue to require fire service, roads, and law enforcement to protect their investments. These perspectives obligate political leadership to balance private interest fairly against the public welfare. Protecting private property and providing public services, however, should not be mutually exclusive activities.

As Adam Smith observed two hundred years ago, private rights and the public good are the dual responsibilities of government. Despite the apprehensions of private interest, there is no inherent conflict between the two.[6] Since public tax policy provides the financial incentives that resolve these conflicts, tax policies are radically politicized by special interest groups. The profitability of many business endeavors is affected by the nature and amount of taxes levied against them.

In West Virginia, state government has failed to identify taxable wealth correctly and to modernize the ideas that underpin revenue-gathering processes. The lucrative business of keeping land out of production or off the real estate market has not been taxed more heavily because the owners of this land have always guided politics within the mountains. Both Virginias historically have unfairly assigned the burdens of public funding to those who have attempted to make land productive, while shielding speculators and industrialists. As the history of the Monongahela region has shown, taxation is an effective tool for accelerating, or delaying, development of land.[7] Beginning in 1831, with Virginia's constitutional revision, land taxation within the mountains has been politically designed to protect the interests of an elite minority. After 1863 brought the admission of West Virginia to the Union, the state's tax classification system continued to be short-sighted because it did not correctly address the value of nonfarm lands. Many other mountainous states implemented similar systems, thus creating a critical inequity. Tax policies did not fully and fairly include the states' total available land supply. The creators of these tax plans did not consider the fact that great amounts of land had moved out of farming and into lower taxation categories. By the 1920s, most of the land within West Virginia had been timbered, mined, burned, or otherwise savagely exploited. Timber and coal were taxed lightly, if at all. Nonfarm land was, indeed, worth very little. Its potential worth, however, can be estimated by the level of taxes levied against farms, which were often located adjacent to timbered areas.

In the 1920s and the 1930s, from the viewpoint of a tax assessor, timbering or fires lowered property values because a negative improvement had taken place. Therefore, more and more acres would be required to amass the basic taxable unit of one hundred dollars in valuation. The land was becoming worth less and less. Coal, oil, and natural gas reserves and production have been "important industries that affect land use and values in many areas of the state."[8] Farmland in West Virginia was aggressively sought for these lucrative competing uses, obliging farmers to consider whether it was economically feasible to keep their farms in agriculture.[9]

West Virginia's taxation policy has provided a disincentive to farm productivity, and at the same time, it has protected a vast taxable resource. Most of the fifty states have abandoned such systems of taxation. Only Alabama, Arizona, Louisiana, Minnesota, Montana, Tennessee, and West Virginia still use the ad valorem system. Their taxation policies actually reduce land value, because the income stream generated by productive land is reduced by the burden of the tax.[10] The system places stresses upon capitalist enterprise and conveys preferential tax status to a specific category of land use.

This practice is at variance with the one-man, one-vote tenet that underpins the American sense of fair play. It more closely resembles the old colonial idea that majorities are dangerous because they pose threats to the upper classes. In the constitutional era, John Jay advocated ideas that were echoed later by John C. Calhoun, the southern theorist. Jay and Calhoun unabashedly defended privilege by arguing that wealthy people have more at stake and should therefore have a greater influence in the workings of government. Virginia conservatives such as Abel Upshur also argued this theory repeatedly.[11] Calhoun fervently believed that wealthy citizens deserved greater political rights than others. This aristocratic view was doomed because it was undemocratic. In its practical application, however, West Virginia's method of land taxation continued to accomplish much the same thing. The land of one group of citizens, by virtue of these owners' efforts and husbandry, was taxed more rigorously than the idle land of other citizens. The system indeed favored the wealthy and elite.

A substantial federal presence has brought additional finance-related woe to the region. The presence of government-owned land prevents local access to tax revenues. The public revenue problem within West Virginia's mountain counties has been further exacerbated by the great disparity between the amount of owner-occupied land and the vast amounts of land owned by lightly taxed absentee owners and the untaxed forest reserve. This monumental difficulty has defeated the region's ability to fund government services adequately and to encourage additional growth and development.

West Virginia's land taxes remain far below national levels, but residents' other personal assets are heavily taxed. The state has become so desperate for revenues that its citizens pay sales tax on food. This is an abject confession of impotence by state government. West Virginia's taxes have not reflected the taxpayers' ability to pay. The state has levied taxes according to benefits received by each taxpayer, yet "this is neither feasible in practice nor generally favored in theory."[12] By poorly defining the real value of absentee-owned land, West Virginia historically has sheltered a vast supply of taxable wealth that could be captured by local governments. Also, the great amount of land owned by the federal government that cannot be taxed weakens the state's long-compromised tax base further.

When the federal government purchased the "lands nobody wanted" beginning in 1911, the Forest Service was in fact sealing the fate of the region. Its citizens would never be able to take charge of their own development and growth, because they would never be able to control or tax enough land to do so. After the transfer of so much of the land to the federal government, the "southern Appalachian farmer did not—indeed could not—buy it back." Within the Monongahela, the dilemma was academic. Even if farmers could have bought the land back, the barren soils would have sustained nothing. Forest fires had burned so hot on the high plateaus of the region that the topsoil was destroyed. Nothing grew in portions of the forest area for decades.[13]

After 1920 the government's husbandry allowed the region depleted by timbering to regain its productivity, but the increasing value of the land cannot ever be adequately addressed by local taxing units. Even though federal payments to local governments are tied to forest production, the formula overlooks the changing potential and changing value of land, thereby keeping the government's payments woefully out of step with the forest land's real value.

Valuable privately owned lands within the Appalachian region continue to be undertaxed and unavailable to local development. In 1983 a retired coal miner put it this way: "The land companies won't let private citizens have the land at any price: a poor person can't deal with them."[14]

Many persons blamed the creation of the national forest system for contributing to the economic distress of the region by undermining the security in land that the agriculturally based local culture relied upon.[15] But in West Virginia, this distress was heightened by land law that has since 1779 allowed for an extreme degree of outside domination of the land and politics within the state. This history greatly exacerbated the difficulties that came with industrialization and federal forest development. Both farm security and economic development have been thwarted by absentee interests for most of the region's history. Disestablishment of the culture

actually was under way—by virtue of absentee landownership—one hundred years before Gilded Age industrialization.
Politically engineered inequities in the land tax system have
worsened the hardship.

The vigilance and ability of absentee landowners is visible
in the land records of the Virginias. Conflicting claims to the
region harken back to the Iroquois wars of the seventeenth
century. They continued into the eighteenth century, as
whites battled Indians for control. Whites also fought among
themselves, and Englishmen ejected Frenchmen. Finally Virginians, having evicted the British, beggared each other in
the writing of state land law and tax policy.

Before industrial development, aggressive speculation in
real estate directed the course of affairs within the mountains. After industrial development, federal patronage froze
the Monongahela region into a pastoral existence that may be
impossible to change. Acquisition of the Monongahela country by the federal government provided some economic stability to the region as it came to the end of an era of
overwhelming industrial exploitation. Federal ownership,
though, brought its own set of problems. There were few, if
any, evictions of local dwellers, because nearly every seller of
land was cooperative, eager to benefit from forest purchases.
The new federal presence defined the region. As the government began ordering the affairs of the national forest, it also
fastened upon the residents a difficult economic distress. Federal ownership removed any hope of diverse economic development within Tucker, Randolph, and Pocahontas counties.
Timbering and tourism will remain the dominant, and low-
paying, industries within the region.

The work of industrialists, speculators, and absentee landowners during the nineteenth century kept the vast wealth of
these counties out of reach of their citizens. As this land re-
turns to productivity in the waning years of the twentieth
century, its resources remain unavailable for local exploitation. The process of industrial transition of the region left its
residents bereft of economic and political power. From earliest settlement to contemporary times, control of the land,
and therefore the resources, was the overarching concern of

Indians, trappers, settlers, speculators, absentees, industrialists, and the federal government. Actual settlers, like the Indians and trappers before them, were not successful in this
quest.

The traditional mountain farm culture was defeated a long
time ago in the Virginian transmontane. Every successful
ejectment or title compromise accomplished by an absentee
or speculator weakened the farmers economically and politically. As this middle class experienced ever-growing demand
for their land, the effectiveness of their political response diminished, despite their resolve. The mountain agricultural
society was not crippled as a result of the industrial transformation of the region; only after defeating land titles held by
the indigenous residents was industry free to flourish. Before
industry could exploit the region's resources, it had first to
control the land. As the region's land records illustrate, the
influence of absent capitalists, speculators, and developers
came hand in hand with white settlement. Ultimately, the
Forest Service did save the region's land, but it abandoned
the region's people to an established economic inferiority.

The state's tax system was designed to facilitate absentee
speculation in land, and it hobbled more productive enterprises. Because industrial owners rarely have lived within the
region, their wealth and incomes have not been subject to the
relatively high taxes that resident West Virginians have traditionally paid on income, personal property, luxuries, and
food. High taxes such as these deter other enterprises from
choosing the mountains for their operations, and economic
growth is consequently stifled. Having lost control of the
land, West Virginians face a more difficult and problematic
future than do residents of those states that tax land more aggressively. West Virginia remains a rich state whose treasury
is impoverished by outside influence.

Notes

Introduction

1. Jack Sosin, *The Revolutionary Frontier, 1763–1783* (New York: Holt, Rinehart, and Winston, 1967), x.
2. Fernand Braudel, *On History*, translated by Sarah Matthews (Chicago: Univ. of Chicago Press, 1980), 27, 33, 38.
3. For example, Ronald D Eller, *Miners, Millhands, and Mountaineers: Industrialization of the Appalachian South, 1880–1930* (Knoxville: Univ. of Tennessee Press, 1982).
4. Minute Book, J.L. Rumbarger Lumber Company, Tucker County Lumber Corporations, A and M 1163, West Virginia and Regional History Collection, West Virginia Univ. Library, Morgantown (depository hereinafter identified as WVU).
5. *William J. Harper v. William W. Parsons, William R. Parsons, and Solomon Parsons*, Tucker County Circuit Court Records, A and M 60, 1858, B1F2, WVU.
6. Gordon McKinney, "Subsistence Economy and Community in Western North Carolina, 1860–65," address presented to the Organization of American Historians, Reno, Nevada, March 1988, p. 10.
7. James M. Callahan, *A Semi-Centennial History of West Virginia* (Charleston, W.Va.: Semi-Centennial Commission of West Virginia, 1913), 49; John E. Selby, *The Revolution in Virginia, 1775–1783* (Williamsburg, Va.: Colonial Williamsburg Foundation, 1992), 255; Van Beck Hall, "The Politics of Appalachian Virginia, 1790–1830," in *Appalachian Frontiers: Settlement, Society, and Development in the Pre-Industrial Era*, edited by Robert D. Mitchell (Lexington: Univ. Press of Kentucky, 1991), 167.
8. Altina L. Waller, "Appalachia's Transition to Capitalism," draft of address presented to the Social Science History Association, Minneapolis, October 1990, p. 13.
9. John Gaventa, *Power and Powerlessness: Quiescence and Rebellion in an Appalachian Valley* (Urbana: Univ. of Illinois Press, 1980), 258–61.

10. Altina L. Waller, *Feud: Hatfields, McCoys, and Social Change in Appalachia, 1860–1900* (Chapel Hill: Univ. of North Carolina Press, 1988), 23.

11. Waller, "Appalachia's Transition," 13; idem., *Feud*, 12–13.

12. Joyce Appleby, "Commercial Farming and the 'Agrarian Myth' in the Early Republic," *Journal of American History* 68 (March 1982): 839; Allan Kulikoff, *The Agrarian Origins of American Capitalism* (Charlottesville: Univ. Press of Virginia, 1992), 103.

13. David Hackett Fischer, *Albion's Seed: Four British Folkways in America* (New York: Oxford Univ. Press, 1989), 406; Rhys Isaac, *The Transformation of Virginia, 1740–1790* (Williamsburg, Va.: Institute of Early American History and Culture, 1982), 90–91.

14. Steven Hahn, "The Unmaking of the Southern Yeomanry," in *The Countryside in the Age of Capitalist Transformation: Essays in the Social History of Rural America,* edited by Steven Hahn and Jonathan Prude (Chapel Hill: Univ. of North Carolina Press, 1985), 179–203.

15. This is not to say that no mountain farmers owned slaves. Many did. But plantations like those in the Tidewater did not exist in the mountains, even when landowners held thousands of acres. Grazing livestock, well managed or not, and raising commercial crops were the major economic pursuits. The 1857 list of tithables for the Horseshoe Bottom region of Tucker County showed 258 white males, 3 free blacks, and 21 slaves. The Parsons, Bonnifield, Goff, and Flanagan families were the slave owners, and they also represented portions of the region's landowning gentry. "List of Tithables, 1857," Jesse Parsons Papers, A and M 731, WVU. Industrial slavery is a separate issue and is discussed in Ronald L. Lewis, *Coal, Iron, and Slaves: Industrial Slavery in Maryland and Virginia, 1715–1865* (Westport, Conn.: Greenwood Press, 1979).

16. Alison Goodyear Freehling, *Drift toward Dissolution: The Virginia Slavery Debate of 1831–1832* (Baton Rouge: Louisiana State Univ. Press, 1982), 228.

17. Ibid., 170–95.

18. Appleby, "Commercial Farming," 839; Wesley Frank Craven, *The Southern Colonies in the Seventeenth Century, 1607–1689* (Baton Rouge: Louisiana State Univ. Press, 1970), 317.

19. D. Alan Williams, "The Small Farmer in Eighteenth-Century Virginia Politics," *Agricultural History* 43 (Jan. 1969): 91.

20. Craven, *Southern Colonies,* 278; Malcolm J. Rohrbough, *The Land Office Business: The Settlement and Administration of American Public Lands, 1789–1837* (London: Oxford Univ. Press, 1968), x–xii.

21. Appleby, "Commercial Farming," 836; Robert D. Mitchell, *Commercialism and Frontier: Perspectives on the Early Shenandoah Valley* (Charlottesville: Univ. Press of Virginia, 1977); Morton Rothstein, "The Antebellum South as a Dual Economy," *Agricultural History* 41 (Oct. 1967): 375; James Henretta, "Families and Farms: Mentalite in Preindustrial America," *William and Mary Quarterly,* 3d ser., 35 (1978): 4; Harry L. Watson, "Conflict and Collaboration: Yeo-

men, Slaveholders, and Politics in the Antebellum South," *Social History* 10 (Oct. 1985): 282.

22. Fischer's *Albion's Seed* may help resolve the Celtic debate, which centers on the concept that because settlers of the mountainous South were of Celtic, not English, origin, their culture and society bear distinct characteristics that are found throughout America's South and in Ireland. Such postbellum developments as enclosure and railroads undermined the old cultural ways, with the result that the reluctant yeomanry declined into peonage and dependency as they lost their land. The argument does not satisfactorily address the actual process by which the yeomen lost their land. Fischer contends that all of America had English antecedents. See Grady McWhiney, *Cracker Culture: Celtic Ways in the Old South* (Tuscaloosa: Univ. of Alabama Press, 1988), and Forrest McDonald and Grady McWhiney, "The South from Self-Sufficiency to Peonage: An Interpretation," *American Historical Review* 85, no. 5 (1980): 1095–118.

23. Gavin Wright, *Old South, New South: Revolutions in the Southern Economy since the Civil War* (New York: Basic Books, 1986), 272.

1. Imperial Politics

1. Patricia Nelson Limerick, *The Legacy of Conquest: The Unbroken Past of the American West* (New York: Norton, 1988), 71.

2. James M. Callahan, *A Semi-Centennial History of West Virginia* (Charleston, W.Va.: Semi-Centennial Commission of West Virginia, 1913), 7–8.

3. George T. Hunt, *The Wars of the Iroquois: A Study in Intertribal Trade Relations* (Madison: Univ. of Wisconsin Press, 1940), esp. map after p. 7, 54; Otis K. Rice, *West Virginia: A History* (Lexington: Univ. Press of Kentucky, 1985), 8–9.

4. Callahan, *Semi-Centennial History*, 14–17.

5. Hunt, *Wars of the Iroquois*, 137–44.

6. Callahan, *Semi-Centennial History*, 17; Warren Hofstra, "Land Policy and Settlement in the Northern Shenandoah Valley," in *Appalachian Frontiers: Settlement, Society, and Development in the Pre-Industrial Era*, edited by Robert D. Mitchell (Lexington: Univ. Press of Kentucky, 1991), 111–12; Stuart E. Brown, Jr., *Virginia Baron: The Story of Thomas, 6th Lord Fairfax* (Berryville, Va.: Chesapeake Book Co., 1965), 90, 100, 117.

7. Callahan, *Semi-Centennial History*, 17.

8. William Wirt, *Sketches of the Life and Character of Patrick Henry*, reprint (Freeport, N.Y.: Books for Libraries, 1970), 146, 147.

9. See William Waller Henning, *The Statutes at Large of Virginia*, vol. 10 (Richmond, 1822), chap. 12, p. 35.

10. Clay County, Deed Book 1; W.E.R. Byrne, *Tale of the Elk* (Richwood, W.Va.: Mountain State Press, 1940), 255–56.

11. Callahan, *Semi-Centennial History*, 6.

12. Ibid., 11.

13. Ibid., 12, 48–49.

14. Ibid., 19.

15. Ibid.

16. Francis Jennings, *Empire of Fortune: Crowns, Colonies, and Tribes in the Seven Years War in America* (New York: Norton, 1988), 37–40.

17. George E. Lewis, *The Indiana Company, 1763–1798: A Study in Eighteenth Century Frontier Land Speculation and Business Venture* (Glendale, Calif.: Arthur H. Clark Co., 1941), 37–38.

18. Jack Sosin, *The Revolutionary Frontier, 1763–1783* (New York: Holt, Rinehart, and Winston, 1967), 6, 9–10. For a local historical account of this rebellion's impact on the Monongahela region, see Hu Maxwell, *History of Randolph County, West Virginia, from Its Earliest Settlement to the Present*, reprint (Parsons, W.Va.: McClain Printing Co., 1961), 36–38.

19. Thomas Perkins Abernethy, *Western Lands and the American Revolution*, Univ. of Virginia Institute for Research in the Social Sciences Monograph 25 (New York: Russell and Russell, 1937), 11.

20. Bernard Bailyn, *Voyagers to the West: A Passage in the Peopling of America on the Eve of the Revolution* (New York: Knopf, 1986), 23.

21. Ibid., 57–60.

22. Callahan, *Semi-Centennial History*, 75; Henry M. Dater, "Albert Gallatin—Land Speculator," *Mississippi Valley Historical Review* 26 (1939–40): 26.

23. Sosin, *Revolutionary Frontier*, 33; Lewis, *Indiana Company*, 37–38, 39.

24. Max Savelle, *George Morgan, Colony Builder* (New York: Columbia Univ. Press, 1932), 78; Lewis, *Indiana Company*, 39–40.

25. Savelle, *George Morgan*, 79; Lewis, *Indiana Company*, 60–61.

26. Savelle, *George Morgan*, 80; Lewis, *Indiana Company*, 92.

27. Bailyn, *Voyagers*, 32–33.

28. Savelle, *George Morgan*, 81–82, 86–87; Lewis, *Indiana Company*, 200–205.

29. Savelle, *George Morgan*, 91; John E. Selby, *The Revolution in Virginia, 1775–1783* (Williamsburg, Va.: Colonial Williamsburg Foundation, 1992), 142; Lewis, *Indiana Company*, 228; Callahan, *Semi-Centennial History*, 17.

30. Savelle, *George Morgan*, 100; Lewis, *Indiana Company*, 228–65; Merrill Jensen, "The Creation of the National Domain, 1781–1784," *Mississippi Valley Historical Review* 26 (1939–40): 332.

31. Sosin, *Revolutionary Frontier*, 58–60; Lewis, *Indiana Company*, 139–40, 149, 176.

32. Abernethy, *Western Lands*, 177; Samuel Eliot Morison, *The Oxford History of the American People*, vol. 1, *Prehistory to 1789* (New York: Mentor, 1972), 266.

33. Abernethy, *Western Lands*, 176, 177; Selby, *Revolution in Virginia*, 142; Sosin, *Revolutionary Frontier*, 163.

34. William Findley, *History of the Insurrection in the Four Western Counties of Pennsylvania in the Year 1794* (Philadelphia: Samuel Harrison Smith, printer, 1794), 18, 19.

35. Sosin, *Revolutionary Frontier*, 60.

36. Sosin, *Revolutionary Frontier*, 60, 163. See Findley, *History of the Insurrection*, 22; and Selby, *Revolution in Virginia*, 256–57.

37. Roy Bird Cook, *Washington's Western Lands* (Strasburg, Va.: Shenandoah Publishing House, 1930), 139.

38. Edgar B. Sims, *Sims Index to Land Grants in West Virginia* (Charleston, W.Va.: Rose City Press, 1952); Cook, *Washington's Western Lands*, 43–68, 75–99; William P. Haymond Notebook, A and M 699, pp. 105–7, WVU.

2. Settler Politics

1. See Henry M. Dater, "Albert Gallatin—Land Speculator," *Mississippi Valley Historical Review* 26 (1939–40): 38. Dater contends that de Valcoulon and Gallatin failed at speculation.

2. Stuart E. Brown, Jr., *Virginia Baron: The Story of Thomas, 6th Lord Fairfax* (Berryville, Va.: Chesapeake Book Co., 1965), 199.

3. Jack Sosin, *The Revolutionary Frontier, 1763–1783* (New York: Holt, Rinehart, and Winston, 1967), 42, 58.

4. Homer Fansler, *History of Tucker County, West Virginia* (Parsons, W.Va.: McClain Printing Co., 1962), 66–67.

5. Ibid., 35–37. Fansler says that the Minear party was returning from Clarksburg, but it seems more likely that they were returning from Morgantown, where the county courthouse was located. For other local accounts of Indian attacks within the Monongahela region, see Hu Maxwell, *History of Randolph County, West Virginia, from Its Earliest Settlement to the Present*, reprint (Parsons, W.Va.: McClain Printing Co., 1961), 185.

6. James M. Callahan, *A Semi-Centennial History of West Virginia* (Charleston, W.Va.: Semi-Centennial Commission of West Virginia, 1913), 36; Samuel Eliot Morison, *The Oxford History of the American People*, vol. 2, *1789 Through Reconstruction* (New York: Mentor, 1972), 64.

7. Sosin, *Revolutionary Frontier*, 171, 167; Warren Hofstra, "Land Policy and Settlement in the Northern Shenandoah Valley," in *Appalachian Frontiers: Settlement, Society, and Development in the Pre-Industrial Era*, edited by Robert D. Mitchell (Lexington: Univ. Press of Kentucky, 1991), 105–6.

8. D. Alan Williams, "The Small Farmer in Eighteenth-Century Virginia Politics," *Agricultural History* 43 (Jan. 1969): 91; Charles S. Sydnor, *American Revolutionaries in the Making: Political Practices in Washington's Virginia* (New York: Free Press, 1952), 60–61; Merrill Jensen, "The American Revolution and American Agriculture," *Agricultural History* 43 (Jan. 1969): 111; James G. Leyburn, *The Scotch-Irish: A Social History* (Chapel Hill: Univ. of North Carolina Press, 1962), 200–210.

9. Sosin, *Revolutionary Frontier*, 21.

10. Hofstra, "Land Policy and Settlement," 107; Sosin, *Revolutionary Frontier*, 21–23; Bernard Bailyn, *Voyagers to the West: A Passage in the Peopling of America on the Eve of the Revolution* (New York: Knopf, 1986), 183–84.

11. Joyce Appleby, "Commercial Farming and the 'Agrarian Myth' in the Early Republic," *Journal of American History* 68 (March 1982): 841, 838–39; Callahan, *Semi-Centennial History*, 49.

12. Robert D. Mitchell, *Commercialism and Frontier: Perspectives on the Early Shenandoah Valley* (Charlottesville: Univ. Press of Virginia, 1977), 3–4.

13. Van Beck Hall, "The Politics of Appalachian Virginia, 1790–1830," in *Appalachian Frontiers: Settlement, Society, and Development in the Pre-Industrial Era*, edited by Robert D. Mitchell (Lexington: Univ. Press of Kentucky, 1991), 166–67, 169; Appleby, "Commercial Farming," 835. For other perspectives, see Richard Hofstadter, "The Myth of the Happy Yeoman," *American Heritage*, 2d ser., 7 (1956): 43–53, and Rodney Loehr, "Self-Sufficiency on the Farm, 1759–1800," *Agricultural History* 26 (1952): 37–42.

14. Appleby, "Commercial Farming," 839, 841.

15. For example, see Altina L. Waller, *Feud: Hatfields, McCoys, and Social Change in Appalachia, 1860–1900* (Chapel Hill: Univ. of North Carolina Press, 1988), and Ronald D Eller, *Miners, Millhands, and Mountaineers: Industrialization of the Appalachian South, 1880–1930* (Knoxville: Univ. of Tennessee Press, 1982).

16. Appleby, "Commercial Farming," 844, 849.

17. Sosin, *Revolutionary Frontier*, 25.

18. Callahan, *Semi-Centennial History*, 6; Thomas Jefferson, *Notes on the State of Virginia*, edited by William Peden (Chapel Hill: Univ. of North Carolina Press, 1955), 119.

19. Callahan, *Semi-Centennial History*, 49.

20. Ibid.

21. Thomas Perkins Abernethy, *Western Lands and the American Revolution*, Univ. of Virginia Institute for Research in the Social Sciences Monograph 25 (New York: Russell and Russell, 1937), 228.

22. Ibid., 218; Nell M. Nugent, *Cavaliers and Pioneers: Abstracts of Virginia Land Patents and Grants, 1623–1800*, vol. 1 (Richmond: Press of the Dietz Printing Co., 1934), x; Edgar B. Sims, *Sims Index to Land Grants in West Virginia* (Charleston, W.Va.: Rose City Press, 1952); surveyor reports, Deakins Family Papers, A and M 197, B1F1, WVU; Sosin, *Revolutionary Frontier*, 31–33. See the listing of land grants culled from Virginia records in Otis K. Rice, *The Allegheny Frontier: West Virginia Beginnings, 1730–1830* (Lexington: Univ. Press of Kentucky, 1970), 137–41.

23. John E. Selby, *The Revolution in Virginia, 1775–1783* (Williamsburg, Va.: Colonial Williamsburg Foundation, 1992), 153–54, 230–31; Abernethy, *Western Lands*, 228; Jefferson, *Notes on the State of Virginia*, 119.

24. Dater, "Albert Gallatin," 26; Abernethy, *Western Lands*, 250, 263.

25. Abernethy, *Western Lands*, 250; copy of survey for Noah Haden, Deakins Family Papers, A and M 197, B1F1, WVU; Eleanor Youst Carter and Kathleen M. Bogdan, comps., *Unpatented Land Records of Monongalia, Yohogania, and Ohio Counties, Virginia, 1766–1794* (Fairmont, W.Va.: Genealogical Club, 1988), 12; Sosin, *Revolutionary Frontier*, 25, 33.

26. Roy Bird Cook, *Washington's Western Lands* (Strasburg, Va.: Shenandoah Publishing House, 1930), 146.

27. Carter and Bogdan, *Unpatented Land Records*, 18; Callahan, *Semi-Centennial History*, 36.

28. Carter and Bogdan, *Unpatented Land Records*, 21, 10; Fansler, *History of Tucker County*, 68.

29. Carter and Bogdan, *Unpatented Land Records*, 10.

30. Reference to treasury warrant 15311, April 2, 1783, Deakins Family Papers, A and M 197, B1F1; treasury warrants 17823 and 19528, and portions of 17822, granted in 1783, in Fansler, *History of Tucker County*, 66.

31. Certified copy of order; McCleery to F. Deakins, May 7, 1790; F. Deakins to Wm McCleery, Oct. 7, 1790; copy of directive, all in Deakins Family Papers, A and M 197, B1F1, WVU.

32. John Compton report to Deakinses, April 3, 1793, A and M 197; warrant 17677, cited, A and M 624; warrant 21187, cited, A and M 197, all in Deakins Family Papers, B1F1, WVU. Carter and Bogdan, *Unpatented Land Records*, 21.

33. Survey, Deakins Family Papers, A and M 197, B1F1, WVU. County records show that Goff claimed one thousand acres in 1781.

34. Maxwell, *History of Randolph County*, 189.

35. From records and field book notations in Deakins Family Papers, A and M 197, B1F1–3, WVU. For an overview of some early Randolph County transactions, see Lee Soltow, "Land Speculation in West Virginia in the Early Federal Period: Randolph County as a Specific Case," *West Virginia History* 44 (Winter 1983): 111–34.

36. Reference to treasury warrant 18085, July 26, 1782, Deakins Family Papers, A and M 197, B1F3–4, WVU.

37. Ibid., B1F3, B1F1, B1F3.

38. Ibid., B2F5.

39. Notation in list of wills, Randolph County Historic Records Survey, microfilm, WVU; Maxwell, *History of Randolph County*, 221, 223.

40. Deakins Family Papers, A and M 197, B2F5, WVU; Maxwell, *History of Randolph County*, 290.

41. Abernethy, *Western Lands*, 217–18, 221–22.

42. Ibid., 217.

43. William Wirt, *Sketches of the Life and Character of Patrick Henry*, reprint (Freeport, N.Y.: Books for Libraries, 1970), 282–85; Abernethy, *Western Lands*, 217.

44. Abernethy, *Western Lands*, 218; Sydnor, *American Revolutionaries in the Making*, 14.

45. Mary Lou Lustig, *Robert Hunter, 1666–1734: New York's August Statesman* (Syracuse, N.Y.: Syracuse Univ. Press, 1983), 99–103; Francis Jennings, *Empire of Fortune: Crowns, Colonies, and Tribes in the Seven Years War in America* (New York: Norton, 1988), 90–92; L. Jesse Lemish, ed., *Benjamin Franklin: The Autobiography and Other Writings* (New York: Signet Classics, 1961), 156, 178–80.

46. Abernethy, *Western Lands*, 217–19; Lemish, *Benjamin Franklin*, 180–81.

47. Abernethy, *Western Lands*, 218–19.

48. Alison Goodyear Freehling, *Drift toward Dissolution: The Virginia Slavery Debate of 1831–1832* (Baton Rouge: Louisiana State Univ. Press, 1982), 69.

49. Appleby, "Commercial Farming," 844.

3. Backcountry Politics

1. Arthur M. Schlesinger, Jr., *The Age of Jackson* (New York: Little, Brown, 1945), 8.

2. Ray Allen Billington, "The Origin of the Land Speculator as a Frontier Type," *Agricultural History* 19 (1945): 204.

3. Eleanor Youst Carter and Kathleen M. Bogdan, comps., *Unpatented Land Records of Monongalia, Yohogania, and Ohio Counties, Virginia, 1766–1794* (Fairmont, W.Va.: Genealogical Club, 1988), esp. preface. The list reveals that settlers in the Monongalia region made attempts to register their claims in a proper manner.

4. J.R. Pole, *Foundations of American Independence, 1763–1815* (New York: Bobbs-Merrill, 1972), 150.

5. The relationship is explored in Charles A. Beard, *An Economic Interpretation of the Constitution* (New York: Macmillan, 1935), and Thomas Perkins Abernethy, *Western Lands and the American Revolution*, Univ. of Virginia Institute for Research in the Social Sciences Monograph 25 (New York: Russell and Russell, 1937), 218–20.

6. Carl Ortwin Sauer, "Homestead and Community on the Middle Border," in *Land and Life: A Selection from the Writings of Carl Ortwin Sauer*, edited by John Leighly (Berkeley: Univ. of California Press, 1963), 33–38.

7. Schlesinger, *Age of Jackson*, 263; Daniel Feller, *The Public Lands in Jacksonian Politics* (Madison: Univ. of Wisconsin Press, 1984), 14–38, xv.

8. Harry L. Watson, "Conflict and Collaboration: Yeomen, Slaveholders, and Politics in the Antebellum South," *Social History* 10 (Oct. 1985): 290, 293; Marvin Meyers, "The Jacksonian Persuasion," *American Quarterly* 5 (Spring 1953): 6, 10.

9. Meyers, "Jacksonian Persuasion," 14–15.

10. Charles H. Ambler, *Sectionalism in Virginia from 1776 to 1861* (New York: Russell and Russell, 1964), 97, 98, 99.

11. *Fairfax's Devisee* v. *Hunter's Lessee*, 7 Cranch 625 (1816); Otis K. Rice, *The Allegheny Frontier: West Virginia Beginnings, 1730–1830* (Lexington: Univ. Press of Kentucky, 1970), 356.

12. Stuart E. Brown, Jr., *Virginia Baron: The Story of Thomas, 6th Lord Fairfax* (Berryville, Va.: Chesapeake Book Co., 1965), 197–200.

13. Ambler, *Sectionalism in Virginia*, 102–3; Brown, *Virginia Baron*, 197–200.

14. William H. Edwards and William Cocoran are two such examples. See Henry Cohen, "Vicissitudes of an Absentee Landlord: A Case Study," in *The Frontier in American Development: Essays in Honor of Paul Wallace Gates*, edited by David Ellis (Ithaca, N.Y.: Cornell Univ. Press, 1968), 192–216.

15. Ambler, *Sectionalism in Virginia*, 118–19.

16. Ibid., 122; Rice, *Allegheny Frontier*, 356–58.

17. Paul Wallace Gates, "The Role of the Speculator in Western Development," *Pennsylvania Magazine of History and Biography* 66 (July 1942): 329.

18. "List of Tithables, 1857," Jesse Parsons Papers, A and M 731, WVU.

19. "List of Tithables, 1858," Jesse Parsons Papers, A and M 731, WVU.

20. Durwood Dunn, *Cades Cove: The Life and Death of a Southern Appalachian Community, 1818–1937* (Knoxville: Univ. of Tennessee Press, 1988), 201.

21. Tucker County Circuit Court Records, A and M 60, 1858, B1F2; 1853, B1F1; and 1855, B1F1, all in WVU.

22. Ibid., 1855, B1F1; 1857, B1F1–2; and 1858, B1F1–2, all in WVU.

23. Acts of Virginia, 1852–53, chap. 7, sec. 3, "An Act Concerning the Assessment and Collection of the Public Revenue."

24. Acts of Virginia, 1860, chap. 121.

25. Morgan H. Dyer, *Dyer's Index to Land Grants in West Virginia* (Charleston, W.Va.: Moses W. Donnally, 1896), 238, 535. This poorly organized accounting of land grants was superseded in the 1950s by the *Sims Index*, which is the general reference. The 1896 publication date of Dyer's work, however, would have given the index significant authority in a time of extreme pressure on land claims. The Dobbinses maintained a resort in the region and by 1884 were holding the mortgage on the Rumbarger Lumber Company lands.

4. Robber Baron Politics

1. Clay County History Book Committee, *History of Clay County* (Salem, W.Va.: Don Mills, 1989), 44; W.E.R. Byrne, *Tale of the Elk* (Richwood, W.Va.: Mountain State Press, 1940), 255–56.

2. Byrne, *Tale of the Elk*, 255; Edgar B. Sims, *Sims Index to Land Grants in West Virginia* (Charleston, W.Va.: Rose City Press, 1952), 359, 370; Kanawha County Deed Book 1, pp. 479, 483.

3. Clay County History Book Committee, *History of Clay County*, 44; see Edwards to David Cochrane, in Clay County, Virginia, Deed Book 1, p. 98.

4. Acts of Virginia, 1837, chap. 235.

5. Phil Conley, *History of the West Virginia Coal Industry* (Charleston: West Virginia Educational Foundation, 1960), 107; Acts of Virginia, 1855–56, chap. 436.

6. Acts of Virginia, 1849–50, chaps. 252, 257; 1852, chap. 325.

7. Clay County, Deed Book 1, p. 343 and thereafter.

8. Clay County, Deed Book 3, pp. 553–82.

9. William Parker Foulke to Samuel Price, Jan. 29, 1849, B1, "Correspondence, 1849, Jan.–March," William Parker Foulke Papers, A and M 3075, WVU.

10. William Parker Foulke to Richard Parker Foulke, Jan. 22, 1849, William Parker Foulke Papers, WVU; Carolyn McCreesh, "The Philadelphia Connection: The Foulke Meadow River Lands in the 18th and 19th Centuries," *West Virginia History* 44 (Summer 1983): 289–320.

11. Alison Goodyear Freehling, *Drift toward Dissolution: The Virginia Slavery Debate of 1831–1832* (Baton Rouge: Louisiana State Univ. Press, 1982), 207.

12. Barrington Moore, Jr., *Social Origins of Dictatorship and Democracy: Lord and Peasant in the Making of the Modern World* (Boston: Beacon Press, 1966), 127, 129.

13. Elizabeth Fox-Genovese and Eugene D. Genovese, *Fruits of Merchant Capital* (New York: Oxford Univ. Press, 1983), 25.

14. Morton Rothstein, "The Antebellum South as a Dual Economy," *Agricultural History* 41 (Oct. 1967): 381–82; Charles Post, "The American Road to Capitalism," *New Left Review* 133 (1982): 38.

15. Moore, *Social Origins of Dictatorship and Democracy*, 127.

16. Ibid., 120, 127; Freehling, *Drift toward Dissolution*, 262–63.

17. Moore, *Social Origins of Dictatorship and Democracy*, 127.

18. Paul Saulstrom, "The Agricultural Origins of Economic Dependency," in *Appalachian Frontiers: Settlement, Society, and Development in the Pre-Industrial Era*, edited by Robert D. Mitchell (Lexington: Univ. Press of Kentucky, 1991), 266.

19. Charles H. Ambler, *Sectionalism in Virginia from 1776 to 1861* (New York: Russell and Russell, 1964), 101.

20. Ibid., 101–2; Charles H. Ambler, *West Virginia: The Mountain State* (New York: Prentice-Hall, 1940), 223-26.

21. Harry L. Watson, "Conflict and Collaboration: Yeomen, Slaveholders, and Politics in the Antebellum South," *Social History* 10 (Oct. 1985): 288, 291. Watson is analyzing Deep South relations, but his argument is eloquently demonstrated by the political disharmony and eventual division of Virginia. See Freehling, *Drift toward Dissolution*, 69–70.

22. Fox-Genovese and Genovese, *Fruits of Merchant Capital*, 5.

23. Freehling, *Drift toward Dissolution*, 77, 79, 53–54; Ambler, *Sectionalism in Virginia*, 267–68.

24. Paul Wallace Gates, "The Role of the Speculator in Western Development," *Pennsylvania Magazine of History and Biography* 66 (July 1942): 328; Deakins Family Papers, A and M 197, B2F6, WVU.

25. Freehling, *Drift toward Dissolution*, 53–55; Ambler, *Sectionalism in Virginia*, 163–65.

26. Freehling, *Drift toward Dissolution*, 70.

27. There was also the Monongahela River Navigation Company (Acts of Virginia, 1816, chap. 50). The state amended the charter in 1817 to increase the stock to $150,000 (1817, chap. 67). This proposal was a response to a growing iron industry in the Monongahela region. The poor-grade iron ore and the eventual location of the Baltimore and Ohio Railroad too far north of the area brought the early iron industry to ruin by 1850. James R. Moreland, "The Early Cheat Mountain Iron Works," unpublished typescript, 1940, p. 148, WVU.

28. Freehling, *Drift toward Dissolution*, 54, 240.

29. Acts of Virginia, 1824, chap. 46; Van Beck Hall, "The Politics of Appalachian Virginia, 1790–1830," in *Appalachian Frontiers*, ed. Mitchell, 182.

30. Conley, *History of the West Virginia Coal Industry*, 95.

31. Ibid., 100–101.

32. Acts of Virginia, 1832, chaps. 116, 119, 156.

33. Ambler, *Sectionalism in Virginia*, 175–80; Thomas Perkins Abernethy, *Western Lands and the American Revolution*, Univ. of Virginia Institute for Research in the Social Sciences Monograph 25 (New York: Russell and Russell, 1937), 217–29.

34. Ambler, *Sectionalism in Virginia*, 166, 173–74.

35. Ibid., 253, 177.

36. Ibid., 260.

37. Ibid., 261.

38. Charles H. Ambler, *West Virginia, the Mountain State* (New York: Prentice-Hall, 1940), 287.

39. Acts of Virginia, Dec. Sess. 1839: Appomatox Mining Company, chap. 146; Bradford Coal Mining Company, chap. 147; Clover Hill Coal Mining Company, chap. 148; Dupuy and Bryant Coal Mining Company, of Powhatan County, chap. 150; and Dutoy and Powhatan Coal Companies, chap. 151.

40. Acts of Virginia, Dec. Sess. 1836–37, chap. 205; Jan. Sess. 1838, chap. 261.

41. The Virginia General Assembly incorporated the following firms with respective acreage allowed: Potomac and Allegheny Coal and Iron Company, twenty thousand acres in Hardy and Hampshire counties (Acts of Virginia, Dec. Sess. 1839, chap. 156); Preston Railroad, Lumber, and Mining Company, ten thousand acres in Preston County (Dec. Ses. 1839, chap. 157); Cheat River Mining, Lumber, Salt, and Iron Company, ten thousand acres in Preston County (Dec. Sess. 1836, chap. 241); Virginia and New York Coal Company, one thousand acres in Morgan County (Dec. Sess. 1836, chap. 219);

Greenville Furnace and Mining Company, ten thousand acres in Monongalia and Preston counties (Dec. Sess. 1836, chap. 226); Preston Mining and Manufacturing Company, one thousand acres in Preston County (Dec. Sess. 1836, chap. 228).

42. Pierpont was a partner of J.O. Watson in the Fairmont area as early as 1855; Francis H. Pierpont Papers, A and M 9, B1F1, WVU. Acts of West Virginia, Jan. Sess. 1867, p. 222, lists Boreman and Pierpont as incorporators of the Boreman Oil Company.

43. David Dare Brown, "Lumbering in Randolph County," paper presented to the Randolph County Historical Society, Jan. 22, 1952, David Dare Brown Notebooks, A and M 1630, B1NB2, WVU.

44. Acts of Virginia, Dec. Sess. 1841, chap. 176: Monongalia Iron Company, 30,000 acres of land, Evan T. Ellicott and Andrew Ellicott, incorporators; North Mountain Mining Company, 44,300 acres of land, Charles Carter Lee, incorporator.

45. Acts of Virginia, Dec. Sess. 1841, chaps. 177, 178.

46. Ibid., Dec. Sess. 1844, chap. 131.

47. Ibid., N. Sess. 1852-53, chap. 376.

48. Ibid., chap. 381.

49. Ibid., chap. 387. The Virginia Coal Company, of Hardy and Hampshire counties, was incorporated on April 3, 1853, with permission to own and mine up to ten thousand acres of land (chap. 425).

50. "The Family Visitor," May 18, 1860, typescript, Francis H. Pierpont Papers, A and M 9, B1F2, WVU.

51. Acts of Virginia, Dec. Sess. 1857: Rowlesburg Lumber and Iron Company, amending 1856 charter (chaps. 399, 400). Acts of Virginia, N. Sess. 1852-53: Fellowsville Mining and Manufacturing Company, by Sylvanus Heermans, Joseph Fellows, Zeno Albro, and others (chap. 393); Dora Coal and Iron Manufacturing Company, by Anastasias Nicholas and Adam Rudolph (chap. 399); North and South Mountain Exploring and Mining Company, by Alexander Hamilton and others (chap. 413). Acts of Virginia, Dec. Sess. 1857: Hardy Coal and Iron Company, by Daniel Bruce, Douglas Percy, Alexander Sloane, Nelson Beal, and J.D. Armstrong (chap. 401); Preston Coal and Iron Company, by F. Pentz, Samuel Mitchell, William Kenson, John C. Erenspritsch, John Witlock, and others (chap. 403); Hampshire Mining Company, by Shepherd Ostrom, Robert Borone, George Potts, Thomas DeVeemon, and George B. Saterlee (chap. 404); Virginia Coal and Iron Company, by John N. Pancake, Joseph C. Pancake, E.M. Armstrong, William Vance, and others (chap. 410); Laurel Iron and coal Company, by Meridith Clymer, John Seymour, Rudolph Winterhoff, and others, (chap. 411). Acts of Virginia, Dec. Sess. 1859: Great Falls Iron and Manufacturing Company, by Harrison, William, and George M. Hagans (chap. 414); Preston Coal and Iron Company, charter extension (chap. 417). Acts of Confederate Virginia, 1863: Hardy Coal Mining Company, by George Lee, George Arents, Charles Hartwell, John Fisher, G.W. Jones, and W. Peterson (chap. 83).

5. Pufferbilly Politics

1. Ronald L. Lewis, "The Use and Extent of Slave Labor in the Virginia Iron Industry: The Ante-Bellum Era," *West Virginia History* 38 (Jan. 1977): 141; idem, *Coal, Iron, and Slaves: Industrial Slavery in Maryland and Virginia, 1715–1865* (Westport, Conn.: Greenwood Press, 1979), 243; James R. Moreland, "The Early Cheat Mountain Iron Works," unpublished typescript, 1940, WVU.

2. Barrington Moore, Jr., *Social Origins of Dictatorship and Democracy: Lord and Peasant in the Making of the Modern World* (Boston: Beacon Press, 1966), 111–55; Eric Foner, *Reconstruction: America's Unfinished Revolution, 1863–1877* (New York: Harper and Row, 1988), 597.

3. See John Alexander Williams, *West Virginia and the Captains of Industry* (Morgantown: West Virginia Univ. Library, 1976), for a synthesis of Williams's earlier studies of these men: "The New Dominion and the Old: Ante Bellum and Statehood Politics as the Background for West Virginia's Bourbon Democracy," *West Virginia History* 33 (July 1972): 317–407; and "The Final Confrontation of H.G. Davis and William L. Wilson in the Election Campaign of 1894," *West Virginia History* 32 (Oct. 1970): 1–10.

4. Eric Foner, "The Causes of the American Civil War: Recent Interpretations and New Directions," *Civil War History* 20 (Sept. 1974): 201; Charles Post, "The American Road to Capitalism," *New Left Review* 133 (1982): 45, 49.

5. Williams, *West Virginia and the Captains of Industry*, 172. Williams eloquently discusses the skill and ruthlessness of the Davis-Elkins-Scott-Camden political domination of the state.

6. Acts of West Virginia, 2nd Sess. 1864, chap. 35.

7. Acts of West Virginia, Jan. Sess. 1866, chap. 85; Williams, "New Dominion and the Old," 360.

8. Charles M. Pepper, *The Life and Times of Henry Gassaway Davis, 1823–1916* (New York: Century, 1920), 36, 33; Williams, *West Virginia and the Captains of Industry*, 172.

9. John A. Caruso, "Henry Gassaway Davis and the Pan American Railway," Ph.D. diss., West Virginia Univ., 1949, p. 12; Williams, "New Dominion and the Old," 359.

10. Pepper, *Henry Gassaway Davis*, 26; Williams, "New Dominion and the Old," 359.

11. Williams, "New Dominion and the Old," 359; Caruso, "Henry Gassaway Davis and the Pan American Railway," 15.

12. Acts of the General Assembly of the Restored Government of Virginia, May Sess. 1862, chap. 11.

13. Acts of Virginia, Dec. Sess. 1850, chap. 233. Incorporators were Benjamin Green, George Maynard, Angus W. McDonald, Richard Clark, and others. The firm was restricted to operating on ten thousand acres of land.

14. The Virginia General Assembly incorporated the Allegheny Mining and Manufacturing Company, by John T. Schermerhorn,

Ernest Snyder, and others, and gave it permission to operate in Allegheny, Pocahontas, and Greenbrier counties and to hold fifteen thousand acres of land (Acts of Virginia, Extra and Reg. Sess. 1849–50, chap. 233). Acts of Virginia, Dec. Sess. 1839, chap. 156: Potomac and Allegheny Coal and Iron Company, by Edward Smith, Samuel Hixon, Jr., Joseph Hixon, Walter Smith, Lyman Moore, Simon Green, limited to twenty thousand acres in Hardy and Hampshire counties. Acts of Virginia, Dec. Sess. 1848, chap. 285: Hampshire Coal and Iron Company, by William Helphenstein, Abelard Guthrie, J.H. Lathrop, Edward Helphenstein, and James Hall, limited to five thousand acres. Acts of Virginia, N. Sess. 1852-53: Hampshire Coal and Iron Company, by Victor DeLaunay, Reuben Johnson, Thomas C. Atkinson, Jerry Cowles, and Rodman Joyce (chap. 381). Acts of Virginia Dec. 1857–Ap. 1858 Sess.: Hampshire Mining Company, by Shepherd Ostrom, Robert Borone, George Potts, Thomas DeVeemon, and George B. Satterlee, limited to ten thousand acres (chap. 404).

15. Gilbert Gude, *Where the Potomac Begins: A History of North Branch Valley* (Washington, D.C.: Seven Locks Press, 1984), 31; Pepper, *Henry Gassaway Davis*, 32.

16. Acts of West Virginia, 1866, chaps. 7, 67.

17. Acts of West Virginia, Jan. Sess. 1868, chap. 76.

18. Williams, "New Dominion and the Old," 359.

19. Homer Fansler, *History of Tucker County, West Virginia* (Parsons, W.Va.: McClain Printing Co., 1962), 28, 69.

20. Acts of West Virginia, Jan. Sess. 1868, chap. 76.

21. Pepper, *Henry Gassaway Davis*, 45; West Virginia, *Manual of the Legislature and of the Executive and Judiciary for 1869* (Wheeling: John Frew, public printer, 1869), 6.

22. West Virginia, Senate, *Journal of the Sixth Session* (Wheeling: John Frew, public printer, 1867–68), Feb. 14, 1868, p. 102.

23. Williams, *West Virginia and the Captains of Industry*, 7.

24. Williams, "New Dominion and the Old," 321, 329; Foner, *Reconstruction*, 423.

25. Williams, *West Virginia and the Captains of Industry*, 174.

26. Pepper, *Henry Gassaway Davis*, 82–83.

27. The railroad announced five subsidiary companies in its 1899 annual report: the Otter Creek Boom and Lumber Company, the Wilson Lumber Company, Otter Creek Mercantile, the Beaver Creek Lumber Company, and the Blackwater Lumber Company. Railroad directors included Davis, Stephen B. Elkins, Augustus Schell, William Keyser, Thomas B. Davis, Alexander Shaw, James G. Blaine, J.N. Camden, A.P. Gorman, W.H. Barnum, and John A. Hambleton. West Virginia Central and Pittsburg Railway Company Annual Report, 1899, WVU.

28. David Luke to Samuel E. Slaymaker, Jan. 4, 1900, Correspondence of Samuel E. Slaymaker, West Virginia Pulp and Paper Company Records, A and M 2134, B1, WVU (hereinafter cited as Slaymaker Correspondence, WVU).

29. Williams, *West Virginia and the Captains of Industry*, 174.

30. Gavin Wright, *Old South, New South: Revolutions in the Southern Economy since the Civil War* (New York: Basic Books, 1986), 270.

31. See the John T. McGraw Papers, A and M 86, B5–6, WVU.

32. Richard Simon, "The Development of Underdevelopment: The Coal Industry and Its Effect on the West Virginia Economy," Ph.D. diss., Univ. of Pittsburgh, 1978, pp. 222–24.

33. Nicholas C. Burckel, "Publicizing Progressivism," *West Virginia History* 17 (Spring–Summer 1981): 222; Wright, *Old South, New South*, 272.

34. Acts of West Virginia, 1867, chap. 22.

35. Ibid., 1869, chap. 141.

36. Ronald D Eller, *Miners, Millhands, and Mountaineers: Industrialization of the Appalachian South, 1880–1930* (Knoxville: Univ. of Tennessee Press, 1982), 234.

37. See, for example, David Luke to Samuel E. Slaymaker, Jan. 4, 1900, Slaymaker Correspondence, WVU.

38. Acts of West Virginia, 1868, p. 186. The State Immigration and Improvement Company of West Virginia was incorporated by Governor Boreman, A.S. Core, J.B. Blair, Moses Sweetser, Thomas Hornbrook, and Joseph H. Diss Debar.

39. John Williams to A.I. Boreman, Jan. 23, 1867, in the Historical Records Survey, Division of Women's and Professional Projects, works Projects Administration, Calendar of the Arthur I. Boreman Letters in the State Department of Archives and History (Charleston, W.Va.: The Historical Records Survey, January 1939) 60; Acts of West Virginia, Jan. 19, 1880, p. 443. Incorporators of the International Real Estate Society were Emanuel Ludwig and Herman Kirchoff of Switzerland, Alexander Matthews of Lewisburg, and Charles C. Lewis, William A. Quarrier, and Clarkson C. Watts of Charleston.

40. Williams, *West Virginia and the Captains of Industry*, 184.

41. Acts of West Virginia, 1870, chap. 108.

42. Ibid., 1873, p. 873; 1867, pp. 185, 201, 222.

6. Farmer Politics

1. John Harvie and James Swan were exceptions. Harvie, a stockholder in the Loyal Company of Virginia, was in charge of Virginia's land office. Swan at one time claimed as much as one-sixth of the present-day state of West Virginia, but he was unsuccessful in patenting his lands. Nothing came of his twenty-one-thousand-acre claim along Little Indian Creek in Monroe County, either. Although Swan died penniless, his investors were repaid. Jim Comstock, ed., *West Virginia Heritage Encyclopedia* (Richwood, W.Va.: Jim Comstock, 1976), 4: 802; 10–11: 382. Harvie was an associate of Robert Morris, Levi Hollingsworth, and other New England investors. His

early and prominent role in Virginia's land businesses is detailed in Thomas Perkins Abernethy, *Western Lands and the American Revolution*, Univ. of Virginia Institute for Research in the Social Sciences Monograph 25 (New York: Russell and Russell, 1937), 7–296 passim.

2. Edgar B. Sims, *Sims Index to Land Grants in West Virginia* (Charleston, W.Va.: Rose City Press, 1952), 513–35; U.S. Department of Commerce, Bureau of the Census, *Thirteenth Census, 1910* (Washington, D.C.: GPO, 1913–14), "Composition and Characteristics of the Population for the State and for Counties," West Virginia, p. 1032.

3. David B. Reger, *West Virginia Geological Survey: Mercer, Monroe, and Summers Counties* (Wheeling, W.Va.: Wheeling News Litho Co., 1926), 749; map, "Important Farmlands of Monroe County, W.Va." (Morgantown, W.Va.: U.S. Soil Conservation Service, 1980).

4. West Virginia, Board of Agriculture, *Second Biennial Report, 1893 and 1894* (Charleston, W.Va.: Moses W. Donnally, 1894), 45; West Virginia, Board of Agriculture, *Third Biennial Report, 1895 and 1896* (Charleston, W.Va.: Moses W. Donnally, 1896), 52.

5. West Virginia, Department of Human Services, "Statement of Expenditures by Area and County Fiscal Year 1975," *Annual Report, 1975* (Charleston: West Virginia Department of Human Services, 1975), 33.

6. Robert Brenner, "The Social Basis of Economic Development," in *Analytical Marxism*, edited by John Roemer (London: Cambridge Univ. Press, 1986), 27.

7. John T. McGraw Papers, B5–6, WVU.

8. Brenner, "Social Basis of Economic Development," 27.

9. Oren Morton, *A History of Monroe County, West Virginia* (Staunton, Va.: McClure Co., 1916; Baltimore: Regional Publishing Co., 1974), 293.

10. Julius DeGruyter, *The Kanawha Spectator*, vol. 1 (Charleston, W.Va.: DeGruyter, 1953), 339, 429; Clay County, Deed Book 3, pp. 553–82.

11. U.S. Department of Agriculture, *Economic and Social Problems and Conditions of the Southern Appalachians*, Miscellaneous Publication no. 205 (Washington, D.C.: GPO, 1935), 70.

12. U.S. Department of Commerce, Bureau of the Census, *Thirteenth Census 1910, vol. 7, Agriculture*, "Table 2, Number, Acreage, and Value of Farms Classified by Tenure, Color, and Nativity of Farmers; and Mortgage Debt by Counties: April 15, 1910"; U.S. Department of the Interior, Census Office, *Ninth Census, 1870* (Washington, D.C.: GPO, 1872), "Table VII—Number and Size of Farms."

13. U.S. census reports, 1880–1910; for 1910 statistics, see U.S. Department of Commerce, Bureau of the Census, *Thirteenth Census*, vol. 7, *Agriculture*, West Virginia, "Table 1, Farms and Farm Property."

14. Bituminous Operators' Special Committee, "A Summary of Statement on Comparative Efficiency of Labor in the Bituminous Coal Industry under Union and Non-Union Operation," *Briefs and*

Other Communications Submitted to the United States Coal Commission, vol. 3 (Washington, D.C., 1923), microfilm, pp. 17, 203.

15. West Virginia, Board of Agriculture, *Second Biennial Report*, 45, 47.

16. Bituminous Operators' Special Committee, "Summary," 16; Damaris Rose, "Homeownership, Subsistence and Historical Change: The Mining District of West Cornwall in the Late 19th Century," in *Class and Space: The Making of Urban Society*, edited by Nigel Thrift and Peter Williams (London: Routledge and Kegan Paul, 1987), 110.

17. The charters of other companies doing business elsewhere in transmontane Virginia are plentiful. The oil and gas fields of Tyler, Ritchie, Wood, and other counties were being opened up by absentee-dominated corporations. The Elk River and Great Kanawha regions were the focus of a developmental frenzy also. Industrialist William H. Edwards was but one of several Philadelphia-based entrepreneurs who would make fortunes extracting West Virginia's natural resources. Nowhere is there more profound evidence of the rush to West Virginia than in the Acts of West Virginia, 1866. Hundreds of absentee firms, mostly based in Philadelphia, were chartered by West Virginia. There is no evidence that these firms were simply rechartering after the division of Virginia; they appear to be new organizations.

18. U.S. Department of the Interior, Census Office, *Ninth Census*, "General Nativity and Foreign Parentage," table 5, West Virginia, p. 324.

19. Ibid., "Population by Counties, 1790–1870," table 2, West Virginia, p. 72; "General Nativity and Foreign Parentage," table 5, p. 324.

20. Ibid., "Selected Statistics of Churches," table 18, West Virginia, p. 559.

21. Ibid., "Selected Statistics of Age and Sex by Counties," table 24, West Virginia, p. 638.

22. U.S. Census Office. *Census Population Schedules*, The National Archives, National Archives and Records Administration, General Services Administration, microfilm, 1910, Randolph, Tucker, and Pocahontas counties, West Viriginia.

23. *Davis News*, Aug. 7, 1913, p. 1.

7. Champagne Politics

1. John Alexander Williams, *West Virginia and the Captains of Industry* (Morgantown: West Virginia Univ. Library, 1976), 195.

2. Ronald D Eller, *Miners, Millhands, and Mountaineers: Industrialization of the Appalachian South, 1880–1930* (Knoxville: Univ. of Tennessee Press, 1982), 57.

3. Minute Books, Tucker County Lumber Corporations (hereinafter cited as TCLC), A and M 1163, WVU.

4. Acts of West Virginia, 1865–92.

5. Minute Book, J.L. Rumbarger Lumber Company, Nov. 2, 1887, and Feb. 20, 1888, TCLC, WVU; Homer Fansler, *History of Tucker County, West Virginia* (Parsons, W.Va.: McClain Printing Co., 1962), 284; David B. Reger, *West Virginia Geological Survey: Tucker County, W.Va.* (Wheeling, W.Va.: Wheeling News Litho Co., 1923), 16.

6. Minute Book, J.L. Rumbarger Lumber Company, Nov. 21, 1888, TCLC, WVU.

7. Minute Book, J.L. Rumbarger Lumber Company, April 2 and Dec. 2, 1897, TCLC, WVU.

8. Minute Book, J.L. Rumbarger Lumber Company, Jan. 17, 1898, TCLC, WVU.

9. Minute Book, J.L. Rumbarger Lumber Company, March 8, 1898, TCLC, WVU.

10. Roy B. Clarkson, *Tumult on the Mountain: Lumbering in West Virginia* (Parsons, W.Va.: McClain Printing Co., 1964), 36.

11. Minute Book, Dry Fork Lumber Company, June 18, 1909, TCLC, WVU; Wilbur Bridges to Henry Gassaway Davis, Oct. 8, 1913, and March 13, 1914, Henry Gassaway Davis Papers, ser. 14, B202, FFB, WVU.

12. Henry Gassaway Davis to R.C. Kerens, Dec. 1, 1885, Henry Gassaway Davis Papers, ser. 14, B201, FI,J,K, WVU.

13. J.R. McPherson to Henry Gassaway Davis, Dec. 7, 1885, Henry Gassaway Davis Papers, ser. 14, B201, FMMc, WVU.

14. T.B. Davis, Jr., president, Blaine Mining Company, to Samuel E. Slaymaker, Nov. 6, 1907, B1, Slaymaker Correspondence, WVU.

15. Stephen B. Elkins, in his own hand, to Henry Gassaway Davis, Nov. 24, 1880, Henry Gassaway Davis Papers, ser. 14, B201, FE-F, WVU.

16. Ibid.

17. Eller, *Miners, Millhands, and Mountaineers*, 12.

18. Brenda K. Walker, Dennis K. Smith, and Anthony Ferrise, *Real Property: Legal Aspects of Fences in West Virginia*, R.D. Publication no. 715 (Morgantown, W.Va.: Center for Extension and Continuing Education, 1983).

19. Gordon McKinney, "Industrialization and Violence in Appalachia in the 1890s," in *An Appalachian Symposium: Essays Written in Honor of Cratis D. Williams*, edited by J.W. Williamson (Boone, N.C.: Appalachian State Univ. Press, 1977); Gavin Wright, *Old South, New South: Revolutions in the Southern Economy since the Civil War* (New York: Basic Books, 1986), 270; Altina L. Waller, *Feud: Hatfields, McCoys, and Social Change in Appalachia, 1860–1900* (Chapel Hill: Univ. of North Carolina Press, 1988); Eller, *Miners, Millhands, and Mountaineers;* and John Gaventa, *Power and Powerlessness: Quiescence and Rebellion in an Appalachian Valley* (Urbana: Univ. of Illinois Press, 1980).

20. Williams, *West Virginia and the Captains of Industry*, 249.

21. "Memo of Coal Rights under Option in the Roaring Creek District," Henry Gassaway Davis Papers, ser. 2, WVU.

22. Acts of West Virginia, 1893, p. 155. Incorporators were S.B. Elkins, H.G. Davis, R.C. Kerens, Col. T.B. Davis, C.M. Hendley, F.B. Lott, and J.A. Hambleton.

23. Acts of West Virginia, 1891, p. 1072.

24. Davis's records indicate that he acquired 110 acres from Parsons and Brown, two-thirds of 3,521 (1,317) acres from Ambler, 122 acres from J. Arnold, one-third of 1,343 (447.66) acres from Dora Ramsburg, 1,935 acres in four tracts from W.F. Deakins, 323 acres from W.B. Maxwell, 1,378 acres from Jane Bonnifield, 239 acres from Jesse Parsons, 316.5 acres from David Goff, 2,537 acres from William Ewin, 310 acres from Evans, 143 acres from Summers, 600 acres from Arnold and Lousdin, and 563.33 acres from Beswick. "H.G. Davis Coal Company Statement of Assets and Liabilities, January 2nd, 1893," Henry Gassaway Davis Papers, ser. 2, B34, WVU.

25. James A. Bent and Wilson B. Maxwell to Henry Gassaway Davis, July 26, 1900, Henry Gassaway Davis Papers, ser. 14, B200, FB, WVU.

26. B.H. Hiner to Henry Gassaway Davis, March 5, 1901, Henry Gassaway Davis Papers, ser. 14, B201, FH, WVU.

27. L. Hansford to Henry Gassaway Davis, Aug. 22, 1901, Henry Gassaway Davis Papers, ser. 14, B200, FF, WVU.

28. William W. Croghan to Henry Gassaway Davis, March 26, 1886, Henry Gassaway Davis Papers, ser. 14, B201, FC, WVU; "Original Land Grants in West Virginia," Correspondence of the Field Office Title Attorney, Letters Received, 1915, B2, Records of the U.S. Forest Service, Record Group 95, National Archives.

29. B.L. Butcher to Henry Gassaway Davis, Sept. 4, 1885, Henry Gassaway Davis Papers, ser. 14, B201, FB, WVU.

30. See Clay County, West Virginia, Deed Book 1; C.F. Moore to Samuel E. Slaymaker, Dec. 9, 1901, B1, Slaymaker Correspondence, WVU.

31. Walker, Smith, and Ferrise, *Real Property*, 1.

32. For example, deed for timber between George Bean and the Buckhannon River Lumber Company, Sept. 8, 1890, Randolph County Deed Book U, p. 494.

33. The Buckhannon River Lumber Company and Hugh Dyer were sued in September 1893 by Levi Leonard, who sought to attach timber purchased from thirty-eight Randolph County farmers. Other powerful creditors who sought to attach the timber, land, and other assets of the Buckhannon company included C.T. Farnsworth, the National Exchange Bank of Weston, the Buckhannon Bank, and the West Virginia and Pittsburg Railroad Company. See memorandum of Lis Pendens, Sept. 1, 1893, Randolph County Deed Book W, p. 588ff.

8. Reform Politics

1. Mayo acquired more than half a million acres of coal lands from friends and neighbors in Kentucky, becoming that state's larg-

est landowner and one of its wealthiest citizens. Ultimately his affairs took him to West Virginia, where he became the major stockholder in the Consolidation Coal Company, whose founders included Fairmont natives A.B. Fleming and James (J.O.) Watson. Ronald D Eller, *Miners, Millhands, and Mountaineers: Industrialization of the Appalachian South, 1880–1930* (Knoxville: Univ. of Tennessee Press, 1982), 60–63.

2. John Alexander Williams, *West Virginia and the Captains of Industry* (Morgantown: West Virginia Univ. Library, 1976), 52–66.

3. E.D. Talbott to John T. McGraw, Sept. 17, 1894, John T. McGraw Papers, A and M 86, B5F6, WVU.

4. Ibid.

5. Charles H. Straub to William L. Key, Sept. 29, 1894, John T. McGraw Papers, B5F6, WVU.

6. Charles Powell to McGraw, Oct. 7, 1894, and E.D. Talbott to McGraw, Oct. 6, 1894, both in John T. McGraw Papers, B5F6, WVU.

7. Festus P. Summers, *William L. Wilson and Tariff Reform* (New Brunswick, N.J.: Rutgers Univ. Press, 1953), 219, 221.

8. Williams, *West Virginia and the Captains of Industry*, 172.

9. Ibid., 245.

10. West Virginia, Tax Commission, *Second Report, State Development* (Wheeling: Charles H. Taney, state printer, 1884), 1.

11. Paul Wallace Gates, "Tenants of the Log Cabin," *Mississippi Valley Historical Review* 49 (June 1962): 9, 17; West Virginia, Tax Commission, *Second Report*, 1.

12. West Virginia, Tax Commission, *Second Report*, 18–19.

13. Ibid.

14. Roy B. Clarkson, *Tumult on the Mountain: Lumbering in West Virginia* (Parsons, W.Va.: McClain Printing Co., 1964), 87; idem, *On Beyond Leatherbark* (Parsons, W.Va.: McClain Printing Co., 1991).

15. Thomas Luke to Samuel E. Slaymaker, April 5, 1900, B1, Slaymaker Correspondence, WVU.

16. Clarkson, *Tumult on the Mountain*, 87.

17. John G. Luke to Samuel E. Slaymaker, Feb. 17, 1900, B1, Slaymaker Correspondence, WVU.

18. Deed, Levi Hollingsworth to Robert Morris, Philadelphia, twenty thousand acres in Ohio County, Virginia, July 3, 1794, Hubbard Family Papers, A and M 755, WVU.

19. Otis K. Rice, *The Allegheny Frontier: West Virginia Beginnings, 1730–1830* (Lexington: Univ. Press of Kentucky, 1970), 143.

20. See Randolph County Deed Book X, pp. 5–14.

21. Pendleton County, West Virginia, Deed Book 29, p. 6. Condon gave Dyer twenty-two thousand dollars in cash and forty-five houses between Pulaski and Smallwood streets in Baltimore for approximately 29,352 acres of the Hollingsworth survey.

22. Although the lands in question were in the Monongahela, the suit was filed in the federal circuit court in Parkersburg. After 1911 that federal court became a court of appeals, and the records of the 1890 case cannot be located. In any case, a U.S. Supreme Court jus-

tice would have presided in the matter. Sale of Maria Shaw's land was ordered by the courts, according to the deed.

23. Randolph County Deed Book X, p. 5-14; Pendleton County Deed Book 29, p. 6.

24. Tucker County Deed Book 8, p. 196. The Longs sold five and a half acres of riverfront property adjacent to Mary Jane and Jesse Pennington for fifteen hundred dollars. The conveyance included permanent access to the site across the Longs' land. Purchasers agreed to be liable for damage caused, "if any," to the Longs' farm. Although the price was high, the advantage to the industrialists was far greater. Jacob Long, in another contract, conveyed a fourteen-acre island, but no additional fee is indicated. See Randolph County Deed Book W, pp. 260–63.

25. Tucker County Deed Book 8, p. 234.

26. Randolph County Deed Book X, pp. 5–14.

27. Eleanor Youst Carter and Kathleen M. Bogdan, comps., *Unpatented Land Records of Monongalia, Yohogania, and Ohio Counties, Virginia, 1766–1794* (Fairmont, W.Va.: Genealogical Club, 1988).

28. William McCleery to [Francis and William] Deakins, July 22, 1781; survey by John Hanway; John Goff to Col. Francis Deakins, Nov. 29, 1790; William McCleery to [Francis and William] Deakins, May 7, 1790, all in Deakins Family Papers, A and M 197, B1F3, WVU.

9. Pulp and Paper Politics

1. David Luke to Samuel E. Slaymaker, Jan. 4 and 12, 1900, B1, Slaymaker Correspondence, WVU. See also Roy B. Clarkson, *On Beyond Leatherbark* (Parsons, W.Va.: McClain Publishing Co., 1991), 30–38.

2. David Luke to Samuel E. Slaymaker, Jan. 4, 1900, B1, Slaymaker Correspondence, WVU.

3. David Luke to Samuel E. Slaymaker, Feb. 12, 1900, and John G. Luke to Samuel E. Slaymaker, Feb. 17, 1900, both in B1, Slaymaker Correspondence, WVU.

4. John F. Wooddell to Samuel E. Slaymaker, March 29, 1900, B1, Slaymaker Correspondence, WVU.

5. E.D. Talbott to Samuel E. Slaymaker, June 14, 1900, B1, Slaymaker Correspondence, WVU.

6. Ibid.

7. John G. Luke to Samuel E. Slaymaker, July 26, 1900, B1, Slaymaker Correspondence, WVU.

8. Ibid.

9. David Luke to Samuel E. Slaymaker, Nov. 1, 1900, B1, Slaymaker Correspondence, WVU; John Alexander Williams, *West Virginia and the Captains of Industry* (Morgantown: West Virginia Univ. Library, 1976), 195.

10. David Luke to Samuel E. Slaymaker, Nov. 1, 1900, B1, Slaymaker Correspondence, WVU.

11. John G. Luke to Samuel E. Slaymaker, Nov. 1, 1900, B1, Slaymaker Correspondence, WVU.

12. Williams, *West Virginia and the Captains of Industry*, 101–3, 109.

13. J.N. Camden to A.B. Fleming, Nov. 7, 1900, Aretas Brooks Fleming Papers, A and M 40, WVU.

14. Williams, *West Virginia and the Captains of Industry*, 109.

15. C.F. Moore to Samuel E. Slaymaker, Jan. 25, 1901, B1, Slaymaker Correspondence, WVU.

16. E.P. Shaffer to Samuel E. Slaymaker, Sept. 25, 1900, B1, Slaymaker Correspondence, WVU.

17. Ibid.

18. John G. Luke to Samuel E. Slaymaker, Dec. 13, 1900, and David Luke to Samuel E. Slaymaker, Dec. 13, 1900, both in B1, Slaymaker Correspondence, WVU; Clarkson, *On Beyond Leatherbark*, 43.

19. John G. Luke to Samuel E. Slaymaker, Jan. 29, 1901, B1, Slaymaker Correspondence, WVU.

20. Ibid.

21. I.A. Allen to Stephen B. Elkins, March 21, 1901, Henry Gassaway Davis Papers, ser. 14, B201, FA, WVU.

22. Thomas Luke to Samuel E. Slaymaker, Nov. 5, 1901, B1, Slaymaker Correspondence, WVU.

23. C.F. Moore to Samuel E. Slaymaker, Dec. 9, 1901, B1, Slaymaker Correspondence, WVU.

24. C.F. Moore to Samuel E. Slaymaker, March 6, 1902, B1, Slaymaker Correspondence, WVU.

25. Albert Thompson to Samuel E. Slaymaker, March 24 and April 30, 1902, B1, Slaymaker Correspondence, WVU.

26. Roy B. Clarkson, *Tumult on the Mountain: Lumbering in West Virginia* (Parsons, W.Va.: McClain Printing Co., 1964), 88; Tom Miller, *Who Owns West Virginia?* reprint from the *Herald-Advertiser* and the *Herald-Dispatch* (Huntington, W.Va., Dec. 1974), pp. 3, 15.

27. "The Last Will and Testament of Henry Gassaway Davis," typescript, WVU. T.B. Davis, Jr., the senator's nephew, was president of the Blaine Mining Company, whose headquarters were at One Broadway Avenue, New York. T.B. Davis, Jr., to Samuel E. Slaymaker, Nov. 6, 1907, B1, Slaymaker Correspondence, WVU.

10. Federal Politics

1. Barbara J. Howe, project director, and Gillian Mace Berman and Melissa Conley-Spencer, *The Monongahela National Forest, 1915–1990*, U.S. Forest Service Bulletin (Washington, D.C., 1992), 82.

2. Shelly Smith Mastran and Nan Lowerre, *Mountaineers and Rangers: A History of Federal Forest Management in the Southern Appalachians*, U.S. Forest Service Bulletin no. 380 (Washington, D.C., 1983), 17.

3. Rudolph Dieffenbach to M.L. Taylor, July 15, 1914, "Correspon-

dence of the Field Office Title Attorney," Monongahela National Forest, Records of the U.S. Forest Service, Record Group 95, National Archives; Wilbur Bridges to Henry Gassaway Davis, Oct. 8, 1913, and March 13, 1914, Henry Gassaway Davis Papers, ser. 14, Box 202, FFB, WVU.

4. Howe, Berman, and Conley-Spencer, *Monongahela National Forest*, 82.

5. Mastran and Lowerre, *Mountaineers and Rangers*, 23, 27.

6. The title of E.J. and W.T. Heishman was "so defective that condemnation is preferred to sale," Francis G. Caffey wrote to Frederick Goshorn on June 11, 1915. "Correspondence of the Field Office Title Attorney," RG 95, National Archives.

7. Monthly Surveyors' Reports, Forest Service Division of Land Acquisition, Box 49, RG 95, National Archives.

8. Ibid.

9. U.S. Congress, *Congressional Record*, 61st Cong., 2d Sess., 1910, vol. 45, pt. 8, June 24, pp. 8974–79; Howe, Berman, and Conley-Spencer, *Monongahela National Forest*, 82.

10. Charles D. Smith, "The Movement for Eastern National Forests, 1899–1911," Ph.D. diss., Harvard Univ., 1956, p. 18.

11. Ronald D Eller, *Miners, Millhands, and Mountaineers: Industrialization of the Appalachian South, 1880–1930* (Knoxville: Univ. of Tennessee Press, 1982), 116–17.

12. Mastran and Lowerre, *Mountaineers and Rangers*, 10, quoting the *Message from the President of the United States Transmitting a Report of the Secretary of Agriculture in Relation to the Forests, Rivers, and Mountains of the Southern Appalachian Region* (Washington, D.C.: GPO, 1902), 24.

13. Mastran and Lowerre, *Mountaineers and Rangers*, v; Eller, *Miners, Millhands, and Mountaineers*, 117; Carl Alwin Schenk, *The Birth of Forestry in America: The Biltmore Forest School, 1898–1913* (Santa Cruz, Calif.: Forest History Society and the Appalachian Consortium, 1974), 92; Ashley L. Schiff, *Fire and Water: Scientific Heresy in the Forest Service* (Cambridge, Mass.: Harvard Univ. Press, 1962), 1–5, 118–23.

14. The indigenous Cherokee Indian culture was disestablished in the 1830s by the quest for land. See James Mooney, *Myths of the Cherokee* (New York: Johnson Reprint Corp., 1970), 130–35; William M. Strickland, "The Rhetoric of Cherokee Indian Removal from Georgia, 1828–32," Ph.D. diss., Louisiana State Univ. and Agricultural and Mechanical College, 1975, pp. 56–140.

15. Stephen B. Elkins died of cancer in Elkins on January 10, 1911, two months before the Weeks Act was passed. His son Davis Elkins was appointed to fill his unexpired term until a successor was named. John Alexander Williams, *West Virginia and the Captains of Industry* (Morgantown: West Virginia Univ. Library, 1976), 242.

16. U.S. Congress, *Congressional Record*, 61st Cong. 2d Sess., 1910, vol. 45, pt. 8, pp. 8974–79.

17. "Correspondence of the Field Office Title Attorney," RG 95, National Archives.

18. C.M. Hendley to William L. Hall, July 13, 1914, "Correspondence of the Forest Service Records Examiner," RG 95, National Archives.

19. Durwood Dunn, *Cades Cove: The Life and Death of a Southern Appalachian Community, 1818–1937* (Knoxville: Univ. of Tennessee Press, 1988), 241–54. Dunn examines the experience of a small and flourishing community of farmers that was forced off the land by federal forestry practices.

20. Thomas Cover to E.D. Clark, March 23, 1915, "Correspondence of the Field Office Title Attorney," RG 95, National Archives.

21. Charles Warren, assistant attorney general, statement, March 12, 1915, "Correspondence of the Field Office Title Attorney," RG 95, National Archives.

22. Two such investigations explore this issue eloquently: John Gaventa, *Power and Powerlessness: Quiescence and Rebellion in an Appalachian Valley* (Urbana: Univ. of Illinois Press, 1980), and Robert Fellmeth, *The Politics of Land* (New York: Grossman Publishers, 1973). Abuse of the railroad's ability to condemn land is hinted at in a May 16, 1887, letter to railroad executive John T. McGraw from West Virginia mine inspector O.A. Veazey. Veazey told McGraw, "If you want to build a road through the *best* mineral and timber region of the state, follow up the main left hand fork of Tygarts Valley to its head, pass around the head waters of Elk River and come down Gauley." John T. McGraw Papers, A and M 86, B5, WVU.

23. Howe, Berman, and Conley-Spencer, *Monongahela National Forest*, 48.

24. Paul Wallace Gates, "The Role of the Speculator in Western Development," *Pennsylvania Magazine of History and Biography* 66 (July 1942): 328.

25. The ten are Mower Lumber Company, 59,787 acres; Neva S. McMullen, 25,000; Coastal Lumber Company, 21,010; J.M. Huber, 19,635; Eastern Associated Coal Company, 15,230; Davis Elkins et al., 14,309; Island Creek Coal Company, 12,772; Sun Lumber Company, 6,000; Pardee and Curtin, 3,406, and Georgia Pacific, 2,810. Tom Miller, *Who Owns West Virginia?*, reprint from the *Herald-Advertiser* and the *Herald-Dispatch* (Huntington, W.Va., Dec. 1974), p. 6.

26. The nine are Chessie System, 49,929 acres; West Virginia Power and Transmission Company, 22,280; Island Creek Coal Company, 6,584; Baltimore Company, 4,031; Monongahela Power Company, 2,775; Baird Catzmer, 1,719; Allegheny Properties Inc., 1,718; Frazee Lumber Company, (est.) 4,650; and Eastern Associated Coal Company, 397. Ibid.

27. The five are Chessie System, 53,623 acres; Savoy Industries, 56,430; Mower Lumber Company, 53,449; Georgia Pacific, 9,000; and Island Creek Coal, 4,230. Ibid., 5.

28. Ibid., 5–6.

29. Appalachian Land Use Task Force, *Who Owns Appalachia? Landownership and Its Impact* (Lexington: Univ. Press of Kentucky, 1983), 75.

30. Miller, *Who Owns West Virginia?*, 5.

31. Appalachian Land Use Task Force, *Who Owns Appalachia?* 75.

32. Mastran and Lowerre, *Mountaineers and Rangers*, 145–46.

33. Si Kahn, *The Forest Service and Appalachia* (New York: John Hay Whitney Foundation, 1974).

34. *U.S. Stat.* 215; 16 *U.S.C.* 528.

35. Robert Dale Miller, "An Examination of Land Use Planning Problems on the Monongahela National Forest," M.A. thesis, West Virginia Univ., 1977, 35.

36. Appalachian Land Use Task Force, *Who Owns Appalachia?* 13.

37. Mastran and Lowerre, *Mountaineers and Rangers*, 146.

38. U.S. Department of Agriculture, *Economic and Social Problems and Conditions of the Southern Appalachians*, Miscellaneous Publication no. 205 (Washington, D.C.: GPO, 1935), 89.

11. Ptolemaic Politics

1. Charles H. Ambler, *Sectionalism in Virginia from 1776 to 1861* (New York: Russell and Russell, 1964), 267–68.

2. Tom Miller, *Who Owns West Virginia?*, reprint from the *Herald-Advertiser* and the *Herald-Dispatch* (Huntington, W.Va., Dec. 1974), 23.

3. David E. White, "The Property Tax in West Virginia: Adequacy, Legitimacy, and Equity," in *Property Taxes in West Virginia*, Institute for Public Affairs Policy Monograph no. 4 (Morgantown: West Virginia Univ., 1991), 43, 44.

4. Gordon C. Bjork, *Life, Liberty, and Property: The Economics and Politics of Land-Use Planning and Environmental Controls* (Lexington, Mass.: Lexington Books, 1980), 21, 22, 30.

5. Georgio De Santillana, *The Crime of Galileo* (Chicago: Univ. of Chicago Press, 1955), 3–4; Ramsey Martin, "Conceptual Obsolescence and Land Use Policy," in *Toward a New Land Use Ethic*, Proceedings of the Piedmont Environmental Council (Warrenton, Va., 1981), 116–23.

6. Richard T. Selden, "Land Use Problems: An Economist's Perspective," in *Toward a New Land Use Ethic*, 95.

7. Ibid., 94.

8. Yue Jin Shi, Timothy T. Phipps, and Dale Colyer, "Agricultural Land Values under Urbanizing Influences," draft typescript, 1993, Department of Agricultural Economics, West Virginia Univ., p. 3.

9. Hettiarachchige Banduratne and Dale Colyer, "Farmland Assessment and Taxation in West Virginia," in *Property Taxes in West Virginia*, Institute for Public Affairs Policy Monograph no. 4 (Morgantown: West Virginia Univ., 1991), 70–71.

10. U.S. Department of Commerce, *Proceedings of the Land Values Workshop*, vol. 2, edited by Gene Wunderlich (Washington, D.C.: GPO, 1982), 23, 19.

11. Virginia, *Proceedings and Debates of the Virginia State Convention of 1829–1830*, 2 vols. (Richmond: S. Shepherd and Co., 1830; Richmond: reprint, New York: DaCapo Press, 1971), 1: 66.

12. U.S. Department of Agriculture, *Economic and Social Problems and Conditions of the Southern Appalachians*, Miscellaneous Publication no. 205 (Washington, D.C.: GPO, 1935), 93.

13. Shelly Smith Mastran and Nan Lowerre, *Mountaineers and Rangers: A History of Federal Forest Management in the Southern Appalachians*, U.S. Forest Service Bulletin no. 380 (Washington, D.C., 1983), 27, v; A.B. Brooks, *West Virginia Geological Survey*, vol. 5, *Forestry and Wood Industries* (Morgantown, W.Va.: Acme Publishers, 1911), 102, 103, 246, 285–86.

14. Appalachian Land Use Task Force, *Who Owns Appalachia? Landownership and Its Impact* (Lexington: Univ. Press of Kentucky, 1983), 38.

15. Mastran and Lowerre, *Mountaineers and Rangers*, 23.

Bibliography

PRIMARY SOURCES

Manuscripts

National Archives and Records Administration, Washington, D.C.
  Records of the U.S. Forest Service, Record Group 95
West Virginia and Regional History Collection, West Virginia University Library, Morgantown, W.Va.
  Aretas Brooks Fleming Papers
  Coal and Coke Railway of West Virginia. First Annual Report, 1905.
  David Dare Brown Notebooks
  Davis Coal and Coke Records
  Deakins Family Papers
  Ezekiel Harper Papers
  Francis H. Pierpont Papers
  George Fairfax Papers
  Gideon Camden Papers
  Hardy and Hampshire County Papers
  Henry Gassaway Davis Papers
  Hubbard Family Papers
  J.N. Camden Papers
  Jesse Parsons Papers
  John T. McGraw Papers
  Minute Book, William Whitmer and Sons, Inc.
  Minute Books, Tucker County Lumber Corporations
  Preston and Virginia Papers, Draper Collection
  Randolph County Historic Records Survey
  Samuel Price Papers
  Stephen B. Elkins Papers
  Tucker County Records
  West Virginia Central and Pittsburg Railway Company Annual Report, 1899.
  West Virginia Pulp and Paper Company Records
  William P. Haymond Notebook
  William Parker Foulke Papers

Maps in the West Virginia and Regional History Collection, West Virginia University Library, Morgantown, W.Va.

A Correct Map of Virginia [By Samuel Lewis. Philadelphia: Carey, 1814]

Henry Gassaway Davis maps [1885]

Important Farmlands of Monroe County, W.Va., Morgantown, W.Va.: U.S. Soil Conservation Service, 1980.

Inventory of Publicly Owned Lands, 1940

A Survey of the Northern Neck of Virginia Being the Lands Belonging to the R^t Honourable Thomas Lord Fairfax Baron Cameron, Bounded By and within the Bay of Chesapoyocke and between the rivers Rappahannock and Potowmack: with the courses of the rivers Rappahannock and Potowmack, in Virginia, as surveyed according to order in the years 1736 and 1737. n.p. n.d.

The Potomac Highlands [1974]

Spruce Knob and Seneca Rocks, 1965

The State of Virginia from the Best Authorities, 1799. (n.p.) I. Low, publisher, [1799]

State of West Virginia, with County Seats. Charleston, W.Va.: West Virginia State Road Commission [1960]

The Ward Lands, Randolph County, n.d.

Map of West Virginia Showing Mother Counties of 1790 and Development of Present Counties, n.d.

West Virginia County and District Map, 1872

West Virginia Principal Railroads. Charleston, W.Va.: West Virginia State Road Commission. [1960]

Government Documents

U.S. Supreme Court *Reports*

Fairfax's Devisee v. *Hunter's Lessee*, 7 Cranch 625 (1816)

Green and others v. *Biddle*, 21 U.S. 1; 8 Wheat. 1 (1823)

Kentucky Union Co. v. *Kentucky*, 219 U.S. 40 (1910)

King v. *Mullins*, 171 U.S. 404 (1897)

King v. *Panther Lumber Co.*, 219 U.S. 437 (1897)

King v. *State of West Virginia and Spruce Coal and Lumber Co.*, 216 U.S. 92 (1910)

King v. *West Virginia and Buskirk*, 216 U.S. 92 (1910)

King v. *West Virginia and Mills*, 216 U.S. 92 (1910)

Other Federal Documents

Bituminous Operators' Special Committee. "A Summary of Statement on Comparative Efficiency of Labor in the Bituminous Coal

Industry under Union and Non-Union Operation." *Briefs and Other Communications Submitted to the United States Coal Commission.* vol. 3. Washington, D.C., 1923. Microfilm.

Brooks, A.B. *West Virginia Geological Survey.* vol. 5, *Forestry and Wood Industries.* Morgantown, W.Va.: Acme Publishers, 1911.

Erwin, Robert B. *West Virginia Gazetteer of Place Names.* West Virginia Geological and Economical Survey, vol. V-24. Morgantown, W.Va.: Mont, Chateau Research Center, 1986.

Gannett, Henry. *A Gazetteer of West Virginia.* U.S. Geological Survey Bulletin no. 233. 1904; Washington, D.C.: GPO, 1975.

Reger, David B. *West Virginia Geological Survey: Tucker County.* Wheeling, W.Va., Wheeling News Litho Co., 1923.

———. *West Virginia Geological Survey: Mercer, Monroe, and Summers Counties.* Wheeling, W.Va.: Wheeling News Litho Co., 1926.

U.S. Census Office. *Census Population Schedules,* The National Archives, National Archives and Records Administration, General Services Administration, microfilm 1870, 1910, Randolph, Tucker, Pocahontas counties, West Virginia.

U.S. Congress. *Congressional Record,* 61st Cong. 2d. Sess., 1910, vol. 45, pt. 8, June 24, 1910.

———. Senate. *Agriculture, Rural Development and the Use of the Land.* Washington, D.C.: GPO, 1974.

U.S. Department of Agriculture. *Economic and Social Problems and Conditions of the Southern Appalachians.* Miscellaneous Publication no. 205. Washington, D.C.: GPO, 1935.

———. Economic Research Service. "Foreign Ownership of U.S. Agricultural Land through December 31, 1988." By Gertrude S. Butler and J. Peter DeBraal. Washington, D.C.: GPO, April 1989.

U.S. Department of Commerce. *Proceedings of the Land Values Workshop.* Edited by Gene Wunderlich. Washington, D.C.: GPO, 1982.

U.S. Department of Commerce. Bureau of the Census. *Thirteenth Census, 1910.* Washington, D.C.: GPO, 1913–14.

U.S. Department of the Interior. Census Office. *Eleventh Census, 1890.* Washington, D.C.: GPO, 1895.

———. *Ninth Census, 1870.* Washington, D.C.: GPO, 1872.

———. *Tenth Census, 1880.* Washington, D.C.: GPO, 1883.

———. *Twelfth Census, 1900.* Washington, D.C.: GPO, 1902.

U.S. Forest Service, Eastern Region. "Final Environmental Impact Statement and Land Management Plan for the Monongahela National Forest." Typescript, 1977.

State and County Documents

Acts of Confederate Virginia, 1863.

Acts of the General Assembly of the Restored Government of Virginia, 1862.

Acts of Virginia General Assembly, 1804–63.

Acts of West Virginia, 1861–1901.

Alexander Shaw v. *H.G. Davis et al.*, 78 Maryland 308 (1893).

Clay County Industrial Development Authority. Archives and Working Papers. 1961. Microfilm.

Henning, William Waller. *The Statutes at Large of Virginia.* Vol. 10. Richmond, 1822.

Virginia. Clay County Deed Books.

———. County Land Entry Books: Index to Records of Commissioners for Adjudication Claims to Unpatented Land.

———. *Journal, Acts and Proceedings of a General Convention of the State of Virginia Assembled at Richmond on Monday, the Fourteenth Day of October, Eighteen Hundred and Fifty.* Richmond: W. Culley, printer, 1850.

———. Land Office Records. Microfilm.

———. Pendleton County Assessment Book.

———. Pendleton County Order Book, 1788–94.

———. Pocahontas County Deed Books.

———. *Proceedings and Debates of the Virginia State Convention, 1829–30.* 2 vols. Richmond: S. Shepherd and Co., 1830; reprint, New York: DaCapo Press, 1971.

———. Randolph County Deed Books.

———. Randolph County Index of Wills.

———. Tucker County Circuit Court Records.

———. Tucker County Deed Books.

West Virginia. Clay County Deed Books.

———. *Debates and Proceedings, First Constitutional Convention, 1861–63.* Edited by Charles H. Ambler, Frances Haney Atwood, and William B. Matthews. Huntington, W.Va.: Gentry Brothers, printers, n.d.

———. Kanawha County Deed Books.

———. Pendleton County Deed Books.

———. Board of Agriculture. *Second Biennial Report, 1893 and 1894.* Charleston, W.Va.: Moses Donnally, 1894.

———. Board of Agriculture. *Third Biennial Report, 1895 and 1896.* Charleston, W.Va.: Moses Donnally, 1896.

———. Department of Human Services. *Annual Report, 1975.* Charleston: West Virginia Department of Human Services, 1975.

———. House of Delegates. *Journal for the Fourth Session.* Wheeling: John Frew, public printer, 1866–68.

West Virginia. *Manual of the Legislature and of the Executive and Judiciary for 1869.* Wheeling, W.Va.: John Frew, public printer, 1869.

———. Senate. *Journal of the Sixth Session.* Wheeling: John Frew, public printer, 1867–68.

———. Tax Commission. *Second Report, State Development.* Wheeling: Charles H. Taney, state printer, 1884.

Willis, Todd C., comp. and ed. *West Virginia Bluebook, 1984.* Charleston, W.Va.: Jarrett Printing Co., 1984.

SECONDARY SOURCES

Books and Pamphlets

Abernethy, Thomas Perkins. *From Frontier to Plantation in Tennessee: A Study in Frontier Democracy,* Chapel Hill: Univ. of North Carolina Press, 1932.

———. *Three Virginia Frontiers.* Baton Rouge: Louisiana State Univ. Press, 1940.

———. *Western Lands and the American Revolution.* Univ. of Virginia Institute for Research in the Social Sciences Monograph 25. New York: Russell and Russell, 1937.

Adams, Henry. *The Education of Henry Adams.* New York: Heritage Press, 1942.

———. *The United States in 1800.* Ithaca, N.Y.: Cornell Univ. Press, 1971.

Ambler, Charles H. *Francis H. Pierpont: Union War Governor of Virginia and Father of West Virginia.* Chapel Hill: Univ. of North Carolina Press, 1937.

———. *George Washington and the West.* Chapel Hill: Univ. of North Carolina Press, 1936.

———. *Sectionalism in Virginia from 1776 to 1861.* New York: Russell and Russell, 1964.

———. *Thomas Ritchie: A Study in Virginia Politics.* Richmond: Bell Book and Stationery Co., 1913.

———. *West Virginia, the Mountain State.* New York: Prentice-Hall, 1940.

Appalachian Land Use Task Force. *Who Owns Appalachia? Landownership and Its Impact.* Lexington: Univ. Press of Kentucky, 1983.

Aptheker, Herbert. *American Negro Slave Revolts.* New York: International Publishers Co., 1963.

Aston, T.H., and C.H.E. Philpin. *The Brenner Debate: Agrarian Class Structure and Economic Development in Pre-Industrial Europe.* New York: Cambridge Univ. Press, 1990.

Atkinson, George, ed. *Bench and Bar of West Virginia.* Charleston, W.Va.: Virginia Law Book Co., 1919.

Bailyn, Bernard. *The Ideological Origins of the American Revolution.* Cambridge, Mass.: Harvard Univ. Press, 1967.

———. *The Peopling of British North America.* New York: Knopf, 1986.

———. *Voyagers to the West: A Passage in the Peopling of America on the Eve of the Revolution.* New York: Knopf, 1986.

Barton, William E. *Hero in Homespun: Tale of the Loyal South.* Boston: Lamson, Wolffe, and Co., 1897.

Beard, Charles A. *An Economic Interpretation of the Constitution.* New York: Macmillan, 1935.

Beard, Charles A., and Mary Beard. *The Rise of American Civilization.* New York: Macmillan, 1930.

194   *Bibliography*

Bergoffen, William W. *100 Years of Federal Forestry.* U.S. Department of Agriculture Bulletin no. 402. Washington, D.C., 1976.

Bjork, Gordon C. *Life, Liberty, and Property: The Economics and Politics of Land-Use Planning and Environmental Controls.* Lexington, Mass.: Lexington Books, 1980.

Blackhurst, W.E. *Riders on the Flood.* New York: Vantage Press, 1954.

Bobbitt, John. *Families of Nicholas County, West Virginia.* Washington, D.C.: John Bobbitt, 1979.

Bosworth, A.S. *A History of Randolph County from Its Earliest Exploration and Settlement to the Present Time.* Elkins, W.Va., 1920.

Braudel, Fernand. *Civilization and Capitalism, 15th–18th Century.* Vol. 1, *The Structures of Everyday Life: The Limits of the Possible.* Translation revised by Siân Reynolds. Berkeley: Univ. of California Press, 1992.

———. *Civilization and Capitalism, 15th–18th Century.* Vol. 2, *The Wheels of Commerce.* Translaion by Siân Reynolds. New York: Harper and Row, 1979.

———. *On History.* Translated by Sarah Matthews. Chicago: Univ. of Chicago Press, 1980.

Breen, T.H., and Stephen Innes. *Myne Own Ground.* New York: Oxford Univ. Press, 1980.

Brooks-Smith, Joan E., comp. *Master Index of Virginia Surveys and Grants, 1774–1791.* Frankfort: Kentucky Historical Society, 1976.

Brown, Stuart E., Jr. *Virginia Baron: The Story of Thomas, 6th Lord Fairfax.* Berryville, Va.: Chesapeake Book Co., 1965.

Bruce, Kathleen. *Virginia Iron Manufacturing in the Slave Era, 1800–1860.* New York: Century, 1931.

Buck, Paul. *The Road to Reunion.* Boston: Little, Brown, 1937.

Byrne, W.E.R. *Tale of the Elk.* Richwood, W.Va.: Mountain State Press, 1940.

Callahan, James M. *A Semi-Centennial History of West Virginia.* Charleston, W.Va.: Semi-Centennial Commission of West Virginia, 1913.

Campbell, John C. *The Southern Highlander and His Homeland.* New York: Russell Sage Foundation, 1921; Lexington: Univ. Press of Kentucky, 1969.

Carter, Eleanor Youst, and Kathleen M. Bogdan, comps. *Unpatented Land Records of Monongalia, Yohogania, and Ohio Counties, Virginia, 1766–1794.* Fairmont, W.Va.: Genealogical Club, 1988.

Caruso, John A. *The Appalachian Frontier: America's First Surge Westward.* New York: Bobbs-Merrill, 1959.

Caudill, Harry M. *Night Comes to the Cumberlands: A Biography of a Depressed Area.* Boston: Little, Brown, 1963.

Clark, Blanche Henry. *The Tennessee Yeoman, 1840–1860.* New York: Octagon Books, 1971.

Clarkson, Roy B. *On Beyond Leatherbark.* Parsons, W.Va.: McClain Printing Co., 1991.

———. *Tumult on the Mountain: Lumbering in West Virginia.* Parsons, W.Va.: McClain Printing Co., 1964.

Clay County History Book Committee. *History of Clay County.* Salem, W.Va.: Don Mills, 1989.

Colyer, Dale, and Anthony Ferrise. *Real Property: Farmland Rental Values in West Virginia and Property Tax Implications.* R.D. Publication no. 721. Morgantown, W.Va.: Center for Extension and Continuing Education, 1984.

———. *Real Property: Questions and Answers on West Virginia's Surface Owners Rights Bill—Oil and Gas.* R.D. Publication no. 722. Morgantown, W.Va.: Center for Extension and Continuing Education [1984?]

Comstock, Jim, ed. *West Virginia Heritage Encyclopedia.* vols. 4, 10–11. Richwood, W.Va.: Jim Comstock, 1976.

Conley, Phil. *History of the West Virginia Coal Industry.* Charleston: West Virginia Educational Foundation, 1960.

Cook, Roy Bird. *Washington's Western Lands.* Strasburg, Va.: Shenandoah Publishing House, 1930.

Core, Earl. *The Monongalia Story: A Bicentennial History.* vol. 2, *The Pioneers.* Parsons, W.Va.: McClain Printing Co., 1976.

Crane, Verner W. *The Southern Frontier, 1670–1732.* New York: Norton, 1981.

Craven, Avery O. *Soil Exhaustion as a Factor in the Agricultural History of Virginia and Maryland, 1606–1860.* Univ. of Illinois Studies in the Social Sciences, vol. 13, no. 1. Urbana: Univ. of Illinois, 1926.

Craven, Wesley Frank. *The Southern Colonies in the Seventeenth Century, 1607–1689.* Baton Rouge: Louisiana State Univ. Press, 1970.

Crumrine, Boyd. *The County Court for the District of West Augusta, Va., Held at Augusta Town, near Washington, 1776–1777.* Washington, D.C.: Washington Historical Society, 1910.

Davis, David Brion. *The Slave Power Conspiracy and the Paranoid Style.* Baton Rouge: Louisiana State Univ. Press, 1969.

Day, John F. *Bloody Ground.* Reprint. Lexington: Univ. Press of Kentucky, 1981.

DeGruyter, Julius. *The Kanawha Spectator.* vol. 1. Charleston, W.Va.: DeGruyter, 1953.

DeHass, Willis. *History of the Early Settlement and Indian Wars of Western Virginia.* Reprint. Parsons, W.Va.: McClain Printing Co., 1960.

De Santillana, Georgio. *The Crime of Galileo.* Chicago: Univ. of Chicago Press, 1955.

Doddridge, Joseph. *Notes on the Settlement and Indian Wars of Western Parts of Virginia and Pennsylvania from 1763 to 1783, Inclusive, Together with a Review of the First State of Society and Manners of the First Settlers of the Western Country.* Pittsburgh: John S. Ritenour and William T. Lindsey, 1912.

Du Bois, W.E.B. *Black Reconstruction: An Essay toward a History of the Part which Black Folk Played in the Attempt to Reconstruct Democracy in America, 1860–1880.* Philadelphia: Harcourt Brace and Co., 1935.

Dumond, Dwight. *Antislavery Origins of the Civil War in the United States.* Ann Arbor: Univ. of Michigan Press, 1939.

Dunn, Durwood. *Cades Cove: The Life and Death of a Southern Appalachian Community, 1818–1937.* Knoxville: Univ. of Tennessee Press, 1988.

Dyer, Morgan H. *Dyer's Index to Land Grants in West Virginia.* Charleston, W.Va.: Moses W. Donnally, 1896.

Dysart, Benjamin, and Marion Clawson. *Public Interest in the Use of Private Lands.* New York: Praeger, 1989.

Eller, Ronald D. *Miners, Millhands, and Mountaineers: Industrialization of the Appalachian South, 1880–1930.* Knoxville: Univ. of Tennessee Press, 1982.

Ellis, David, ed. *The Frontier in American Development: Essays in Honor of Paul Wallace Gates.* Ithaca, N.Y.: Cornell Univ. Press, 1968.

Ergood, Bruce, and Bruce Kuhre. *Appalachia: Social Context, Past and Present.* Dubuque, Iowa: Kendall/Hunt Co., 1983.

Erikson, Kai. *Everything in Its Path.* New York: Simon and Schuster, 1976.

Fansler, Homer. *History of Tucker County, West Virginia.* Parsons, W.Va.: McClain Printing Co., 1962.

Feller, Daniel. *The Public Lands in Jacksonian Politics.* Madison: Univ. of Wisconsin Press, 1984.

Fellmeth, Robert. *The Politics of Land.* New York: Grossman Publishers, 1973.

Findley, William. *History of the Insurrection in the Four Western Counties of Pennsylvania in the Year 1794.* Philadelphia: Samuel Harrison Smith, printer, 1794.

Fischer, David Hackett. *Albion's Seed: Four British Folkways in America.* New York: Oxford Univ. Press, 1989.

Fogel, Robert A., and Stanley L. Engerman. *Time on the Cross: The Economics of American Negro Slavery.* Boston: Little, Brown, 1974.

Foner, Eric. *Reconstruction: America's Unfinished Revolution, 1863–1877.* New York: Harper and Row, 1988.

Fox-Genovese, Elizabeth, and Eugene D. Genovese. *Fruits of Merchant Capital.* New York: Oxford Univ. Press, 1983.

Freehling, Alison Goodyear. *Drift toward Dissolution: The Virginia Slavery Debate of 1831–1832.* Baton Rouge: Louisiana State Univ. Press, 1982.

Gaventa, John. *Power and Powerlessness: Quiescence and Rebellion in an Appalachian Valley.* Urbana: Univ. of Illinois Press, 1980.

Geiger, George Raymond. *The Theory of the Land Question.* New York: Macmillan, 1936.

Geisler, Charles C., and Frank J. Popper, eds. *Land Reform American Style.* Totowa, N.J.: Rowman and Allanheld, 1984.

Genovese, Eugene D. *The Political Economy of Slavery: Studies in the Economy and Society of the Slave South.* New York: Vintage Books, 1965.

Giffin, Keith B. *Land Concentration and Rural Poverty.* New York: Holmes and Meier, 1976.
Gilbert, L. *The Land Warrant Swindle.* New Martinsville, W.Va.: Daniel Long, [1874].
Gray, L.C. *History of Agriculture in the United States to 1860.* Reprint. Clifton, N.J.: A.M. Kelly, 1973.
Green, Jack P. *Colonies to Nation, 1763–1789: A Documentary History of the American Revolution.* New York: Norton, 1975.
Gude, Gilbert. *Where the Potomac Begins: A History of North Branch Valley.* Washington, D.C.: Seven Locks Press, 1984.
Haga, Pauline, comp. *Miscellaneous Records of Monroe County.* vol. 1, to 1799. Crab Orchard, W.Va., n.d.
Hahn, Steven. *The Roots of Southern Populism: Yeoman Farmers and the Transformation of the Georgia Upcountry, 1850–1890.* New York: Oxford Univ. Press, 1983.
Hahn, Steven, and Jonathan Prude, eds. *The Countryside in the Age of Capitalist Transformation: Essays in the Social History of Rural America.* Chapel Hill: Univ. of North Carolina Press, 1985.
Hall, Granville Davisson. *The Rending of Virginia.* Chicago, 1901.
Hill, David S. *Landlord and Tenant Law.* St. Paul, Minn.: West Publishing Co., 1980.
Hilliard, Sam. *Hogmeat and Hoecake: Food Supply in the Old South, 1840–1860.* Carbondale: Southern Illinois Univ. Press, 1972.
Historical Records Survey. Division of Women's and Professional Projects, Works Progress Administration. *Calendar of the Arthur I. Boreman Letters in the State Department of Archives and History.* Charleston, W.Va.: The Historical Records Survey, January 1939.
Hofstadter, Richard. *America at 1750: A Social Portrait.* New York: Vintage Books, 1971.
Howe, Barbara J., project director, and Gillian Mace Berman and Melissa Conley-Spencer. *The Monongahela National Forest, 1915–1990.* U.S. Forest Service Bulletin. Washington, D.C., 1992.
Hunt, George T. *The Wars of the Iroquois: A Study in Intertribal Trade Relations.* Madison: Univ. of Wisconsin Press, 1940.
Inscoe, John. *Mountain Masters, Slavery, and the Sectional Crisis in Western North Carolina.* Knoxville: Univ. of Tennessee Press, 1989.
Isaac, Rhys. *The Transformation of Virginia, 1740–1790.* Williamsburg, Va.: Institute of Early American History and Culture, 1982.
Jefferson, Thomas. *Notes on the State of Virginia.* Edited by William Peden. Chapel Hill: Univ. of North Carolina Press, 1955.
Jennings, Francis. *Empire of Fortune: Crowns, Colonies, and Tribes in the Seven Years War in America.* New York: Norton, 1988.
Jones, E. *Principles of Railroad Transportation.* New York, 1924.
Kahn, Si. *The Forest Service and Appalachia.* New York: John Hay Whitney Foundation, 1974.
Kenny, Hamill Thomas. *West Virginia Place Names, Their Origin and Meaning, Including the Nomenclature of the Streams and Mountains.* Piedmont, W.Va.: Place Name Press, 1945.

Kenyon, Cecelia M., ed. *The Antifederalists*. Boston: Northeastern Univ. Press, 1985.

Kephart, Horace. *Our Southern Highlanders*. New York: Macmillan, 1922.

Klein, Rachel N. *Unification of a Slave State: The Rise of the Planter Class in the South Carolina Backcountry, 1760–1808*. Chapel Hill: Univ. of North Carolina Press, 1990.

Koontz, Louis K. *The Virginia Frontier*. Baltimore: Johns Hopkins Univ. Press, 1925.

Kulikoff, Allan. *The Agrarian Origins of American Capitalism*. Charlottesville: Univ. Press of Virginia, 1992.

Lemish, L. Jesse, ed. *Benjamin Franklin: The Autobiography and Other Writings*. New York: Signet Classics, 1961.

Lewis, George E. *The Indiana Company, 1763–1798: A Study in Eighteenth Century Frontier Land Speculation and Business Venture*. Glendale, Calif.: Arthur H. Clark Co., 1941.

Lewis, Ronald L. *Coal, Iron, and Slaves: Industrial Slavery in Maryland and Virginia, 1715–1865*. Westport, Conn.: Greenwood Press, 1979.

Leyburn, James G. *The Scotch-Irish: A Social History*. Chapel Hill: Univ. of North Carolina Press, 1962.

Limerick, Patricia Nelson. *The Legacy of Conquest: The Unbroken Past of the American West*. New York: Norton, 1988.

Lustig, Mary Lou. *Robert Hunter, 1666–1734: New York's August Statesman*. Syracuse, N.Y.: Syracuse Univ. Press, 1983.

McKinney, Gordon. *Southern Mountain Republicans, 1865–1900: Politics and the Appalachian Community*. Chapel Hill: Univ. of North Carolina Press, 1978.

McWhiney, Grady. *Cracker Culture: Celtic Ways in the Old South*. Tuscaloosa: Univ. of Alabama Press, 1988.

Main, Jackson Turner. *The Antifederalists*. New York: Norton, 1961.

Malone, Dumas. *Jefferson and the Ordeal of Liberty*. Boston: Little, Brown, 1962.

———. *Jefferson and the Rights of Man*. Boston: Little, Brown, 1951.

Mastran, Shelly Smith, and Nan Lowerre. *Mountaineers and Rangers: A History of Federal Forest Management in the Southern Appalachians*. U.S. Forest Service Bulletin no. 380. Washington, D.C., 1983.

Maxwell, Hu. *History of Randolph County, West Virginia, from Its Earliest Settlement to the Present*. Reprint. Parsons, W.Va.: McClain Printing Co., 1961.

Miles, Emma Bell. *The Spirit of the Mountains*. Reprint. Knoxville: Univ. of Tennessee Press, 1975.

Miller, Tom D. *Who Owns West Virginia?* reprinted from the *Herald-Advertiser* and the *Herald-Dispatch*. Huntington, W.Va., Dec. 1974.

Mitchell, Robert D. *Commercialism and Frontier: Perspectives on the Early Shenandoah Valley*. Charlottesville: Univ. Press of Virginia, 1977.

————. ed. *Appalachian Frontiers: Settlement, Society, and Development in the Pre-Industrial Era.* Lexington: Univ. Press of Kentucky, 1991.

Mooney, James. *Myths of the Cherokee.* New York: Johnson Reprint Corp., 1970.

Moore, Barrington, Jr. *Social Origins of Dictatorship and Democracy: Lord and Peasant in the Making of the Modern World.* Boston: Beacon Press, 1966.

Moreland, J. Kenneth, ed. *The Not So Solid South: Anthropological Studies in a Regional Subculture.* Proceedings of the Southern Anthropological Society, no. 4. Athens: Univ. of Georgia Press, 1971.

Morison, Samuel Eliot. *The Oxford History of the American People.* vols. 1–3. New York: Mentor, 1972.

Morton, Oren. *A History of Monroe County, West Virginia.* Staunton, Va.: McClure Co., 1916; Baltimore: Regional Publishing Co., 1974.

Mott, Pearl G. *History of Davis and Canaan.* Parsons, W.Va.: McClain Printing Co., 1972.

North, E.L. *The 55 West Virginias: A Guide to the State's Counties.* Morgantown: West Virginia Univ. Press, 1986.

Nugent, Nell M. *Cavaliers and Pioneers: Abstracts of Virginia Land Patents and Grants, 1623–1800,* vol. 1. Richmond, Va.: Press of the Dietz Printing Co., 1934.

Olmsted, Frederick Law. *The Cotton Kingdom: A Traveller's Observations on Cotton and Slavery in the American Slave States.* Edited by Arthur M. Schlesinger. New York: Knopf, 1953.

Otto, John Solomon. *The Southern Frontiers, 1607–1860: The Agricultural Evolution of the Colonial and Antebellum South.* New York: Greenwood Press, 1989.

Owsley, Frank. *Plain Folk of the Old South.* Baton Rouge: Louisiana State Univ. Press, 1949.

Paludan, Phillip Shaw. *Victims: A True Story of the Civil War.* Knoxville: Univ. of Tennessee Press, 1981.

Pepper, Charles M. *The Life and Times of Henry Gassaway Davis, 1823–1916.* New York: Century, 1920.

Plunkett, H. Dudley, and Mary Jean Bowman. *Elites and Change in the Kentucky Mountains.* Lexington: Univ. Press of Kentucky, 1973.

Pole, J.R. *Foundations of American Independence, 1763–1815.* New York: Bobbs-Merrill, 1972.

Public Land Law Review Commission. *Study of Public Land Timber Policy.* vol 1, *Report and Summary.* Washington, D.C., 1969.

Raine, James Watt. *The Land of Saddle-Bags: A Study of the Mountain People of Appalachia.* New York: Council of Women for Home Missions and Missionary Education Movement of the United States and Canada, 1924.

Ransom, Roger, and Richard Sutch. *One Kind of Freedom: The Economic Consequences of Emancipation.* New York: Oxford Univ. Press, 1985.

Remini, Robert. *Andrew Jackson*. New York: Twayne, 1966.
———. *Andrew Jackson and the Course of American Empire, 1767–1821*. New York: Harper and Row, 1977.
Reynolds, Michael M. *Forests and Forestry in West Virginia: A Bibliography*. Morgantown: West Virginia Univ. Library, 1962.
Rice, Otis K. *The Allegheny Frontier: West Virginia Beginnings, 1730–1830*. Lexington: Univ. Press of Kentucky, 1970.
———. *West Virginia: A History*. Lexington: Univ. Press of Kentucky, 1985.
Rohrbough, Malcolm J. *The Land Office Business: The Settlement and Administration of American Public Lands, 1789–1837*. London: Oxford Univ. Press, 1968.
Rose, Willie Lee. *Rehearsal for Reconstruction: The Port Royal Experiment*. New York: Oxford Univ. Press, 1976.
Sauer, Carl Ortwin. *Land and Life: A Selection from the Writings of Carl Ortwin Sauer*. Edited by John Leighly. Berkeley: Univ. of California Press, 1963.
Savelle, Max. *George Morgan, Colony Builder*. New York: Columbia Univ. Press, 1932.
Schenk, Carl Alwin. *The Birth of Forestry in America: The Biltmore Forest School, 1898–1913*. Santa Cruz, Calif.: Forest History Society and the Appalachian Consortium, 1974.
Schiff, Ashley L. *Fire and Water: Scientific Heresy in the Forest Service*. Cambridge, Mass.: Harvard Univ. Press, 1962.
Schlesinger, Arthur M., Jr. *The Age of Jackson*. Boston: Little, Brown, 1945.
Selby, John E. *The Revolution in Virginia, 1775–1783*. Williamsburg, Va.: Colonial Williamsburg Foundation, 1992.
Shackelford, Laurel, and Bill Weinberg. *Our Appalachia: An Oral History*. New York: Hill and Wang, 1977.
Shamsuden, Noor Bin. *Mineral Rights and Property Taxation in West Virginia*. Morgantown: Division of Resource Management, College of Agriculture and Forestry, West Virginia Univ., 1979.
Shapiro, Henry D. *Appalachia on Our Mind: The Southern Mountains and Mountaineers in the American Consciousness, 1870–1920*. Chapel Hill: Univ. of North Carolina Press, 1978.
Sims, Edgar B. *Making a State: Formation of West Virginia, Including Maps, Illustrations, Plats, Grants, and the Acts of the Virginia Assembly and the Legislature of West Virginia Creating the Counties*. Charleston, W.Va.: Matthews Printing and Lithography Co., 1956.
———. *Sims Index to Land Grants in West Virginia*. Charleston, W.Va.: Rose City Press, 1952.
Slaughter, Thomas P. *The Whiskey Rebellion: Frontier Epilogue to the American Revolution*. New York: Oxford Univ. Press, 1986.
Sosin, Jack. *The Revolutionary Frontier, 1763–1783*. New York: Holt, Rinehart, and Winston, 1967.
Smith, Newlin Russell. *Land for the Small Man: English and Welsh Experience with Publicly Supplied Small Holdings, 1860–1937*. New York: King's Crown Press, 1946.

Stampp, Kenneth M. *The Peculiar Institution: Slavery in the Ante-Bellum South*. New York: Vintage Books, 1956.

———, ed. *The Causes of the Civil War*. New York: Simon and Schuster, 1974.

Stephenson, John B. *Shiloh: A Mountain Community*. Lexington: Univ. Press of Kentucky, 1968.

Still, James B. *River of Earth*. New York: Viking Press, 1940.

Stutler, Boyd. *West Virginia in the Civil War*. Charleston: West Virginia Educational Foundation, 1966.

Summers, Festus P. *William L. Wilson and Tariff Reform*. New Brunswick, N.J.: Rutgers Univ. Press, 1953.

Sydnor, Charles S. *American Revolutionaries in the Making: Political Practices in Washington's Virginia*. New York: Free Press, 1965. [Originally published as *Gentlemen Freeholders* Chapel Hill: University of North Carolina Press, 1952.]

Tate, Thad, and David L. Ammerman, eds. *The Chesapeake in the Seventeenth Century: Essays on Anglo-American Society*. New York: Norton, 1979.

Teeter, Don. *Goin' Up Gandy: A History of the Dry Fork Region of Randolph and Tucker Counties, West Virginia*. Parsons, W.Va.: McClain Printing Co., 1977.

Toynbee, Arnold. *A Study of History, II*. New York: Oxford Univ. Press, 1947.

Tucker, St. George. *A Dissertation on Slavery with a Proposal for the Gradual Abolition of It in the State of Virginia*. Philadelphia: Matthew Carey, 1796.

Wainwright, Nicholas B. *George Croghan: Wilderness Diplomat*. Chapel Hill: Univ. of North Carolina Press, 1959.

Walker, Brenda K., Dennis K. Smith, and Anthony Ferrise. *Real Property: Legal Aspects of Fencers in West Virginia*. R.D. Publication no. 715. Morgantown, W.Va.: West Virginia University Cooperative Extension Service, 1983.

Waller, Altina L. *Feud: Hatfields, McCoys, and Social Change in Appalachia, 1860–1900*. Chapel Hill: Univ. of North Carolina Press, 1988.

Weatherford, Willis D., ed. *Religion in the Appalachian Mountains: A Symposium*. Berea, Ky.: Berea College, 1955.

Weller, Jack. *Yesterday's People: Life in Contemporary Appalachia*. Lexington: Univ. Press of Kentucky, 1965.

Whisnant, David E. *All That's Native and Fine: The Politics of Culture in an American Region*. Chapel Hill: Univ. of North Carolina Press, 1983.

Wiener, Jonathan M. *The Social Origins of the New South*. Baton Rouge: Louisiana State Univ. Press, 1978.

Williams, Harold A. *The Western Maryland Railway Story: A Chronicle of the First Century, 1852–1952*. Baltimore: Western Maryland Railway Company, 1952.

Williams, John Alexander. *West Virginia: A History*. New York: Norton, 1984.

————. *West Virginia and the Captains of Industry.* Morgantown: West Virginia Univ. Library, 1976.

Wirt, William. *Sketches of the Life and Character of Patrick Henry.* Reprint. Freeport, N.Y.: Books for Libraries, 1970.

Wood, Gordon S. *The Creation of the American Republic, 1776–1786.* New York: Norton, 1969.

Woodward, C. Vann. *Origins of the New South, 1877–1913.* Baton Rouge: Louisiana State Univ. Press, 1951.

Wright, Gavin. *Old South, New South: Revolutions in the Southern Economy since the Civil War.* New York: Basic Books, 1986.

————. *The Political Economy of the Cotton South: Households, Markets, and Wealth in the Nineteenth Century.* New York: Norton, 1978.

Young, Alfred, ed. *The American Revolution: Explorations in the History of American Radicalism.* Dekalb: Northern Illinois Univ. Press, 1976.

Articles and Chapters

Allen, James Lane. "Through Cumberland Gap on Horseback." *Harper's* 73 (June 1886): 50–66.

Appleby, Joyce. "Commercial Farming and the 'Agrarian Myth' in the Early Republic." *Journal of American History* 68 (March 1982): 833–49.

Anderson, James Donald. "Vandalia, the First West Virginia." *West Virginia History* 40 (Summer 1979): 375–92.

Bailey, Kenneth. "A Judicious Mixture: Negroes and Immigrants in the West Virginia Mines, 1880–1917." *West Virginia History* 34 (Jan. 1973): 141–61.

Banduratne, Hettiarachchige, and Dale Colyer. "Farmland Assessment and Taxation in West Virginia." In *Property Taxes in West Virginia,* 69–90. Institute for Public Affairs Policy Monograph no. 4. Morgantown: West Virginia Univ., 1991.

Beale, G. William. "Annals of the Northern Neck." *Northern Neck of Virginia Historical Journal* 42 (Dec. 1967): 1620–57.

Beale, Howard. "On Rewriting Reconstruction History." *American Historical Review* 45 (July 1940): 807–27.

Bean, William Gleason. "The Ruffner Pamphlet of 1847, An Anti-Slavery Aspect of Virginia Sectionalism." *Virginia Magazine of History and Biography* 61 (July 1953): 260–82.

Bestor, Arthur. "The American Civil War as a Constitutional Crisis." *American Historical Review* 69, no. 2 (1964): 327–52.

Billings, Dwight, Kathleen Blee, and Louis Swanson. "Culture, Family, and Community in Pre-Industrial Appalachia." *Appalachian Journal* 13 (Winter 1986): 154–69.

Billington, Ray Allen. "The Origin of the Land Speculator as a Frontier Type." *Agricultural History* 19 (1945): 204–13.

Brand, Irene B. "Dunmore's War." *West Virginia History* 40 (Fall 1978): 28–46.

Brenner, Robert. "The Social Basis of Economic Development." In *Analytical Marxism*, edited by John Roemer, 23–53. London: Cambridge Univ. Press, 1986.

Brooks, Douglas. "Land Use in Economic Theory: Principles and Prospects." U.S. Department of Agriculture Economic Research Service Report no. AGE870806. Washington, D.C., 1987.

Buck, Paul. "The Poor Whites of the Antebellum South." *American Historical Review* 31 (Oct. 1925): 41–54.

Burckel, Nicholas C. "Publicizing Progressivism." *West Virginia History* 42 (Spring–Summer 1981): 222–48.

Colyer, Dale, and Anthony Ferrise. "West Virginia Agriculture: 1987 Census of Agriculture: Selected Data from the Advance State Report." Morgantown: West Virginia Univ. Extension Service, 1989.

Conference on Housing as a Land Use Issue. *Housing, the Threshold Problem: A Synopsis of a Conference on Housing as a Land Use Issue.* Morgantown, W.Va.: Center for Extension and Continuing Education, 1978.

Cox, LaWanda, and John H. Cox. "Negro Suffrage and Republican Politics: The Problem of Motivation in Reconstruction Historiography." *Journal of Southern History* 33 (Aug. 1967): 303–20.

Dater, Henry M. "Albert Gallatin—Land Speculator." *Mississippi Valley Historical Review* 26 (1939–40): 21–38.

Foner, Eric. "The Causes of the American Civil War: Recent Interpretations and New Directions." *Civil War History* 20 (Sept. 1974): 197–214.

Ford, Thomas R. "Status, Residence and Fundamentalist Religious Beliefs in the Southern Appalachians." *Social Forces* 39 (1960): 41–49.

Formisano, Ronald P. "Deferential Participant Politics: The Early Republic's Political Culture, 1789–1840." *American Political Science Review* 68 (1974): 473–87.

Friedmann, John. "Poor Regions and Poor Nations: Perspectives on the Problem of Appalachia." *Southern Economic Journal* 32 (April 1966): 465–73.

Frost, William Goodell. "Our Contemporary Ancestors in the Southern Mountains." *Atlantic Monthly* 83 (March 1899): 311–19.

———. "The Southern Mountaineer: Our Kindred of the Boone and Lincoln Type." *American Monthly Review of Reviews* 21 (March 1900): 303–11.

Gates, Paul Wallace. "The Federal Lands: Why We Retained Them." In *Rethinking the Federal Lands*, edited by Sterling Brubaker, 35–73. Washington, D.C.: Resources for the Future, 1984.

———. "Research in the History of Public Lands." *Agricultural History* 48 (Jan. 1974): 31–50.

———. "The Role of the Speculator in Western Development." *Pennsylvania Magazine of History and Biography* 66 (July 1942): 314–33.

———. "Tenants of the Log Cabin." *Mississippi Valley Historical Review* 49 (June 1962): 3–31.

Genovese, Eugene D. "Yeomen Farmers in a Slaveholder's Democracy." *Agricultural History* 49 (April 1975): 331–42.

Gerrard, Nathan L. "Churches of the Stationary Poor in Southern Appalachia." In *Change in Rural Appalachia: Implications for Action Programs,* edited by John D. Photiadis and Harry K. Schwarzweller, 99–114. Philadelphia: Univ. of Pennsylvania Press, 1970.

Harney, Will Wallace. "A Strange Land and Peculiar People." *Lippincott's Magazine* 12 (Oct. 1873).

Henretta, James. "Families and Farms: Mentalite in Preindustrial America." *William and Mary Quarterly,* 3d ser., 35 (1978): 3–32.

Hofstadter, Richard. "The Myth of the Happy Yeoman." *American Heritage,* 2d ser., 7 (1956): 43–53.

Holmes, William F. "Moonshining and Collective Violence: Georgia, 1889–1895." *Journal of American History* 67 (Dec. 1980): 589–611.

Holt, John B. "Holiness Religion: Cultural Shock and Social Reorganization." *American Sociological Review* 5 (Oct. 1940): 740–47.

Isaac, Rhys. "Evangelical Revolt: The Nature of the Baptists: Challenge to the Traditional Order in Virginia, 1765–1775." *William and Mary Quarterly* 32 (1974): 345–68.

Jensen, Merrill. "The American Revolution and American Agriculture." *Agricultural History* 43 (Jan. 1969): 107–24.

———. "The Creation of the National Domain, 1781–1784." *Mississippi Valley Historical Review* 26 (1939–40): 323–42.

Julian, Ralph. "Our Appalachian Americans." *Harper's* 107 (June 1903): 32–46.

Kane, Steven M. "Ritual Possession in a Southern Appalachian Religious Sect." *Journal of American Folklore* 87 (Oct.–Dec. 1974): 293–302.

Klingberg, Elizabeth Wysor. "Glimpses of Life in the Appalachian Highlands." *South Atlantic Quarterly* 14 (Oct. 1915): 371–78.

Kulikoff, Allan. "The Transition to Capitalism in Rural America." *William and Mary Quarterly,* 3d ser., 46 (1989): 120–44.

Lemon, James T. "Household Consumption in 18th Century America and Its Relationship to Production and Trade: The Situation among Farmers in Southwestern Pennsylvania." *Agricultural History* 41 (Jan. 1967): 59–70.

Lewis, Ronald L. "The Use and Extent of Slave Labor in the Virginia Iron Industry: The Ante-Bellum Era." *West Virginia History* 38 (Jan. 1977): 141–56.

Loehr, Rodney. "Self-Sufficiency on the Farm, 1759–1800." *Agricultural History* 26 (1952): 37–45.

MacClintock, S.S. "The Kentucky Mountains and Their Feuds." *American Journal of Sociology* 7 (July–Sept. 1901): 1–28, 171–87.

McCreesh, Carolyn. "The Philadelphia Connection: The Foulke Meadow River Lands in the 18th and 19th Centuries." *West Virginia History* 44 (Summer 1983): 289–320.

McDonald, Forrest, and Grady McWhiney. "The South from Self-Sufficiency to Peonage: An Interpretation." *American Historical Review* 85, no. 5 (1980): 1095–118.

McKinney, Gordon. "Industrialization and Violence in Appalachia in the 1890s." In *An Appalachian Symposium: Essays Written in Honor of Cratis D. Williams*, edited by J.W. Williamson, 131–44. Boone, N.C.: Appalachian State Univ. Press, 1977.

Martin, Ramsey. "Conceptual Obsolescence and Land Use Policy." In *Toward a New Land Use Ethic*, 116–23. Warrenton, Va.: Piedmont Environmental Council, 1981.

Meyers, Marvin. "The Jacksonian Persuasion." *American Quarterly* 5 (Spring 1953): 3–15.

Moore, George E. "Slavery as a Factor in the Formation of West Virginia." *West Virginia History* 18 (Oct. 1956): 5–90.

Morrison, Charles. "Early Land Grants and Settlers along Patterson Creek." *West Virginia History* 40 (Winter 1979): 164–99.

Nichols, Roy F. "The Kansas-Nebraska Act: A Century of Historiography." *Mississippi Valley Historical Review* 43 (Sept. 1956): 187–212.

Nobles, Gregory H. "Breaking into the Backcountry: New Approaches to the Early American Frontier, 1750–1800." *William and Mary Quarterly*, 3d ser., 46 (Oct. 1989): 641–70.

———. "Capitalism in the Countryside: The Transformation of Rural Society in the United States." *Radical History Review* 4 (1988): 163–76.

Photiadis, John D., and B.B. Maurer. "Religion in an Appalachian State." Research Report no. 6, West Virginia Univ. Appalachian Center. Morgantown, W.Va., 1974.

Post, Charles. "The American Road to Capitalism." *New Left Review* 133 (1982): 30–51.

Pudup, Mary Beth. "The Boundaries of Class in Preindustrial Appalachia." *Journal of Historical Geography* 15, no. 2 (1989): 139–62.

———. "The Limits of Subsistence: Agriculture and Industry in Central Appalachia." *Agricultural History* 64 (Winter 1990): 61–89.

Robinson, Morgan P. "Virginia Counties: Those Resulting from Virginia Legislation." *Bulletin of the Virginia State Library* 9 (1916): 5–283.

Rodd, Thomas Whitney. "Tracing West Virginia's Constitution." *West Virginia Public Interest Law Report* (Summer 1982): 12–21.

Rose, Damaris. "Homeownership, Subsistence and Historical Change: The Mining District of West Cornwall in the Late 19th Century." In *Class and Space: The Making of Urban Society*, edited by Nigel Thrift and Peter Williams. London: Routledge and Kegan Paul, 1987.

Rothstein, Morton. "The Antebellum South as a Dual Economy." *Agricultural History* 41 (Oct. 1967): 373–82.

Selden, Richard T. "Land Use Problems: An Economist's Perspective." In *Toward a New Land Use Ethic*, 90–96. Warrenton, Va.: Piedmont Environmental Council, 1981.

Simon, Richard. "Uneven Development and the Case of West Virginia: Going Beyond the Colonialism Model." *Appalachian Journal* 8 (Spring 1981): 164–86.

Soltow, Lee. "Land Speculation in West Virginia in the Early Federal Period: Randolph County as a Specific Case." *West Virginia History* 44 (Winter 1983): 111–34.

Stampp, Kenneth M. "Lincoln and the Strategy of Defense in the Crisis of 1861." *Journal of Southern History* 11 (Aug. 1945): 227–323.

Swierenga, Robert P. "Land Speculation and Frontier Tax Assessments." *Agricultural History* 44 (July 1970): 253–66.

Taylor, George Rogers. "The National Economy before and after the Civil War." In *Economic Change in the Civil War Era*, edited by David T. Gilchrist and W. David Lewis, 1–22. Greenville, Del.: Hagley Foundation, 1965.

Thomas, John L. "Romantic Reform in America, 1815–1865." *American Quarterly* 17, no. 4 (Winter 1965): 656–81.

Thompson, E.P. "Eighteenth-Century English Society: Class Struggle without Class?" *Social History* 3 (May 1978): 133–65.

———. "The Moral Economy of the English Crowd in the Eighteenth Century." *Past and Present* 50 (1968): 76–136.

———. "Patrician Society, Plebian Culture." *Journal of Social History* 3 (Summer 1970): 383–405.

———. "Time, Work-Discipline and Industrial Capitalism." *Past and Present* 38 (Dec. 1967): 56–97.

Vincent, George. "A Retarded Frontier." *American Journal of Sociology* 4 (July 1898): 1–20.

Vogeler, Ingolf. "The Peasant Culture of Appalachia and Its Survival." *Antipode* 5 (March 1973): 17–24.

Wallace, Michael. "Changing Concepts of Party in the United States: New York, 1815–1828." *American Historical Review* 74 (1968): 453–91.

Watson, Harry L. "Conflict and Collaboration: Yeomen, Slaveholders, and Politics in the Antebellum South." *Social History* 10 (Oct. 1985): 273–98.

Weiman, David F. "Families, Farms and Rural Society in Preindustrial America." In George Grantham and Carol S. Leonard, Eds., *Agrarian Organization in the Century of Industrialization: Europe, Russia and North America*, 255–78. Research in Economic History 5. Greenwich, Conn.: JAI Press, 1989.

———. "Farmers and the Market in Antebellum America: A View from the Georgia Upcountry." *Journal of Economic History* 47 (Sept. 1987): 627–47.

Weisberger, Bernard A. "The Dark and Bloody Ground of Reconstruction Historiography." *Journal of Southern History* 25 (Nov. 1959): 427–47.

White, David E. "The Property Tax in West Virginia: Adequacy, Legitimacy, and Equity." In *Property Taxes in West Virginia*, 31–67. Institute for Public Affairs Policy Monograph no. 4. Morgantown: West Virginia Univ., 1991.

Williams, D. Alan. "The Small Farmer in Eighteenth-Century Virginia Politics." *Agricultural History* 43 (Jan. 1969): 91–99.

Williams, Harry. "An Analysis of Some Reconstruction Attitudes." *Journal of Southern History* 12 (Nov. 1946): 470–86.

Williams, John Alexander. "The Final Confrontation of H.G. Davis and William L. Wilson in the Election Campaign of 1894." *West Virginia History* 32 (Oct. 1970): 1–10.

———. "The New Dominion and the Old: Ante Bellum and Statehood Politics as the Background for West Virginia's Bourbon Democracy." *West Virginia History* 33 (July 1972): 317–407.

Woodson, Carter G. "Freedom and Slavery in Appalachian America." *Journal of Negro History* 1 (April 1916): 132–50.

Dissertations, Theses, Addresses, and Unpublished Papers

Atkins, Paul. "Henry A. Wise and the Virginia Secession Convention, February 13–April 17, 1861." M.A. thesis, Univ. of Virginia, 1950.

Caruso, John A. "Henry Gassaway Davis and the Pan American Railway." Ph.D. diss., West Virginia Univ., 1949.

Cubby, Edwin Albert. "The Transformation of the Tug and Guyandotte Valleys: Economic and Social Change in West Virginia." Ph.D. diss., Syracuse Univ., 1962.

Curry, Richard Orr. "A House Divided: A Study of Statehood Politics and the Copperhead Movement in West Virginia during the Civil War." Ph.D. diss., Univ. of Pennsylvania, 1961.

Ferrell, Barbara Ann. "West Virginia and the Election of 1896." M.A. thesis, West Virginia Univ., 1967.

Goodall, Elizabeth Jane. "History of the Development of the Charleston Industrial Area." M.A. thesis, West Virginia Univ., 1937.

Irons, J.C. "History of Horton-Whitmer." Unpublished typescript, Sept. 1936. West Virginia and Regional History Collection, West Virginia Univ. Library.

Isserman, Andrew. "The West Virginia Economic and Demographic Picturebook." Draft of a report to be submitted to the University President's Committee on the Year 2000. West Virginia Univ. Regional Research Institute, 1989.

McKinney, Gordon. "Subsistence Economy and Community in Western North Carolina, 1860–65." Address presented to the Organization of American Historians, Reno, Nevada, March 1988.

Mayola, Peter Louis. "Whiskey Insurrection of 1794 in Fayette County, Pa." M.A. thesis, West Virginia Univ., 1949.

Miller, Robert Dale. "An Examination of Land Use Planning Problems on the Monongahela National Forest." M.A. thesis, West Virginia Univ., 1977.

Moreland, James R. "The Early Cheat Mountain Iron Works." Unpublished typescript, 1940. West Virginia and Regional History Collection, West Virginia Univ. Library.

Shi, Yue Jin, Timothy T. Phipps, and Dale Colyer. "Agricultural Land Values under Urbanizing Influences." Draft typescript, 1993. Department of Agricultural Economics, West Virginia Univ.

Shiflett, Crandall. "Culture, Economy, and the Stable Ideal: Demographic and Economic Change in the Appalachian South, 1830–1915." Address presented to the American Historical Association, San Francisco, December 1989.

Simon, Richard. "The Development of Underdevelopment: The Coal Industry and Its Effect on the West Virginia Economy." Ph.D. diss., Univ. of Pittsburgh, 1978.

Smith, Charles D. "The Movement for Eastern National Forests, 1899–1911." Ph.D. diss., Harvard Univ., 1956.

Strickland, William M. "The Rhetoric of Cherokee Indian Removal from Georgia, 1828–32." Ph.D. diss., Louisiana State Univ. and Agricultural and Mechanical College, 1975.

Sturm, Theodore. "The Jumonville Incident." M.A. thesis, West Virginia Univ., 1961.

Summers, Festus P. "The Baltimore and Ohio Railroad: A Study in the Civil War." Ph.D. diss., West Virginia Univ., 1933.

Turner, Ian Bruce. "Antislavery Thought in the Border South, 1830–1860." Ph.D. diss., Univ. of Illinois, 1977.

Turner, William Patrick. "From Bourbon to Liberal: The Life and Times of John T. McGraw." Ph.D. diss., West Virginia Univ., 1960.

Waller, Altina L. "Appalachia's Transition to Capitalism." Draft of address presented to the Social Science History Association, Minneapolis, October 1990.

Widen Community Report. "Wild Wonderful Widen, W.Va." Typescript, Dec. 1980. West Virginia and Regional History Collection, West Virginia Univ. Library.

Williams, John Alexander. "Davis and Elkins of West Virginia: Businessmen in Politics." Ph.D. diss., Yale Univ., 1967.

Wilson, Donald Edward. "Joseph H. Diss Debar in West Virginia." M.A. thesis, West Virginia Univ., 1961.

Woodward, Isaiah A. "Arthur Ingram Boreman: A Biography." Ph.D. diss., West Virginia Univ., 1970.

Woofter, Perry. "History of Clay County, West Virginia." Typescript. n.d. West Virginia and Regional History Collection, West Virginia Univ. Library.

Newspapers

The Davis News, 1913
La Sentinella del West Virginia (Thomas, W.Va.), 1905–11
The Mineral Daily News, 1913
The Pocahontas Times, 1900–1901
The Tucker Democrat (St. George, W.Va.), 1883–92

Index

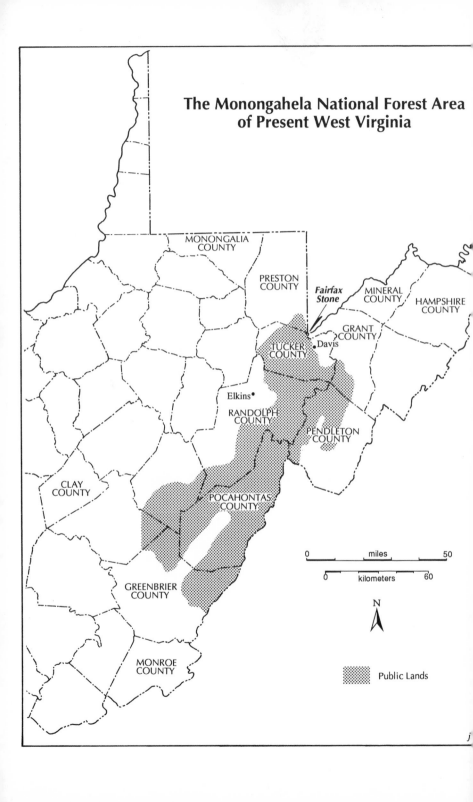

The Monongahela National Forest Area
of Present West Virginia

MONONGALIA
COUNTY

PRESTON
COUNTY

*Fairfax
Stone*

MINERAL
COUNTY

HAMPSHIRE
COUNTY

GRANT
COUNTY

TUCKER
COUNTY

•Davis

Elkins•

RANDOLPH
COUNTY

PENDLETON
COUNTY

CLAY
COUNTY

POCAHONTAS
COUNTY

0   miles   50

0   kilometers   60

GREENBRIER
COUNTY

N

MONROE
COUNTY

Public Lands

j